INTERNATIONAL RELATIONS
IN A CONSTRUCTED WORLD

INTERNATIONAL RELATIONS IN A CONSTRUCTED WORLD

VENDULKA KUBÁLKOVÁ,
NICHOLAS ONUF, PAUL KOWERT
Editors

M.E. Sharpe
Armonk, New York
London, England

Library of Congress Cataloging-in-Publication Data

International relations in a constructed world /
edited by Vendulka Kubálková, Nicholas Onuf, and Paul Kowert.
p.   cm.
Includes bibliographical references and index.
ISBN 0-7656-0297-0 (cloth : alk. paper). —
ISBN 0-7656-0298-9 (pbk. : alk. paper)
1. International relations.   2. Constructivism (philosophy).   I. Kubálková, V.
II. Onuf, Nicholas Greenwood.   III. Kowert, Paul, 1964–
JZ1305.I575   1998
327—dc21   97-46968
CIP

Printed in the United States of America

The paper used in this publication meets the minimum requirements of
American National Standard for Information Sciences—
Permanence of Paper for Printed Library Materials,
ANSI Z 39.48-1984.

BM (c)   10   9   8   7   6   5   4   3   2   1
BM (p)   10   9   8   7   6   5

Contents

About the Editors and the Contributors

Harry D. Gould received an M.A. in International Studies from Florida International University. He is pursuing doctoral studies in the Department of Political Science, Johns Hopkins University.

Henry L. Hamman received his Ph.D. from the University of Miami in International Relations. He is president of Sociocybernetics Inc., a systems research company based in Miami. He is the author and editor of a number of books on international relations.

Paul Kowert is an assistant professor in the Department of International Relations at Florida International University. He is the author of recent studies on foreign policy decision making and social identity in international politics.

Vendulka Kubálková is a professor of international studies in the School of International Studies at the University of Miami and the author, among other works, with A.A. Cruickshank, of *Marxism and International Relations*.

Nicholas Onuf is a professor in the Department of International Relations at Florida International University. His most recent book is *The Republican Legacy in International Thought*.

Elisabeth Prügl is an assistant professor in the Department of International Relations at Florida International University and the author of recent studies in feminist international relations theory.

Craig Simon is a database application specialist. He is a Ph.D. candidate at the School of International Studies at the University of Miami, and is writing a dissertation "Bandwidth Rules: Standards and Structure in Global Internet Governance."

Preface

Prefaces are really postscripts. Authors write them at the very end, grateful that their labors are really over. They acknowledge the assistance of institutions, colleagues, and relatives, and explain the circumstances under which the book was written. It is also the last opportunity to reprise some of the book's themes.

It is in the nature of this particular project that we have many afterthoughts. We did not want to write yet another book on the parlous state of theory in the field of International Relations (IR). The dominant approaches and theories in any field of study are seldom without critics. The "third debate" in IR has been especially ferocious, as anyone who takes the trouble to understand its technically difficult language can confirm. Some critics have indicted mainstream theorists for fraud, finding them guilty by association with the "Enlightenment project." On the evidence of great changes in the world during the past decade, other critics have been content to show that the theoretical mainstream failed in its own terms.

In this book, we do not enter into the debate, except to the very limited extent required to situate ourselves. Instead, we try to do something different: to develop an alternative way of studying international relations *as* social relations, and in the process reconceptualize the field in relation to other fields.

The opportunity to try something different arose when Nicholas Onuf came to teach in Miami several years after he had written *World of Our Making* (1989). In this systematic and technically demanding book, Onuf developed a "constructivist" framework from a broad range of theoretical materials as a way beyond what was then emerging as the third debate. Vendulka Kubálková greeted Onuf's arrival across town by proposing that they convene the "Miami International Relations Group" as a running seminar for their colleagues and students. Kubálková soon prevailed on Onuf to present an accessible version of his constructivist framework to the Miami Group, and other participants followed suit with papers variously relevant to that framework. In 1996, several members of the Miami Group presented their papers together at the joint conference of the International Studies Association and the Japan Association of International Relations. At that time the editors began the process of forming the work of the Miami Group into a coherent volume.

Since Onuf introduced "constructivism" in 1989 it has generated growing interest, and many scholars have adopted the name for their approaches. There are, in fact, not one but several "constructivisms" in the literature. The appeal of the name should come as no surprise in a decade that has witnessed epochal political and economic rearrangements. The bipolar Cold War system and the entire Soviet bloc collapsed. The world plunged into turmoil with an unprecedented number of nations and ethnic groups demanding sovereign statehood, political subdivision, or at least redrawn frontiers. The world is abuzz with economic and diplomatic activities as new geopolitical, geoeconomic, and geostrategic changes take place. These "international" changes occur against the backdrop of the vast part of the planet also changing "internal" ways of running political, economic, and social affairs. No part of the world can avoid these changes or their consequences; the entire world is continuously "under construction." The choice of the term "constructivism" therefore seems particularly apposite.

Mainstream IR failed to anticipate these changes: in theory, nothing much was supposed to change. Many critics saw this failure as evidence against the possibility of theory. Some critics even saw it as confirming that the world is never what it seems. Constructivism points to the limitations of mainstream thinking, but it rejects the conclusion that theory about the world—or a coherent description of the world—is impossible.

Instead, constructivism offers a way how to go about redescribing the world. Mainstream theorists and their critics leave *people* out. Constructivism puts people and their activities at the forefront. It is indeed an irony that at the turn of millennium, when people have achieved wondrous technological feats, scholars do not see how people construct the world as a consequence of their social relations.

Many other constructivists have also pointed out that the scope for people in the agent-structure relation must be enlarged. It is one thing of course to say that people make the world or that state identities influence the international structure. It is quite another to be specific and explain by what mechanism this "making" or "influencing" works. The inability to figure out how these processes work so that they can be empirically explored has been a blindspot in many forms of constructivism. What binds people to each other and to the material world around them? Onuf's constructivism identifies the main element through which this "construction" takes place: *rules*. Rules provide the medium for human interactivity. Our species is inherently social, defined by the social arrangements we create. Endowed with free will, people (agents) are thus seen as knowledgable participants in the reproduction of social rules, and thus free from the assumed determinism of immaterial, inanimate, factors (structure).

Onuf begins with people, understanding first of all the simple social relations they have with each other. Only then does he work his way up to complex relations, practices, institutions, "structures," or social arrangements that are called states and IR. The axioms "saying is doing," "rules make rule," and "rules put resources into play" distinguish Onuf's school of constructivism from positivist and Marxist philosophies such as realism, neoliberalism, and historical materialism as well as from others who claim the constructivist mantle. Those approaches look first at the ways resources determine structure, and then at specific social outcomes. Mainstream IR specialists try to see a single world by standing outside, looking for that which is "objectively given": measurable structural variables that can be said to cause human behaviors. The traditional mainstream research interest is the extent to which material structure makes social behavior involuntary and predictable. Constructivists, on the other hand, see human behavior and social structure as inseparable, simultaneous, co-constituted.

Constructivism provides a template for viewing the world in a fundamentally different way from that offered in the standard IR literature. Instead of introducing a vocabulary of states, balances of power, anarchies, and other IR terms, constructivism begins its first lesson on international relations with an analysis of speech acts, rules, practices, agents, agencies, and social arrangements. These are the building blocks of society and its institutional structure. States, balances of power, hegemonies, and so forth are specific instances. As Onuf put it, constructivism paints a picture of "staggering complexity and constant change" within the interwoven patterns of overlapping social arrangements. The complexity of the constructivist redescription of the world, however, does not preclude the possibility of focusing on any single aspect of human relations, international or otherwise. Different types of rules, different social arrangements, institutions, conventions and societies can all be subjected to this type of analysis. Rules hold the key to understanding.

In this reading, the different political systems, ideologies, religions, or worldviews, of North and South, of East and West, and of civilizations throughout history are built on narratives that can be broken down and analyzed according to the types of speech acts that sustain them. All narratives consist of instruction-rules, directive-rules, and commitment-rules that work in distinctive ways. Depending on which of the three types is more strongly represented, and on how it is mixed with the others, one might classify societies and institutions. International relations is itself a complex institution based on a mixture of these rules. To study international relations as constructivists requires that we study rules rather than imaginary, artificially reified entities such as states or structures. Rules have ontological substance; they are there for anybody to see.

Constructivism is not a theory, it does not claim to explain why things work as they do. Constructivism is simply an alternative ontology, a redescription of the world. Thus it does not carry any inherent ideological stance. Constructivism is not an "ism" to be added to the list dominated in the IR studies by neorealism and neoliberalism.

We promised the publisher that this book would have several qualities that are usually considered mutually exclusive: the book was to introduce something original; it was to be scholarly and educational and yet easy to read. As we struggled to lighten our prose—which came more naturally in some chapters than in others—we discovered just how hard it is to write something "easy."

In Chapter 1 we try to explain some of the most difficult terms, such as epistemology, methodology, ontology, and positivism, in a straightforward way. This difficult task was necessary in order to be able to place our book against the backdrop of current controversies in the IR discipline, the third debate in particular. Yet we stay out of the actual debate. Our purpose is only to distinguish constructivism from other approaches with which it is often confused, such as postmodern, deconstructionist, post-structuralist, and critical approaches discussed briefly in Chapter 2 and the other forms of constructivism discussed in Chapter 4. Chapter 3 is central to the project. It is written by Professor Onuf in a deliberately straightforward fashion, setting out the ABCs of constructivism. It introduces a different way of thinking about the world and IR. The reader should approach this chapter as one would approach learning a new language with a different alphabet, grammar, range of sounds, and meanings. As in learning a new language it might be difficult at first for readers to get "their tongues around" the constructivist language and begin to think along the constructivist lines. The remaining chapters are concerned with the payoff of this effort. Their authors do occasionally revisit the main features of Onuf's framework, but their main purpose is to show the empirical and conceptual utility of the framework by applying it to topics of contemporary relevance such as political identity (Chapter 5), social movements (Chapter 6), the Information Age (Chapter 7), and even the profession of IR scholarship itself (Chapter 9). These are but a few examples of the ways constructivism can be applied. Chapters 5 and 6 also reveal the facility with which constructivist research can proceed using case historical methods, and Chapter 7 shows how constructivists might grapple with even the "newest" topics such as the implications of Internet expansion. Chapter 8 introduces the reader to some of the recent advances in physical sciences which replaced conceptual instruments that still form a bedrock of positivism in social sciences. It shows conceptual compatibility of constructivism with these new developments.

As we contemplate the finished volume the daunting question remains whether we have succeeded in our goal and have managed to present Onuf's constructivism as an alternative way to view the world. Will the reader get it? How soon into the book will the reader realize what a radical a change we advocate? Irrespective of the answers to these questions, we hope that the book will be as rewarding to read as it was to write.

It now remains only to thank all those that made this project possible. First is the University of Miami (in particular Provost Luis Glaser and Professor Haim Shaked) for helping us to go as a group to Japan in 1996. The prospect of a "school trip" provided the incentive for completion of the initial papers. M.E. Sharpe Executive Editor Patricia Kolb and Project Editor Steve Martin extended us invaluable encouragement and help. Craig Simon, one of the contributors to this volume, put our diversely formatted chapters into digital conformity with the publisher's specifications. Gonzalo Porcel-Quero helped this project as research assistant throughout its development. Our thanks go also to the graduate students and faculty of the Miami IR theory group. They read many parts of this book and pointed out places where we lapsed into the customarily obscure prose of professional academics. Their enthusiasm has made the work on this book worthwhile. It is to them that we dedicate this project.

Part I
Introduction

Constructing Constructivism

Vendulka Kubálková, Nicholas Onuf, and Paul Kowert

". . . so that they will not understand one another's speech . . ."

The Tower of Babel

"And thus what was written was fulfilled," and a common language was lost. Books, articles, and conference papers explaining the world at the turn of the millennium are a Tower of Babel (Genesis 11). For half a century, English has been the unofficial but universal language of scholarly exchange. Today, scholars speak in many, highly specialized English languages, and they barely manage to understand each other. Specialized languages have always characterized *disciplines*, the subjects of study that scholars have delimited among themselves, *as if* these subjects were the natural and inevitable way to arrange the production and dissemination of knowledge. What is unusual and has reached truly biblical proportions is the way that specialized languages have swept across traditional disciplinary boundaries. International Relations (for convenience, IR) is a conspicuous case, in part because its status as a discipline is not secure, in part because its subject matter (international relations, in this book always spelled out in the lower case) has undergone a spectacular transformation within a decade's time.

Indeed, the contributors to this book do not even agree among themselves on whether IR is a discipline in its own right, an interdisciplinary undertaking, or merely a field (or subdivision) of political science. Perhaps changes in the world make the traditional ways that scholars have divided up the world seem increasingly arbitrary and irrelevant. Perhaps the Babel of scholarly languages signifies the dismantling of the current arrangement of disciplines conventionally known as the social sciences. The editors do agree that a common language of scholarship is both desirable and possible for the subject of international relations; that this language should also suit social relations in general; *and* that this language should never be made deliberately obscure just to maintain disciplinary boundaries or, for that matter, to keep people who are not scholarly specialists in the dark.

IR scholars speak in many voices. They regularly propose new "approaches" to the subject, and proponents engage in "great debates" over their merits. They feel obliged to propose schemes for classifying an ever larger number of approaches. Their students spend an increasing, and perhaps inordinate, amount of time reprising these debates and memorizing classificatory schemes.

This volume grew out of the pedagogical concerns of a group of teachers and students at two universities in Miami. Although our backgrounds and interests vary, our discussions have increasingly centered on "constructivism," in which the discipline as a whole has taken a great deal of interest since Nicholas Onuf (one of the group's members) introduced the term in 1989. As we considered the version of constructivism that he had developed in *World of Our Making* and began to think about our other scholarly interests in constructivist terms, this book gradually took form. Onuf's essay (see Chapter 3) sets out his version of constructivism in language that any serious-minded reader can understand. Other contributors explain and refine constructivism, and apply it to a variety of important topics in international relations. In the process, they help to dispel some myths and misunderstandings that have already attached themselves to a term that scholars have begun to use rather casually. One myth is that constructivism is closely related to the "post-modern" practice of "deconstruction"; a second is that constructivism mandates an "emancipatory" or "critical" politics; a third is that constructivism, being "post-positivist," is indifferent to empirical research and antithetical to "positivist" science. (We shall consider these and many other terms more fully in this introductory chapter.)

This book shows that constructivism offers an unfamiliar but systematic way of thinking about social relations in general and international relations in particular. The book also shows the relevance of constructivism to the empirical investigation of important topics in contemporary international relations, such as national identity, gender in political economy, and the emerging information age. In sum, the volume addresses these questions:

What is constructivism? Where does it fit in the discipline? How it can help the discipline to move on?

In this introductory chapter, we undertake several preliminary tasks. We look briefly into the relatively short history and currently confused state of the discipline. We discuss disciplinary boundaries, external influences, and endless debates as sources of confusion. We show that the ways IR scholars categorize approaches and stake out positions for debate have led them to underestimate constructivism as an alternative to received ways of thinking. Finally, and perhaps most important, we explain a considerable number of concepts that scholars often use but rarely give sufficient thought to, and that readers unschooled in the scholarly languages of philosophy and the social sciences will find utterly baffling.

The purpose of this book is not to pronounce on the state of the discipline, to assess all sources of confusion, or to pass judgment on every debate. Part I of the book does so only as necessary to discuss the intellectual context from which constructivism has grown. Nor is our purpose to discredit the efforts of IR scholars to learn from other disciplines. Our purpose, rather, is to show that constructivism can make sense of international relations by making sense of social relations, and that constructivism offers IR a way beyond the impasse of many discordant languages and distracting debates.

Disciplines and Dialects

Insular and protected as a discipline, IR is overwhelmingly the work of scholars from just two countries: Britain and the United States. Just as IR has finally begun to open itself to other disciplines and their languages, it is ironic that the subject matter of international relations came to the attention of scholars in those other disciplines. All of a sudden, "global concerns" are on everyone's agenda. At the same time, scholars from all over the world have begun to identify themselves with IR as a discipline. IR has become a major importer of ideas and authors—ideas to be applied to IR and authors to cite as sources of inspiration. It is especially unsettling for an older generation of IR scholars to see other names than their own sprinkled in the footnotes of their younger colleagues.

As a discipline, IR has accumulated a huge intellectual balance of trade deficit. Little produced in the discipline has found its way into other disciplines. IR scholars do not seem to lead or influence public debate. The past decade was characterized by tumultuous and far-reaching changes that exposed the irrelevance of the discipline's accumulated knowledge about international relations. Any number of politicians, intellectuals, and journalists have declared the end of the Cold War, communism, modernity, and history, and the beginning of some new epoch, with no help whatsoever from IR scholars. Furthermore, most of these scholars are only slowly adjusting to a new agenda of concerns—global warming, environmental degradation, overpopulation, ethnic conflict—identified by somebody outside the discipline. Everything allegedly new and different is "post": post-communist, post–international relations, post-modern, post-positivist, post-realist, post-Soviet, post-structural, post-theory. As a universal prefix, "post" indicates more clearly what has been transcended or rejected than what may be expected in the future.

IR is hardly alone in its bewilderment. The division of knowledge by disciplines no longer seems convincing. There are so many bodies of knowledge, each couched in its own arcane language, that reaching across disciplines brings huge costs in translation, dissipating intellectual resources that could otherwise be used to address new concerns. Because IR combines global pretensions with an exceptionally insular perspective on itself and its subject, it suffers more than most disciplines from this state of affairs.

The creation and accumulation of knowledge in the last two hundred years advanced hand in hand with the multiplication of specializations and their institutionalization as disciplines. Since there is nothing natural or inevitable about the way scholars define their substantive concerns and parcel them out among themselves, some of these concerns—especially the ones now popularly called "global"—are shared, but the way they are studied is not. Even if scholars were able to overcome their parochial tendencies, disciplinary "dialects" make it difficult for them to share anything across disciplines. Indeed, the more something passes muster as knowledge within a discipline, the less likely it is to "translate" to other disciplines.

Dialects develop because the same words used in several disciplines or their subfields begin to carry different meanings in each. When scholars introduce and debate new concepts, they give new meaning to old words. They separate synonyms, realign antonyms, and invent new words. As worlds of scholarship, disciplines are never completely sealed off from each other. The words themselves drift across disciplinary boundaries like snippets of conversation for which an eavesdropper has no context. They tantalize scholars dissatisfied with the state of their own disciplines, who borrow them with minimal care and adapt them to new uses.

To give a few examples relevant to our concerns, *structure*, *agent*, and *realism* mean very different things in different disciplines. The structuralism of anthropologist Claude Lévi-Strauss has little to do with the structural Marxism of Louis Althusser and even less to do with the structural realism of IR's Kenneth Waltz. Economists and sociologists mean quite different things by the term *agent*. Realism in philosophy is far removed from realism in international relations. (See Chapter 4 for a discussion of "scientific realism.")

The term *critical* is another, instructive example. Philosophers have used the term in a specialized sense that goes back to Immanuel Kant. In the hands of Marxist theorists, it acquired a different, though still specialized, meaning. Other scholars had always used the term to refer to the "ability to find defects and faults," once regarded as a critical faculty of every scholar. Thanks to the diffusion of a specifically neo-Marxist dialect, scholars in several disciplines now use the term in ways that neither Kant nor any ordinary person would understand. The antonym of the term *critical* is not *uncritical* but, in some cases, *positivist* (a term itself carrying several meanings) and in others, *problem-solving*. Not all scholars are critical (although this does not mean that they are "uncritical"). Not being critical might mean that a scholar is positivist or interested only in proposing policies to solve narrowly defined problems.

There are powerful incentives to perpetuate the confusion. Who would not want to be a critical scholar if it reflects on one's intellectual abilities? Yet becoming "critical" carries certain implications: for some scholars being critical means openly acknowledging a connection to Marx, while other critical scholars go out of their way to deny such a connection. The distinctions are not often appreciated. Some scholars quote post-structuralists and critical theorists in support of the same argument, overlooking vehement disagreements between the two groups (Kratochwil 1984). The same argument may once be described as leftist or Marxist, and another time as right-wing and conservative. The same words point in altogether different directions.

Often scholars and students blithely use words, such as *discourse* and *the other*, for their sophisticated and contemporary flair. The word *problematique* (with appropriate French pronunciation) is used instead of *problem* or *hypothesis* in total ignorance of the very special meaning that the French term is intended to convey. Similarly *project* is no longer just an exercise for schoolchildren. In the history of ideas, some antecedents are more controversial than others, and the genesis of many currently fashionable terms in earlier leftist ideas is still a sensitive subject. *Practice* is just such a term, only somewhat separated from the Marxist notion of *praxis* by translation into English. In fact, this is a term to which constructivists are partial, and readers will find it used in this book.

Words are imported from all over the place, including meteorology, physics, and mathematics. Terms such as *turbulence*, *chaos*, and *cascade*, which natural scientists and mathematicians have adopted from ordinary language for their own very specific use, have been borrowed by social scientists, including IR scholars, and used metaphorically. With so many casual appropriations and mixed signals, it is not surprising that many IR scholars are casting about for terms to describe themselves that simultaneously seem right for disciplinary purposes, flatter them in their ordinary meaning, and suggest a connection to other disciplinary conversations (*conversation* is another term that scholars have favored with a specialized meaning). Just as some scholars feel that they ought to make sure that they are *critical* in some sense of the term, many are now self-proclaimed *constructivists*. They often use the term to suggest what they are not: they are not realists or positivists in any narrow sense. They do not practice "deconstruction." Taking the middle path, as they see it (Adler 1997), they are protected on both sides by the fuzzy use of language.

International Relations as a Discipline

The Enlightenment's celebration of reason unleashed a tremendous range of intellectual activities previously restricted by the medieval acceptance of God's revelation as the truth. By the end of the eighteenth century, two previously synonymous terms, *science* and *philosophy*, had been redefined and separated. Thereafter, science dealt with the material world and included such pursuits as astronomy, chemistry, and physics. Scientists made innumerable discoveries that had a cumulatively staggering effect on the material conditions of daily life. Overshadowed by the dazzling successes of science, philosophy was left with "metaphysical" questions that no one could hope to answer convincingly.

In the nineteenth century, between the growing edifice of science and the shrinking edifice of philosophy, ground was broken by one of the "inventors" of positivism, Auguste Comte, for an ambitious new undertaking. The new edifice of the "social sciences" was to be built to the image of the highly successful "natural sciences." Sustaining this development was a belief, known as *naturalism*, that nature and society do not fundamentally differ. In positivist terms, any phenomenon, no matter how complex in appearance, can be broken down into units that can be studied scientifically. Cumulative knowledge will faithfully represent the world as it is, explain how it works, predict its future unfolding, and allow humanity to control its own destiny.

Late in the nineteenth century, the separation of political economy into politics (mainly government and public law) and economics, and the separation of sociology from the other two disciplines, followed the liberal practice of separating state, economy, and society. Anthropology came in tandem with colonial administration, while history occupied an ambiguous position between the humanities and the social sciences.

IR came late and developed slowly, in the shadow of the other social sciences, especially political science. World War I endowed it with a subject matter that other disciplines had relegated to the margins of systematic inquiry: the study of war and ways to avoid it. The first IR scholars were, for the most part, international lawyers and diplomatic historians. Diplomats and journalists mattered, and professional journals were devoted to policy issues and current events. Students of politics concerned themselves with the subject from the point of view of international law and international organizations (chiefly the League of Nations). Other social scientists were conspicuously absent, and the positivist idea of science was almost unheard of. (A British meteorologist, statistician, and Quaker, L.F. Richardson, is the most interesting exception to this generalization; his work went largely unnoticed until after World War II.)

Between the two world wars, many IR scholars were closely connected to the governments of the day in Britain and the United States. To the extent that the discipline can be said to have existed at all, its dominant concerns reflected the liberal internationalism of English-speaking political elites. A Continental tradition of concern for statecraft—*Realpolitik*—figured little in the discipline. Marxist concerns mattered even less.

After World War II, IR gained disciplinary momentum. The United States assumed an active stance toward the world commensurate with its power, universities in the United States expanded rapidly, and German Jewish expatriates brought a Continental concern for statecraft to the fore. What seemed like a new and very powerful way of thinking, styled *realism*, transformed the discipline.

Realists fostered the impression that war is a permanent feature of human experience because human communities had always been organized to expect the worst from each other. They dismissed the liberal internationalist project of progressive pacification as dangerously naive. States, they reasoned, are here to stay, and relations of states demand constant attention, skillful statecraft, and an unswerving commitment by every state's leaders to the "national interest."

Furthermore, realists argued that human experience at the level of states and their relations is distinct from behavior at other levels. IR's subject matter was to be uniquely its own, as guaranteed by the principle of sovereignty. Despite recurrent debates over the most appropriate "level of analysis," IR was overwhelmingly state-centric. IR's *raison d'être* was the study of states, and thus the study of *raison d'état*. Always haphazard about levels of analysis, the first generation of realists still showed traces of concern for national character. The behavior of states reflected their distinctive histories and geographical positions; the behavior of their leaders reflected the inevitable flaws of human character. Starting in the 1960s, however, realist scholars sought to make the new discipline scientific.

The credibility of science depends on findings that are themselves credible by scientific criteria *and* cumulative. After two decades of science, IR had precious little to show in the latter respect. Some scholars counseled patience, and have diligently continued with the job of science. Others began to doubt that realism provided science with an adequate basis for cumulative findings. As a matter of *theory*, attention to the characteristics of states, no matter how scientific, missed the point that states might behave alike because of a common situation that none of them can hope to escape. In this situation, readily associated with Thomas Hobbes's state of nature, states need only respond rationally to the radical insecurity engendered by their collective, unregulated existence.

The rationality postulate permitted a rigorous theory of international relations, analogous to price theory in microeconomics—or so Kenneth Waltz proclaimed in his immensely influential book, *Theory of International Politics* (1979). Instead of an equilibrium of supply and demand, the theory predicted (frequently unstable) equilibria of power and security. Redirecting attention to the structure of the international system, Waltz attributed the "long peace" after World War II to the simplicity of a bipolar equilibrium of states. Structuralist realists then resumed a familiar debate over the relative merits of bipolar and multipolar arrangements.

Observing that no set of conditions consistent with a state of nature anticipates genuinely harmonious relations among states, other scholars attributed the long peace instead to the United States' international hegemony. The term *hegemony* had long been used to describe the efforts of leading states to best their peers through diplomacy and war. The use of this term to describe the dominant position of Britain in the nineteenth century and the United States after World War II signaled two tendencies in the discipline that emerged more or less simultaneously with the project to rationalize realism. One was a revival of liberal institutionalism, fostered by recognition that these countries held their positions in good measure by virtue of having institutionalized a liberal world economy. In short order, application of the rationality postulate to the circumstances of liberal hegemony had the effect of joining *structural realism* and *structural liberalism* (both often called "neo-") as the discipline's competing but closely related orthodoxies.

A second tendency signaled by the term *hegemony* stemmed from its use by the Italian Marxist Antonio Gramsci to refer to the importance of ruling ideas rather than formal institutional arrangements. In the context of the world economy, liberal ideas made the dominance of Britain and then the United States easy. Until the Vietnam War, IR had developed in almost complete isolation from the many forms of Marxist thought that had proliferated over the decades. Even then, IR scholars were slower than their colleagues in the other social sciences to explore the intellectual legacy of the Left. As a ritual, IR scholars often asked their students to read a little bit of Lenin. While sociologists and diplomatic historians strenuously discussed imperialism during the Vietnam era, nothing comparable took place in IR. Only through dependency theory, which Latin American writers proposed to explain the persistence of international inequality, did the Left make its first real contribution to the discipline. Thereupon followed world systems theory and the Gramscian interpretation of hegemony.

Recognition that writers on the left had something to say took the form of an *ad hoc* scheme sorting approaches to international relations into three categories—realist (including mercantilist), pluralist (meaning liberal), and radical (or globalist, sometimes even called Marxist)—on what amounted to an ideological spectrum. The radical category was, however, far removed from decades of discussion among European Marxists, which began a great reconsideration of Enlightenment premises on philosophical as well as ideological grounds. Only gradually over the last twenty years have IR scholars begun to appreciate the challenge that this reconsideration of the "modern project," as it is often called, represents for their own discipline, for positivist science, for the way that they think about language and its uses, and for the very idea that knowledge is possible.

As Vendulka Kubálková makes clear in the next chapter, confronting the challenge of "post" thinking has had a cathartic effect on many IR scholars. Whether it has had a comparable effect on the discipline as such is harder to say. In the short term, structural realists and their liberal look-alikes have succeeded in maintaining their disciplinary hegemony, especially in the major graduate institutions in the United States. Indeed, rational choice theory holds sway at Harvard University, the University of Chicago, and the University of California at Berkeley. The longer term may prove to be a different story, especially as the discipline becomes as global as its subject matter.

The Forest Fire

Until the "post" movement prompted the emergence of new ways of thinking in IR, including constructivism, debates in the discipline were relatively simple—and practically continuous. One debate never took place. When David Singer directed attention to the level of analysis problem, he used the imagery of trees (read "states") and forest (read "the international system") (Singer 1961, 77). Actual forests contain many different species of trees, depending on terrain, soil conditions, human intrusion, and so on. Yet Singer's forest is perfectly homogeneous, no doubt because realists have always dismissed a liberal concern for differences among societies and forms of government within states. In a minor debate that still rumbles on, liberals tried to find a place for "deer or birds, also denizens of the forest," as K.J. Holsti (1985, 38) suggested in a useful extension of the imagery, but they failed to persuade most realists, for whom war, or "forest fire," is the only reason to pay attention to the forest or to think of it as composed of trees. Perhaps, from a realist point of view, "Smokey the Bear" can alert us to the danger of forest fires, but bears living in the forest cannot prevent them. We too will use the metaphorical language of the forest throughout the rest of this introductory chapter.

The power of this imagery is obvious when we stop to consider the terrifying speed with which people have been burning up and cutting down tropical forests. Faced with this sort of threat, forest rangers scanning the horizon for signs of smoke are beside the point. Liberal scholars have always looked for ways of eliminating fire from the forest, while realists rule out elimination of fires and concentrate their attention on damage control. Dependency theorists are happy to explain that people destroy their forests because their position in the world economy leaves them no choice. The issue is not the forest as such, but a structure of planetary relations that force African women to walk miles for firewood while IR scholars furnish their studies with mahogany bookcases. True to Marx, dependency theorists would also admonish us to beware of scholars who claim that they have no ax to grind.

Back to Basics

The metaphorical language of forest, trees, and fire helps to clarify the sorts of debates in IR that have—or might have—taken place. It can also show what scholars in the discipline have taken for granted in conducting their debates, at least until they confronted the arrival of "post" influences from other disciplines. Everyone took for granted scholars' ability to represent the world (or the forest) as it is. Objective knowledge seemed a feasible goal.

To put it differently, *epistemology* (how do we know what we know?) was not an issue. We know what we know, because we—as scholars, and as children of the Enlightenment—have been in the business of systematically knowing more for a long time and we have gotten better and better at it. In particular, we know how to separate our knowing selves, and our wishes, from the world that we know more and more about. At issue and much debated was *methodology* (how should we go about the business of knowing?). *Methodology* differs from *epistemology* in that the former inquires into procedures for attesting to knowledge, while the latter is concerned with the basis for knowledge—the conviction that our sensory experience is systematically related to the world outside ourselves.

Ontology (what is it that we know?) was an issue, though rarely discussed as such. We do know that there is a world out there, independent of our efforts to know more about it. We even know that our efforts affect the world; we are only provisionally outside of it. At issue is the fundamental nature of the world: Is it in the end a simple matter to explain how the world works once we have broken it down into its smallest parts? Or is it finally a matter of great complexity, perhaps even more than we can imagine? Convinced that the world will reveal its simplicity to us once we know enough, positivists claimed that science cleared the way for ever more powerful theories. On the defensive, historicists treated these claims with skepticism, only to be described, or dismissed, as traditionalists for doing so.

Metaphysical issues were off limits. Scholars had no business asking what it all meant—what higher purpose our earthly existence might serve. These were private matters of faith or speculation. *Ethical* issues were public business, but the public consisted of consumers of knowledge, not producers. Scholars were both. As teachers, consultants, or occasional policy makers, scholars could speak their minds on what people should do and what the world ought to be like, but even then scholarly norms urged a balanced and detached public demeanor.

Of the debates that *did* occur in IR, the first "great debate" ruled questions of ethics out of order, establishing the primacy of realists over so-called idealists. The second "great debate" ratified the methodological assumption that scientific testing should prevail over historical reconstruction. Although the terms of the debate were methodological, the underlying issue was ontological: Is the world ultimately very simple, or is it irreducibly complex? The debate itself gradually petered out in quibbles over method. At the same time, philosophers and social theorists began to challenge the epistemological consensus that sustained all such debates. Eventually these challenges precipitated a far deeper and more divisive debate than the discipline had previously experienced, which was heralded in the 1980s as the "third debate." Many scholars began to suspect that there was nothing actually to debate. The incompatibility of epistemological positions, and the refusal to believe that a common position was even possible, meant choosing sides and going separate ways. It was in this context that *constructivism* emerged.

Even the simplest of statements can be used to reinforce the understanding of some of these issues. In everyday conversation, we do not examine everything that we say in order to understand its philosophical implications, but we could. To illustrate this, let us start with a simple claim about the world: "There is a fire in the forest." An examination of this claim takes us to ontology.

Ontology deals with essence and appearance, the nature of things and how they are related, and how this affects the way that things appear to us. The statement "there is a fire in the forest" claims to tell us what "it" is that we are talking about, what "it" consists of, and how "its" parts are related. An examination of this claim requires us to introduce categories into which the object we are talking about can be meaningfully placed: the forest in question is but one possible member of a class of objects called *forests*, and its placement in that class may be subject to confusion or controversy. The same goes for the fire.

The statement "there is a fire in the forest" ought not to be confused with the statement "the forest is on fire." Both statements are commonsense shorthand representations of a series of different propositions, themselves based on assumptions that anyone hearing these statements must share in order to understand them. The term *fire* probably refers to a common chemical reaction that takes place under certain conditions, with a readily observable result (namely, that combustible objects burn). It is unclear, however, whether the speaker intends hearers to believe that the whole forest is burning all at once; such a situation is unlikely and such an interpretation seems too literal. Indeed, the statement "the forest is on fire" could simply be intended to convey an image of the forest on the occasion of a particularly magnificent sunset.

Even if the statement "there is a fire in the forest" is less likely to be misconstrued, at least in English, it still depends on context for meaning. The person reporting the fire must assume that hearers know that a forest is an extensive, unenclosed tract of land (its Latin root, *foris*, means "outside"), that particular kinds of chemical reactions called *fires* are frequent events in forests, that forests contain a great deal of combustible material, and that immediate conditions (such as wind and relative humidity) will have a significant effect on the combustibility of that material. The prepositional phase "in the forest" is ontologically significant because it tells us to think about the properties and relations of particular trees, and not, at least initially, about the forest as a whole.

Furthermore, the person shouting "fire" believes that a series of empiri-

cal generalizations cover the situation. Flickering light, intense heat, volumi-
nous smoke, or crackling noises generally mean fire; beyond a certain size,
fires are generally hard to control; big fires in the forest are generally undesirable; it is generally responsible to report untended fires in the forest; and other
people will generally believe the report of fire if it is appropriately conveyed.
To report that the forest is "on fire" invites disbelief, even if the intention is to
report, quite specifically, that an untended fire in the forest is growing rapidly
and is possibly already out of control. To report "there is a fire in the forest"
invites hearers to participate in the process of empirical generalization from
which shared knowledge results. Others will ask: "Where is the fire? How big
is it? What direction is it moving? What should we do now?"

As this discussion shows, any statement can be broken into a chain of
propositions about the world. It may be that none of these propositions is
"true." As the person shouting "fire," I may be mistaken about the smoke or
the crackling noise. I may not realize that the fire is under control, or indeed
that it was set for the desired goal of burning away underbrush. Craving
attention, I may have cried "fire" so often in the past that no one believes
me any longer. When others agree with my claims about the world, and acts
that we take on the basis of these claims have the effects that we generally
expect them to, I think that I have spoken truly. If others confirm that there
is a fire, if we all take what we believe are the appropriate actions to put the
fire out, and if a number of us then report that the fire is no longer burning,
then I may rest assured that I had reported the truth.

In the first instance, speaking truly is a methodological matter. If others
have doubts about the accuracy or relevance of my claims, I will tell them
how I figured out that there is a fire in the forest. Sticking my hand in it,
looking at the flames, and smelling the smoke, I have relied on my senses
and compared the results with what I already know about fires. I am
obliged, at least in principle, to show that I have chosen a method suited to
the circumstances and then used it properly before others are obliged to
grant that my claims are true. If we consider the complexity of any claim
that I might make about the outbreak of war in international relations, it is
clear how difficult it is to verify such claims.

Ever since the Enlightenment, we have assumed that we can stand apart
from the world in order to "see" it clearly and formulate statements that
correspond to the world as it truly is. Seeing the world even more clearly
depends on improving our observational techniques and making our empirical generalizations more precise. The more we are able to offer propositions
about the world, and the more we can identify relations between them, the
better able we are to capture the truth of the world. All these activities
vouch for our epistemological convictions.

If we wished, we could break down even further our propositions about forest fires, identifying various physical and chemical processes, specifying the circumstances under which they take place, measuring and classifying them by reference to their properties, and generalizing about them on the basis of observed regularities. Ontologically speaking, this endeavor is *positivism*, which holds that the world consists of many things held together by many fewer sets of relations. Methodologically speaking, this is *science*, consisting of better and better explanations for what we observe, buttressed by more and better data.

Questions

As yet, nothing in this discussion challenges the epistemological consensus that has prevailed since the Enlightenment. The relationship between me, as observer, and the fire, as an objective, observable condition, is something that I and the others to whom I am speaking take for granted. I observe the fire at a specifiable distance, and my report of fire will affect the fire in a way that I or another observer can also, in principle, specify: for example, we all put the fire out. If anyone were to raise questions about my assumptions, then my belief that I can speak truly has become a matter of epistemology. I can know the truth, given certain assumptions about the world. I cannot know whether these assumptions are true, however, precisely because they are assumptions. How do I know that I am not deluded in thinking that I see the world out there? How do I know whether we have not together invented a world that exists (as a discernible whole in many parts) only in, or inseparably from, the shared meanings that we give to it? Even if my propositions about the world are true, is not the truth of the world dependent on the linguistic properties of these propositions?

The first of these questions is ageless. Many a child has asked it. Treating the question as pointless or silly, or as something for philosophers to worry about, allows us all to get on in a world that does *seem* to exist pretty much as we sense it. If we are deluded, then delusions have their advantages.

The second question challenges the naturalism that most positivists espouse. The physical world may exist more or less as we sense it, but the social world exists because we participate in it and bring our wishes to bear upon it. Detaching ourselves from the social world to observe it is something that we can only do provisionally, in a weak approximation of the requirements of science. Framing the problem this way raises the possibility that the positivists are right, after all, to insist on the unity of the physical and social worlds, but wrong to think about it in "natural" terms. Perhaps the physical world is nothing apart from what we say it means to us, and meaning is always social.

The third question is as old as the study of rhetoric, but with rhetoric out of fashion for centuries, it strikes us as the newest and most challenging. It makes language the central issue for epistemology: is truth contingent on the way we speak? Philosophers and social theorists who ask this question have taken the "linguistic turn," as they call it, and their answers helped to launch the "post" movement. One answer, "truly" radical in its implications, holds that the truth of our propositions is strictly limited to those propositions; there is no world apart from them. In effect, language can only represent itself. At best, such a position allows us to think of the world as a "text" and fosters an interest in "deconstructing" the propositions making it up to show how truths are fabricated and for whose benefit. A second answer to the question suggests that language can never represent the world completely accurately, because language is implicated in making the world it purports to represent. Such a position treats most truths as provisional and the world as a complex process of social construction. Standing back and observing this process is a useful activity, often to be undertaken with scientific rigor, but not an activity that can produce the comprehensively true picture of the world to which positivists aspire.

The Challenge of the "Post" Movement

By now the reader should be able to appreciate that IR as a social science is based upon a more or less unexamined set of assumptions, most of which define positivist science as a major undertaking of the modern world. Positivist assumptions have locked IR onto a particular point on a broad spectrum of philosophical possibilities that many scholars in the discipline might not even have been aware of. When a few scholars began to discuss these possibilities, often rather tendentiously, the tone and substance of IR debates completely changed. Having shaped realism with positivist zeal, the young radicals of an earlier generation suddenly found themselves described as reactionary disciplinary guardians—or, in keeping with our earlier imagery, as forest rangers patrolling a burned-out, desolate landscape in magnificent ignorance of the irrelevance of their vocation.

For most scholars, and certainly for the discipline's leading figures, experiencing the "post" challenge was disagreeable and often mystifying. What is one to make of the preposterous claim that none of us stand on the same "ground" when we speak of forests? The epistemological challenge to foundations made demolition of the discipline or dismissal of the challenge seem like the only possibilities. Even issues that seem thorny enough in ontological terms took a radical, epistemological turn. How do I know that you and I mean the same thing by "fire" or "war"? Is my world generally commensurable with Aristotle's, a Chinese villager's, yours? Some "post" challengers would argue that there are as many worlds as there are beholders, and that these worlds are impossible to compare or relate to each other. For most scholars, any such argument simultaneously mocks us for our delusions and demeans us as social beings. It hardly matters whether I go walking in the forest with you or with my dog. Each of us senses the world as entirely, unrecognizably different. Our only satisfaction comes from the prospect that you, I, and the dog can at least enjoy the walk, however incommensurable our reasons!

If the radical impulse of the "post" challenge brought cries of outrage from the discipline's leading figures, another predictable response also quickly made its presence felt. Perhaps the challenge could be domesticated by taking it inside the discipline and giving it a name. Since most of the challengers had made the linguistic turn, a label reflecting their preoccupation with language would seem to have been an appropriate choice. *Hermeneutics* was a good candidate. Named after Hermes, the Greek god of messengers and interpreters of messages, hermeneutics referred to a quest for the correct theological interpretation of the Bible and later to the interpretation of any text. As a name, however, it suggested a rather too specific intellectual genealogy and a too narrow concern with meaning.

Interpretive and its cognate *interpretivist* offered a better choice. Widely used in sociology, *interpretivist* attracted considerable attention in IR when Friedrich Kratochwil and John Ruggie used it in 1986 to criticize positivist assumptions. While the term itself suggests an epistemological concern with the status of the knower, Kratochwil and Ruggie's exposition was concerned more with what we know (that is, ontology) was not especially radical. For them, an interpretivist stance suits the multiplicity of meanings that complex, normatively freighted social processes inevitably engender (Kratochwil and Ruggie 1986).

Two years later, Robert Keohane used his presidential address to the International Studies Association as an occasion to pronounce on the subject. Setting on one side scholars with *rationalistic* inclinations, including himself, he thought the term *interpretive* left too much out on the other side. He proposed *reflective* instead to indicate a stress on "human reflection" (Keohane 1988, 382). It was a stroke of genius for Keohane to choose a flatteringly empty term—who wouldn't want to be thought of as reflective?—to deflect attention from the epistemological thrust of the "post" challenge. In effect, he resuscitated the earlier debate between positivists and historicists, and suggested that "reflection" is the appropriate method for historicist inquiry. Many scholars with Keohane's rationalist sensibilities adopted the term *reflectivist* to describe their "post" challengers.

Yosef Lapid (1989) offered the challengers (himself among them) a more attractive alternative. They are *post-positivists*, whom he set against positivists in what he called the "third debate." Given the ferocity of the challenge and the befuddled response to it, styling this situation a "great debate" granted the challengers a certain legitimacy. In exchange, Lapid softened the epistemological challenge by calling it *perspectivism*, skipped over ontology as such, and went on to discuss the move toward *methodological pluralism* (1989, 241–44).

The term *post-positivism* is undoubtedly better than its alternatives, including *critical* (which we criticized above). Nevertheless, the simple symmetry of the paired terms *positivism* and *post-positivism* unduly rationalizes a moment of controversy and obfuscation in the discipline's short history. In these introductory pages, we refer to the challenge of the "post" movement. We do so for convenience, and in full recognition that scholars have attached the prefix "post" to so many, diverse nouns that it captures the flavor of that turbulent moment, not to mention a continuing sense of disorientation in the discipline.

At the same time, Onuf proposed *constructivism* as a framework for social theory. Taking the linguistic turn, he settled for the second, less radical answer to the epistemological question "Is truth contingent on the way we speak?" Language is indeed implicated in the world it purports to represent. This answer implies an affirmative answer to the ontological question "Is the world something that we have invented?" He then developed an additional claim about language. We use language to represent the world to ourselves, just as we have always thought, and we use language quite deliberately to bring our representations of the world—as we think it is and as we want it to be—to bear upon that world. Language is the most powerful tool available to us for social construction as an ongoing, largely unpremeditated activity in which everyone is inevitably and perpetually engaged. Constructivism effectively leaves epistemology to the philosophers, and takes the linguistic turn back to ontology (Onuf 1989, 36–43). Onuf thus avoided choosing sides in the third debate; he dissociated himself from post-structuralism and its repudiation of foundations, while conceding that such foundations as we have may be nothing more than "the rubble of construction" (1989, 35).

Onuf's subsequent concern with modernity resembles Jürgen Habermas's in the latter's debate with the post-moderns, and Onuf's debts to Habermas are substantial. Nevertheless, Onuf does not see constructivism as a recipe for emancipation, which has always been the goal for Habermas as a critical theorist. Constructivism is normative in the sense that it takes normative phenomena—rules—as the foundation of society, but Onuf's claim that rules always result in a condition of rule has earned him criticism from scholars who believe that a post-positivist position is necessarily "critical." Onuf shares with liberal theorists (and Keohane's rationalistic positivists) an interest in the unintended consequences of individual choices and acknowledges their importance for social construction without succumbing to the ingenuous claim that a harmony of interests or balance of power is likely to result. As a label, *constructivism* conjures up an image of intentional activity on a grand scale, of concrete being poured and buildings and malls going up, or the Stalinist practice of giving out medals to those constructing the bright socialist future. Onuf shares with Marxist theorists an interest in the materials of social construction (they are never simply "raw" materials), but again without becoming a historical materialist who dismisses the importance of human agency.

If Onuf's constructivism is indeed a third way in the third debate, it is hardly the path of least resistance. Constructivism accepts the unity of nature and society, as positivists do, but does not deny society its distinctive ontological character by doing so. Instead, constructivism sees nature as irrevocably social. From a constructivist point of view, the "forest" is not so much a metaphor as a misrepresentation: the forest should never be thought of as an extensive piece of nature that is somehow "outside" society. Onuf's constructivism offers an alternative ontology, a redescription of the scenery. If we were to force the metaphor, the forest, as an ensemble of trees and much else, is everywhere, and we are always in it, making the trees and the forest what they are.

About This Book

Constructivism is a constructive response to the challenge of the "post" movement. It rejects the "slash-and-burn" extremism of some post-modern thinkers who leave nothing behind them, nowhere to stand, nothing even for themselves to say. Constructivism tries to make sense of social relations in general in order to get beyond the pointless posturing that passes for debate in a discipline that cannot even defend its claim to a distinctive subject matter called "international relations." While constructivists join the "post" movement in calling into question much of the orthodoxy of postwar IR scholarship, they reject neither empirical research nor social science as such. Instead, constructivism maintains that the sociopolitical world is constructed by human practice, and seeks to explain how this construction takes place.

Four objectives guided the contributors to this book. First, they try to make Onuf's "construction" of constructivism accessible to a broad audience that may not wish to read his technically demanding *World of Our*

Making. Onuf himself offers a comprehensive overview in simple language. Second, several of the contributors situate constructivism in the context of IR's tormented recent history, the constructivist claims of other scholars in the discipline, and recent trends in the philosophy of science. Third, several contributors explore the relevance of constructivism for empirical research and offer new ways of conceptualizing key issues of contemporary international politics. Fourth, the book concludes by considering the implications of constructivism for teaching international relations, inasmuch as teaching is itself an act of social construction.

Throughout, the contributors show that constructivism is a powerful, systematic way of thinking about social relations in general and international relations in particular. Once familiar with constructivism, few readers will continue to be comfortable with the world as portrayed in academic textbooks. More to the point, they will see themselves in a new light—as agents in a world that makes them what they are, and as agents in a world that they are responsible for making in everything that they do.

Bibliography

Adler, Emanuel. 1997. "Seizing the Middle Ground: Constructivism in World Politics." *European Journal of International Relations* 3 (September): 319–63.

Holsti, K.J. 1985. *The Dividing Discipline: Hegemony and Diversity in International Theory*. Boston: Allen & Unwin.

Keohane, Robert O. 1988. "International Institutions: Two Approaches." *International Studies Quarterly* 32 (December): 379–96.

Kratochwil, Friedrich. 1984. "Errors Have Their Advantage." *International Organization* 38 (Spring): 303–20.

——— and John Gerard Ruggie. 1986. "International Organization: A State of the Art on an Art of the State." *International Organization* 40 (Autumn): 753–75.

Lapid, Yosef. 1989. "The Third Debate: On the Prospects of International Theory in a Post-Positivist Era." *International Studies Quarterly* 33 (September): 235–54.

Onuf, Nicholas Greenwood. 1989. *World of Our Making: Rules and Rule in Social Theory and International Relations*. Columbia: University of South Carolina Press.

Singer, J. David. 1961. "The Level-of-Analysis Problem in International Relations." *World Politics* 14 (October): 77–92.

Waltz, Kenneth N. 1979. *Theory of International Politics*. Reading, MA: Addison-Wesley.

Part II
Constructivism in Context

2

The Twenty Years' Catharsis: E.H. Carr and IR

Vendulka Kubálková

This chapter is an academic mystery story with a twist: the mystery isn't just about whodunit, but about who is the victim, who was the villain, and what is the meaning of the message that was left behind? And at the heart of it all lies the question: "Who was Mr. Carr?" To start out, some background is necessary. This much we know:

Few historical personalities or philosophers can boast of adherents and disciples of all stripes, including adversaries engaged in deadly combat against each other. Edward Hallett Carr (1892–1982) is one of that small band; he has been acclaimed as one of the intellectual founders, both of the mainstream in the International Relations (IR) discipline and of the approaches of its fiercest critics. Carr has been seen as the forefather of realism and of the "post" movement, as well as a " 'proto' constructivist" who helped to develop the approach introduced in this book (Dunne 1995, 373). This means that were he alive, Carr could do a circus act at IR conferences by sitting alone at a roundtable discussing three positions at the same time. Or, was he really the victim of an academic mugging?

Carr wrote a book, published in 1939, called *The Twenty Years' Crisis 1919–1939: An Introduction to the Study of International Relations* (hereafter referred to as *Twenty Years' Crisis* and cited from the 1962 printing of the second edition). The twenty years Carr referred to was the interwar period, during which, in his view, the IR discipline took a wrong turn. One of the purposes of this chapter is to show that the "twenty years' crisis" has in fact turned out to be a crisis lasting more than sixty years and that, only now, long after his death, Carr's crisis might be ending. The past twenty years have seen, I will argue, the ultimate, cathartic, stage of that crisis. The main purpose of this chapter (apart from solving the mystery) is to place constructivism, its intellectual sources, and its origin in the context of these tumultuous twenty years to which Carr holds the key.

Who Was E.H. Carr?

In his *Twenty Years' Crisis*, Carr labeled the main approach to IR as "realism." He also coined a distinction between "realists" and "idealists" (the latter were also referred to as "utopians"). He said they were locked in a debate, known thereafter as the great debate. Scholars ever since have sought to identify something that would constitute another debate to follow in the footsteps of E.H. Carr. A few have been lucky: Hedley Bull identified the second great debate and Yosef Lapid the third debate. The third debate, still in progress, is a part of the catharsis with which this essay deals. But Carr started the idea of having "great debates." His book has been described as "the first 'scientific' treatment of modern world politics" (Hoffmann 1977, 43). To complicate the matter, however, in one of the most influential pieces anticipating the third debate, Carr was named an intellectual progenitor of a "critical approach" to IR when other, much more deserving candidates such as Habermas surprisingly did not make the cut (Cox 1981).[1] Carr received applause and eulogies from the most prominent Trotskyists (Isaac Deutscher 1955; Tamara Deutscher 1983). What are we to make of this?

Carr, the historian, made it onto the 1997 *Foreign Affairs* list of the best books of the last seventy-five years with his twelve-volume *History of Soviet Russia* (Legvold 1997, 230). Carr the journalist and publicist occasioned political controversy as one of the editorial writers of *The Times* of London, where his political views were attacked for a variety of reasons, including his being too pro-Soviet. Among the strongest critics of his political views were prominent British politicians and scholars, including the historian Hugh Trevor-Roper and Carr's co-founder of IR realism, Hans Morgenthau (Jones 1996).

Were it not for the continuation of his twenty-year crisis and had the developments of the last twenty years not taken place, the political controversy about Carr would have been long forgotten and historians of the IR discipline would not be confused about him. Until recently, the central fact of Carr's IR legacy appeared to be his role as the key figure of the realist approach. Admittedly, a number of his distinguished colleagues from the IR discipline were critical of his work and found in it minor or major defects (Morgenthau 1948; Trevor-Roper 1962; Bull 1969; K.W. Thompson et al.

1980; Fox 1985). The number of citations endorsing Carr as the founder of realism, however, far outnumbers those commenting on his various inconsistencies. Because of the increasing visibility of the approval of Carr by the "post" movement (Cox 1981, 131; Linklater 1990, 7; Booth 1991; Linklater 1992; Howe 1994; Jones 1996; Linklater 1997), the "paternity" issue will have to be addressed and realists will have to decide whether they still want to claim him as a founding father.

The paradox is that Carr is now praised and celebrated for what earlier were regarded as serious defects. Errors in his judgment were not accidental but "rooted in a more fundamental weakness in his political philosophy" (K.W. Thompson et al. 1980, 77). In sharp contrast to this view, a critical writer asserts that Carr's "reputation for Realism . . . served to distort [his] relevance to contemporary debates" (Linklater 1997, 321). While earlier such labels were derogatory, they are now flattering and it is a compliment when Carr is called a "utopian realist" (Howe 1994) or an "ambivalent realist" (Jones 1996). In a book on "post-realism," Carr is used as an example of a major IR figure who took what the authors call a "rhetorical turn" (Beer & Hariman 1996). Whatever that might mean exactly, the drift of the detailed "post-realist" rhetorical deconstruction of his texts concludes that Carr played games with his readership and, in a subtle use of rhetorical contradictory statements, tried to please, tease, or fool everybody. While this explanation might go some way to explain the attitude of the IR discipline toward Carr, it seems to be a bit of a stretch to impute to Carr a Machiavellian genius that connived to deceive the discipline on a gigantic scale. Besides, even if he had had the means and opportunity to do this, what would the motive have been?

The Overlooked Clue?

Carr agrees with Lord Acton, who said that "few discoveries are more irritating than those which expose the pedigree of ideas" (Carr 1962, 71). Perhaps Carr did not mind the misunderstanding. But there is, in my view, a much less sophisticated, much simpler reading of Carr, which to a considerable extent reconciles the seeming contradiction of Carr's *Twenty Years' Crisis*. In formal logic, A and non-A cannot be true at the same time. Therefore, a realist could not at the same time be an antirealist or an idealist. However, there is a form of thought called dialectics and in dialectical logic a realist could be a nonrealist. Perhaps then Carr was a dialectician. One of the important members of the "post" movement in Australia, Jim George, briefly noted Carr's dialectical inclinations but did not think Carr was consistent even at that (George 1994, 78). I will argue that Carr *was* a dialectician.

Carr's *Twenty Years' Crisis* reveals a strong influence of Marx's thought as modified by Engels and Lenin, particularly his use of the concept of dialectics. If his *Twenty Years' Crisis* is reread with an understanding of dialectics, it becomes clear that, far from being playful or conniving, intellectually dishonest, sloppy, or inconsistent, Carr was simply using dialectical reasoning. It is easily recognizable by anybody familiar with the concept of dialectics of the genre of Soviet Marxist-Leninist textbooks. Over the years only a few IR authors noted Carr's thinking as a rather puzzling, mild case of Marxism. Carr has been referred to as a "Marxist of sorts" and "a Marxist-realist" (Brown 1992, 25, 69). Carr's Marxism is clearly non-Marxist Marxism "Westernized" by Carr himself with no help from the "Western Marxists." Carr's nonrelationship with Western Marxists is an important reason why the Marxist elements in his thought have been overlooked. But the Western Marxists have played an important role in the emergence of the IR "post" movement. Again, it is curious to note that some of his contemporary admirers believe that Carr did parallel or anticipate Western Marxists or post-Marxists, Habermas, and Foucault (Linklater 1997).

"Western Marxists," initially the Hungarian Georg Lukacs (1885–1971), the German Karl Korsch (1886–1961), and the Russian Leon Trotsky (1879–1940), were so named by Maurice Merleau-Ponty (1905–1961) exactly so as not to be mistaken for the Soviet version of Marxism-Leninism. The term *Western Marxism* normally refers also to the Italian Antonio Gramsci (1891–1937) and the German Frankfurt School. I refer to them by nationalities to explain the contemporary custom of referring to them also as "Continental European." By the mid-1930s, the Western Marxists were united in their rejection of the Soviet Union's practice and theory. Despite disclaimers that they had nothing to do with the Soviet Union, the members of the famous German Frankfurt School, undoubtedly the most influential center of Western Marxism in this century, adopted in 1937 the term *critical* as a code word for Marxism, so as not to use the term *Marxism*. Even so, the entire school had to flee to the United States from the anti-communist and anti-Semitic Hitler Germany. Carr wrote his *Twenty Years' Crisis* only a couple years later, in the United Kingdom There is no visible connection between Carr and Western Marxists. On the contrary, Carr's sort of Marxism is very different from the distinct form of Western Marxism already established at the time.

Western Marxists, influenced not only by Marx but by many other thinkers, changed their writing style to an idiom of tremendous technical difficulty, accessible only to fellow academics. Since then, Western Marxism has stayed in the hands of academics and the difficult idiom has become a characteristic feature of social sciences generally. Carr refers disapprovingly to academics without practical experience as "armchair students of international politics" (1962, 38), using exactly the same words as did Lenin.

Carr's style does not suffer from the opacity of prose of Western Marxism. It is more reminiscent of the Soviet version of Marxism, which met with an opposite fate. As can be seen from the standard textbooks of Marxism-Leninism from which the populace was taught at school and in refresher courses throughout their adulthood, Soviets made out of Marxism a fairy tale in which the good characters always won over the bad characters. It was accessible and understandable to all and for many decades was highly attractive in its promises and its comforting moral justifications. In the gigantic experiment of social construction, Marxist-Leninist textbooks were published in millions of copies across the Soviet empire, achieving a circulation second only to the Bible.

If anything, Carr's prose and his definition of realism and idealism have been found too simple (Brown 1992, 25). If we reread Carr's *Twenty Years' Crisis* with the help of dialectics, we get a different picture and a different message altogether. The message becomes more complex once we realize that he related realism *dialectically* to idealism. We can then see that Carr strongly advocated realism, but as a transition, a station on the way. IR scholars of the postwar period generally missed this point, which is hardly surprising since the discipline was already permanently embedded in realism, like a fly in amber. Only in the last decade has the discipline had to reopen itself enough to reconsider its historical legacy and the true views of its father figure.

A Case of Mistaken Identity?

There are many telltale signs of Carr's exposure to some sort of Marxism. Carr approvingly quotes Marxist classics and even includes Marx among key representatives of "modern realism" (1962, 65). Marx did write extensively about the foreign policy of his time, but Carr is not referring to Marx in that sense. Carr does not talk about revolutions, class struggles, and the proletariat. Nor is he an economic determinist. Carr, however, uses dialectics, at the minimum to organize his thinking and to organize his argument. The celebrated passages of his rejection of utopianism constitute much less than half of the story contained in Carr's book. I will briefly overview some key elements of Carr's reasoning and concepts such as dialectics, not only as they relate to Carr, but as a useful introduction in simple terms to the language required for the understanding of the "post" movement.

The Mysterious Formula

Dialectics has a quite respectable, if limited, place in Western philosophy; its progenitors include not only Marx, Engels, and Lenin, but also Aristotle, Heraclitus, and Hegel. American Marxist Bertell Ollman uses it as the key concept of his version of Marxism, and Hayward Alker, who is by no means a Marxist, defines *dialectics* as one of the three approaches to IR (Alker and Biersteker 1984). Alker alone published a number of pieces about the application of dialectics to IR with a large cooperative project in progress dealing with the subject of dialectics (Alker 1981, 1982, 1996). Dialectical thinking is not unheard of in Western sociology (Ritzer 1983). Dialectics has been used in mathematical modeling (Mitroff and Mason 1982 and Rescher 1977).

Using dialectics alone does not make one into a Marxist. The choice of dialectics simply indicates a rejection of the monocausal approach and the notion of unilinear development in favor of the dynamic, multicausal, and multidirectional. Where a liberal thinker sees harmony as the normal state of affairs and views conflict as a deviation; for a dialectician it is the other way around. Dialecticians regard conflict as normal and harmony as only temporary. (Soviets referred to détente as *peredyshka*, meaning "breathing space," between stretches of peaceful coexistence which had little to do with peace.) Preoccupied with conflict and contradiction, those applying the dialectical method seek to understand change through a study of the past and the present that establishes a connection between future developments and the present. Dialecticians therefore study history and look for change over time. Dialectics sees things as inevitably interconnected and interdependent. Dialecticians are by definition holistic in their approach, arguing that events cannot be torn out of context. Dialecticians never see cause and effect as isolated, but perceive reciprocal causalities in which both events and processes exert influence and are influenced by each other. In other words, dialecticians believe that each part influences the whole just as much as the whole influences each individual part. Dialecticians see things and processes in a state of constant flux and change.

Dialecticians think in terms of related pairs of concepts; let us say A and B, where these pairs are construed in a binary thesis-antithesis way. A is in a causal relation to B, but the relation is reciprocated since B is also in a causal relation to A. Realism and utopianism, or idealism, in Carr's book are in this relationship. The tension leads to a resolution which contains both A and B in a transcended form in a resulting synthesis. The synthesis in turn becomes a thesis in contradiction to an antithesis, and so the process goes not in a straight line but—as it were—on a spiral. It then follows that if A and B are in a dialectical contradiction, then B could not simply vanish leaving A intact. Nothing remains intact. Everything is in some sort of dialectical relationship. So A cannot be separated permanently from B or B from A. Such an outcome is not conceivable, nor would it represent a resolution of the contradiction. Dialectics can represent an *ontological* position, finding mutually contradictory relationships between things and processes "out there," in the world and history. The standard Soviet textbooks used Friedrich Engels's (1820–1895) butterflies cavorting in the butterfly mating season to convey the point. The mating of the first butterfly ("thesis") with the second ("antithesis") gives rise to thousands of butterflies.

Dialectics, however, need not be fatuous. Apart from its ontological claims, dialectics can be used also as an *epistemological* theory concerning the nature of knowledge of the material world. It can also be used as a *method*, a tool whose understanding advances the quest for truth and knowledge. In what Marx's closest friend and coauthor, Engels, called dialectical materialism (which means in ordinary language simply "Marxist philosophy"), dialectics has both ontological and epistemological substance. Both the material world and the human mind are believed to follow dialectical rules. This is important for our argument. Marx conceives of man as a "real, active man." Cognitive action is material and practical, and thus knowledge is not merely a cognitive reflection upon an external world, but becomes the means for shaping, constructing, and changing reality. To simplify it even further, formulating thoughts, analyzing, because it is going on in one's mind and the mind is a part of the world, means that, as the thought is formulated, the world undergoes a change. Thus thinking is doing, making or changing the world. Theory fuses with practice, values with facts, and man in his thinking alters the world. Or, as Carr put it, "in the process of analyzing the facts, Marx altered them" (1962, 4). Carr hints here at Marx's notorious *Eleventh Thesis on Feuerbach*, so well known in certain circles that he did not need even to cite it. And Carr adds, "Nor is it only the thinking of professional or qualified students of politics which constitutes a political fact" (41).

Deciphering Carr

Like the thinking of a contemporary IR dialectician, Professor Hayward Alker, who spells out the relationship more clearly (1981, 1982), Carr's understanding is based on perceiving the effect of one party to a contradiction interpenetrating the other in such a way that the original distinguishing features of both parts of the contradiction are blurred. To Carr what was wrong with idealism is that it developed without realism. Realism is the necessary corrective to the "exuberance of utopianism, just as in other periods, utopianism must be invoked to counteract the barrenness of realism. Immature thought is predominantly purposive and utopian. Thought which rejects purpose is the thought of old age. . . . Utopia and reality are thus the two facets of political science. Sound political thought and sound political life will be found only where both have their place" (1962, 10). Or, more bluntly, "the characteristic vice of the utopian is naivety; of the realist, sterility" (12). By that logic, having suppressed much of what Carr would call idealist thought, the IR discipline, until recently, has been geriatric and sterile.

Carr's whole book is based upon a series of dialectically related pairs of concepts, like realism and idealism. Parallel to realism and idealism, Carr construes a chain of binary dialectical relationships. The point is the parallel construction: A and B, C and D, and X and Z. There is a link between the first of the pairs, A, C, X, on the one hand, and the second of the pairs B, D, Z, on the other hand. Carr calls these "antitheses" and argues that "these antitheses reproduce themselves in different forms." As he puts it, the "most fundamental utopia-reality antithesis is rooted in a different conception of the relationship of politics and ethics, the world of value and the world of nature, purpose and fact" (1962, 20–21). Other than this sequence that leads to the utopian-realist distinction, he sees the same theme, as it were, metamorphosed into relationships between theory and practice, voluntarism and determinism, Left and Right, intellectual and practitioner (bureaucrat), radical and conservative, ideals and institutions, immature and old, inexperienced and experienced, and many others. He links theory, voluntarism, Left, intellectual, radical, ideals, immature, inexperienced. He links practice, determinism, Right, bureaucrat, conservative, institutions, old, experienced.

The Message: "It Is All in E.H. Carr"

Carr's impressions of the nascent IR discipline were derived from his experience with it in the late 1930s. He did not know either structural realism or logical positivism and empiricism in their full-blown forms in IR. However, the current philosophical debates in the IR discipline would appear to him long overdue and trivial. The essence of the last twenty years could be summarized as idealism-utopianism correcting realism and thus man and his mind being returned to the world and to the theory now cleansed of its positivist distortions. Neither realism nor idealism would be the outcome of this process. One of the leading contemporary British critical IR theorists, an admirer of Carr, suggests that

Carr himself provides "outlines of the third way" (Linklater 1997, 323). Carr was neither realist nor idealist.

Thus, just as realists maintain about their wisdom that "it is all in Thucydides," it can be claimed with even greater justification that, as far as the current debate is concerned, "it is all in E.H. Carr." Carr anticipates an application of the dialectical approach to IR. Carr champions intellectual pluralism. Carr anticipated the creation of the International Political Economy. Having had a go at both practice (as a diplomat and journalist) and theory (as a professor of IR in Aberystwyth and a Cambridge University Fellow), Carr calls for more stress on policy relevance of theoretical efforts. Carr strongly urges an inclusion of Leftist thought in any academic pursuit. "The Right is weak in theory and suffers through its inaccessibility to ideas," while the Left suffers from a lack of practical experience and a failure "to translate its theory into practice." However, he says, "the intellectual superiority of the Left is seldom in doubt. The Left alone thinks out principles of political action and evolves ideals for statesmen to aim at" (1962, 19). If it would be too early to describe Carr as postpositivist, then he is certainly antipositivist. For Carr, positivism in the form he knew in the 1930s was unacceptable, mainly because of the disagreement he would have with the totally nondialectical separation of man and nature as subject and object, and treating social phenomena as if they were natural phenomena. As he put it, "By an easy analogy, the Newtonian principles were applied to the ethical problems . . . once these laws were determined, human beings would conform to them just as matter conformed to the physical laws of nature." In natural sciences "facts exist independently of what anyone thinks of them. In the political sciences, which are concerned with human behavior, there are no such facts. The investigator is inspired by the desire to cure some ill of the body politic" (22). "The purpose is not, as in the physical sciences, irrelevant to the investigation and separable from it; it is itself one of the facts" (3–4). Theory, says Carr, is for a purpose. R.W. Cox, another of the contemporary critical theorists of IR, became celebrated for saying something very similar fifty years after Carr (Cox 1981, 128). Carr distinguishes three interdependent categories of "political power in the international sphere": "military, economic and over opinion" (108). No doubt the members of the "post" movement will cringe at the suggestion, but it can be argued that the main and lasting contribution of the "post" movement is to be found in the attention it has drawn precisely to what perhaps Carr clumsily calls "power over opinion." The "post" movement has shifted IR concerns to include the fundamental human mental processes of people, both IR theorists and states, which are made of people.

The Missing Pieces

In very simple terms Carr alluded to central philosophical issues debated in
the field of IR today. In a variety of esoteric ways and in a technically
difficult idiom they became catapulted into prominence in the social sciences and, in the last twenty years, also in the discipline of International
Relations.

But what do these questions have to do with the affairs of states and
statecraft? As we argued in the introduction, the answer is, in the view of
the "post" movement (and also of Carr), a great deal. The "post" movement
does not pick an argument about specific issues and international relations
per se. Instead, the targets of criticism are the philosophical foundation of
how, in the IR discipline, the world is viewed; how what we call knowledge
is put together; and for what purpose that knowledge is used. All of the
strands of the "post" movement have in common an assertion that the
philosophical foundations of IR lead to misinterpretation and misrepresentation of the world including international relations. In that view, not only
did IR get stuck at a stage of permanent realism; it is also based on a
fundamentally flawed understanding of the relationship between man and
the world—"reality"—in the usual parlance. Some, of course, argue that it
is deliberate. This is where the argument begins to be too difficult to simplify, but the points that the "post" movement makes are too important to
set them aside just because they are made in a difficult language.

Did Waltz Do It?

None of this was ever considered of any relevance to the IR discipline. Why
and how did the situation change, and how did these topics get introduced?
In the IR discipline there was an increasing dissatisfaction with the positivist portrayal of reality as reflected in man's mind in an "objective" way. The
positivism of this position has been further compounded in the work of
Kenneth Waltz, particularly in his book *Theory of International Politics*
(published in 1979) but circulating around through the earlier publications
of its parts (Waltz 1979; Waltz in Polsby and Greenstein 1975). If previously positivism was objected to because of its disregard for the human
mind under the guise of objectivity, then Waltz's new theory of realism, to
be known as "neorealism" or "structural realism," made this characterization even more valid. Waltz added a component of structuralism to positivism. It has been this particular mix of positivism and structuralism added to
realism that has stirred a more effective opposition to realism in IR than
ever before. In my view, it also set off the processes I describe as catharsis

and the creation of the "post" movement. To make at least a dent on the new form of what appeared to be indestructible realism, IR authors started wheeling into IR studies intellectual weaponry of the Left from all over humanities and social sciences, and the "post" movement came into existence.

Structuralism was nothing new. It had been used in different fields many times before. The term refers to a distinct approach to social phenomena. As its critics claim, structuralism pushes man even further out of the picture. Man is lost as "systems and subsystems, elements and structures are drilled up and down the pages [of history] pretending to be people" (Ashley 1984, 226–27, quoting E.P. Thompson 1978). Structuralists assert that only by looking into that which is hidden and underpins the apparent can we reach beyond the study of self-conceptions and motives of individuals (or individual entities such as states). Structuralists look for a structure and structural forces because they believe that individuals, or in this case, states, are constrained by structural forces over which they have no control. Structuralism, in other words, sharpens some of the features of positivism.

It is worth mentioning that the line cited above about structures being drilled into the pages of history was a quotation used by an IR scholar to attack the structuralism of Waltz. Characteristically, however, this scholar borrowed it, together with the overall argument, from an attack on a structural Marxist. The early pieces of this genre were characterized by extremely eclectic borrowing, in which Ashley typically spends page after page explaining at length to the IR audience concepts quite well known elsewhere.

Kuhn as an Accomplice

Waltz was by no means solely responsible for the turmoil in the discipline. He had a helper named Thomas Kuhn. Kuhn himself did nothing, but his slim volume (Kuhn 1970), not even intended for the IR discipline or social sciences, played a role. His concept of "paradigm" was enthusiastically used in the IR discipline. Why would that make any difference?

Because of the way the IR discipline has been constituted, it has proved extraordinarily difficult to challenge the reigning approach. When the concept of paradigm was introduced to the IR discipline, a subtle terminological substitution took place. IR scholars talked suddenly not about "theories" or "approaches" but about "paradigms," a term that Kuhn used. They did not always explain what was the difference in this terminology, giving an impression that the three terms are more or less synonymous, and many scholars in fact used them interchangeably.

Kuhn's concept of paradigm, however, has a very special meaning. Kuhn wrote about physics and not about social sciences but—as in the case of Carr—it is what was made of Kuhn rather than what he himself said that was important. The slow arrival of the concept of paradigm and IR as "paradigmatic discipline" is fascinating to follow in a sequence of writing spanning more than a decade (Phillips 1974; Inkeles 1975; Lijphart 1981; Banks 1978; Rosenau 1979; Pettman 1981; Alker and Biersteker 1984; Holsti 1985; Banks 1985).

Those IR scholars impatient with realism and its staying power obviously found solace in the use of the term. There were several very attractive points about the concept of paradigm, which undoubtedly explains why IR discipline so enthusiastically embraced Kuhnian analysis: first, the content of the term *paradigm* runs counter to the basic premises of positivism. Thus as soon as the term is used, those that understand its meaning know that an attack on positivism and its belief in the value-free nature of knowledge is taking place. Second, according to Kuhn, the term *paradigm* conveys that any theoretical effort is only of temporary nature. Thus there can be no continuity of knowledge but instead a succession of paradigms offering different ways of viewing the world. Third, since there is an element of contingency in the creation of a paradigm (via consensus in the discipline), additional doubt is cast on the proclaimed goal of an objective search for truth. Fourth, thus knowledge on which paradigms are based is not regarded as certain, but as fallible and open to refutation. Fifth, hence the apparent monopoly of one approach in the discipline is taken into question. Sixth, out goes the axiom that realist knowledge has been accumulating since Thucydides. And finally, since it is reasonable to anticipate the demise of any paradigm, that of realism and positivism shall one day also pass. The use of the expression *interparadigmatic* for IR simply institutionalized an acceptance of a plurality of approaches as the discipline's feature, if a replacement of a paradigm turned out to be out of reach. The door was left ajar for an introduction of influences unheard of in the discipline before.

Carr: "Power Over Opinion"

Cox quoted mainly Gramsci, and Ashley quoted Habermas and Foucault, authors who did not write specifically on the subjects of international relations. In fact, Foucault's work ranges from such unlikely subjects as prison systems and psychiatry to the history of sexuality. The Italian communist Gramsci also seems to be an unlikely candidate for extension to IR. He wrote his major work in a fascist jail pondering the failure of Marxist strategies in Western Europe in the aftermath of World War I. Both his concerns and those of the German Frankfurt School, either in Germany or in exile in the United States, would appear to be far removed from anything remotely relevant. How could Ashley, Cox, or any of the later scholars working in this genre stretch any of these apparently unrelated ideas to international relations?

Except in the new Soviet Union, the dream of a revolution was quashed. Only in Soviet Russia was there a likelihood of man "constructing reality" in his image as envisaged by Marx in his concept of praxis. The first generation of Marx's heirs had different concerns to address: namely, why the fiasco of Bolshevik-style revolutions everywhere other than in the Soviet Union and, generally, why a permanent retreat and pessimism were warranted in contrast with the optimism of Marx. Both Gramsci and particularly the contemporary German critical sociologist Jürgen Habermas turned their attention to the pathology of Western societies and the pathology of the human mind, problems that Marx envisaged would be swept away in what he wrongly predicted to be forthcoming revolutions.

When we examine Gramsci's concept of hegemony, Habermas's knowledge of constitutive interests, and even post-structuralist, post-Marxist Foucault's idea of power-knowledge and discourse, Carr's idea of "power over opinion" comes to mind. Carr's concept sounds primitive compared to the sophisticated conceptualizations of contemporary social science. His concept, however, resonates with the image of the ideas conveyed in the more sophisticated terminology: the world of distorted social construction designed to subordinate, dominate, and oppress under the veil of positivist philosophies that present it as objectively given. Overt coercion need not be resorted to; full consensus and cooperation of the population is achieved, ironically without so much as a murmur of protest from the targets of oppression and domination. This feat is accomplished not by overt military or economic power, the two forms of power Carr identifies in the finale of his dialectical reasoning. It is accomplished through the third form of power, which Carr calls "power over opinion." To Gramsci and his followers, and to those that espouse the critical approach, this situation is still reversible: to Gramsci by means of revolution; to the critical school by means of what they call emancipation. For post-structuralists and post-modernists, there seems to be no way out.

All approaches of the "post" movement see the societies of the twentieth century as based on social construction, though the particular labels attached to the idea may vary. Although the movement is eclectic, its originality and creativity lie in applying the borrowed concepts to international relations. To understand just how difficult this "stretch" might be, let me briefly summarize some of the main concepts before they were introduced in a duly "internationalized" form to IR.

Gramsci argued that the defeat of the Marxist revolution in Western Europe in the early 1920s and its victory in the Soviet Union were due to different stages of development of the respective societies. In the Western societies it was not possible to replicate the Bolshevik success and violently overthrow governments as it was done in 1917 in Russia and tried with disastrous results in Hungary, Slovakia, and the Weimar Republic. Over-throwing government would only show that the state was but "an outer ditch" within which lay "civil society." *Civil society* in the Gramscian sense (the same term used with different meanings in other social sciences) con-sists of people—those that are subject to oppression and domination above all. Civil society is a social construction designed in such a way that the oppression is disguised and is made easy with the active participation of its victims. By a skillful use of cultural and ideological instruments which Gramsci called *hegemony* (again used in a different sense in the IR discipl-ine) the society at large was deflected from its true path and—not to put a fine point on it—fooled. The only strategy for overthrowing the "hege-monic" rule proposed by Gramsci was to devise a "counterhegemony" that would use the same method as "hegemony": construction and manipulation of a consensus in society. European Eurocommunism, inspired by this idea, cooperated with any available group of the civil society, including the Church, as a part of its counterhegemonic strategy. I argued elsewhere that Gorbachev's "new thinking" had distinct features of Gramscian coun-terhegemony, a point confirmed by the heightened interest in Western Marxist and radical thought at the time by Gorbachev and his appeal to Western civil societies (Kubálková and Cruickshank 1989b).

None of these strategies worked. Beyond this point social construction has ceased to be a romanticist celebration of man's creativity. It is now creativity perverted, an indictment of man as a social being, man divided and bent on ruthless domination of whomever he can through the clever construction of knowledge, consciousness, and manipulation of minds.

There are variations and subtleties in different sources, but the theme remains the same: how could this giant fraud have been gotten away with? The answer is consistent with Carr's phrase: by exercising "power over opinion" in a much more profound way than the propaganda that Carr refers to. In 1939, when he wrote his *Twenty Years' Crisis*, the major Western Marxist, post-Marxist, and post-structuralist and critical works were still to be written. None of the other more subtle ways of expressing "power over opinion" were in circulation. However, in their work Western Marxists now focus on this general direction: namely, on stripping the facade of objectivity and analysis of how and in whose interests and for whose purpose the twenti-eth-century Western social world has been constructed. To those few critical theorists, in IR and outside, who still believe in *emancipation*, the term often means no more than a full realization and understanding of the oppressive nature of the social construction of societies in this century. The corollary of unveiling the pathologies of contemporary societies is an absolute denial that anything to do with social reality, or any of its representations or theories, can ever be objective. Theory is always constructed for someone, and for someone's purpose. As Carr says, "Purpose, whether we are conscious of it or not, is a condition of thought; and thinking for thinking's sake is as abnormal and barren as the miser's accumulation of money for its own sake" (1962, 3–4). Or, in Habermas, class domination takes place through the medium of distorted ideologies. In his theory of distorted communication, Habermas alleges that those that are subjugated are encouraged to subordinate their interests to those representing the social order, whose injustices remain hidden and repressed. They are hidden behind the veil of objectivity, objective science, appeal to the common good, the nation, and so on.

A similar theme appears through the work inspired by structuralist theories of linguistics and post-structuralist theories. Language has now broken loose from reality and become autonomous (Callinicos 1983, 25). The "power over opinion" of Carr reaches another height. Foucault's *episteme* (his parallel to Vanguihelm's, Bachelard's, and Althusser's *problematique*, to Kuhn's *paradigm*, and to Lakatos's *research program*) is in fact an autonomous theoretical structure determining how we perceive the world and how we identify and organize its elements. To put it more simply, we see the world through lenses artificially implanted in our eyes that we do not even know we have. Foucault now studies not how we know what we know, but how these lenses are distorting our vision and how they were inserted into our eyes. Foucault's antiepistemology, his archaeology of knowledge, unlike epistemology, now tries to determine the conditions that permit (or require) certain statements to be uttered and to exclude the utterance of others (Callinicos 1983, 100). This way of thinking culminates in Foucault's concept of power-knowledge and discourse. Not only is the relationship between reality and knowledge suspended, but the pursuit of knowledge and truth is rendered impossible, because knowledge is inseparably wedded to power. Statements, the constituent elements of what Foucault calls "discourses," do not derive at all from objective reality, but are constructed on the basis of power-relations. There is, in fact, no power without the correlative constitution of a field of knowledge; nor, conversely, is there any knowledge that does not presuppose or constitute at one and the same time power-relations (Foucault 1977, 27–28).

This line of reasoning reaches even further when we come to those scholars who, like Gadamer, believe that the world is created by words. We have now moved to the last stop, the post-modernists. The language is, in the hands of post-modernists, reduced only to text. The real world is constituted like a text because one can only refer to interpretative experience. Attention turns to time and space and their suffocating effect. As Anderson describes Derrida's work,

> Derrida often evades comprehension. But this is part of the point he wants to get us to see. Clarity is not the only virtue in writing, and at times it may even be a disadvantage since clarity of expression and ease of comprehension encourage the belief that language is under control. . . . [He] also refuses to be bound by the conventions of normal academic reading. He is determined to challenge our expectations and so highlight what we do when we give text a reading. (1986, 120)

To Derrida no accurate representation of reality in thought is possible. "Modes of writing," interpretations, and the textual interplay refer to mutually constitutive relations between different interpretations in the representation and constitution of the world. This conclusion is uncovered through *deconstruction*—an interpretive technique aimed at a radical unsettling of stable concepts. The author of the text is dead. If the era of modernity is connected firmly to man, then it is possible to agree with post-modernists that modernity built around man has come to an end.

The Historiography of the Last Twenty Years in the IR Discipline

These thoughts, duly applied to international relations, have been introduced to the IR discipline in the course of the last twenty years. There are certain milestones that suggest stages of this period. Roughly I see two stages: 1977–1987 and from 1987 on. I take for the starting point approximately the year 1986. Many important books and articles were published around that year. In 1977 R.O. Keohane and J.S. Nye staged an unsuccessful coup intended to unseat the dominant realist approach. Their book, *Power and Interdependence: World Politics in Transition*, according to some reviewers, was to become the new Bible, replacing in that role Hans Morgenthau's *Politics Among Nations* (1948) and, as the title suggests, replacing a concept of "power" with "interdependence." In that same year (1977) Stanley Hoffmann published his "An American Social Science: International Relations" article in *Daedalus*, chastising IR discipline in the United States for excessive parochialism and isolationism and warning that the discipline will decay if certain changes are not adopted. Also published in 1977 was a codification of the English School wisdom in Hedley Bull's *Anarchical Society*. Also in 1977, Robert Tucker's *International Inequality* was an eloquent response and rebuttal to the neo-Marxist and radical liberal theories of imperialism and dependency on behalf of mainstream realism. Most important, however, as mentioned earlier, Kenneth Waltz published his *Theory of International Politics*. Although that book came out in 1979, an earlier version of the theory was published as a chapter in an edited volume in 1975 (Polsby and Greenstein 1975).

The watershed separating the two stages of the last twenty years is around the years 1986–87, the naming of the new approaches that we refer to as the "post" movement (Kratochwil and Ruggie 1986; Keohane 1988; and Lapid 1989).The "nameless" first stage then was over. It is interesting that the two prominent founders of the "post" movement, Cox (1981) and Ashley (1984), returned the favor and coined two names for Waltz's approach: "neorealism" and "structural realism." Both labels have stuck. Though the two articles naming Waltz's approach were published in 1981 and 1984, respectively, they reached a wider audience when they were reprinted in an edited volume by R.O. Keohane entitled *Neorealism and Its Critics* and published in 1986. Ashley and Cox were now granted a "status of critics."

The Pedigree

When we add the main intellectual sources that have come to play in assisting the formation of the "post" movement and put them into one family tree, we get a pedigree more impressive than any European royal house or racehorse can boast (Figure 2.1).

Figure 2.1 is divided into four horizontal rows, numbered 1–4. The philosophical lineage of the mainstream IR literature (and what is called *realist* and *pluralist* approaches) is at the top, in row 1. To realists and pluralists most classifications of approaches add *globalists*, whose roots come from row 4. The lineage of the two bottom rows of the figure, namely the determinist and nondeterminist and post-Marxist rows 3 and 4, are consistent not only with Perry Anderson's magisterial accounts of the Left's intellectual history (Anderson 1976, 1983) but with a similarly construed pedigree of Leftist sociology (Burawoy 1982, S5ff.). Figure 2.1 shows the contemporary divisions and currents as they can be traced along approximately horizontal lines. For lack of space, not all names that ought to be are included. The figure is intended to show how difficult it is to attach labels. If the cross-referencing and influences were to be marked with arrows, the page would be black and illegible. As Perry Anderson once put it, lateral bourgeois influences make Marx just one of the names among others. The

Figure 2.1

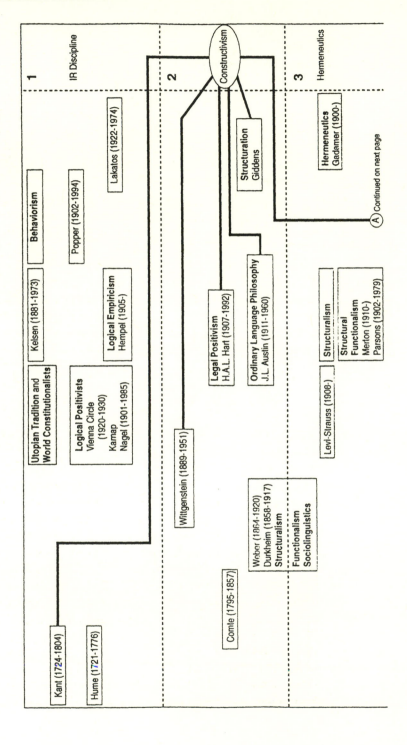

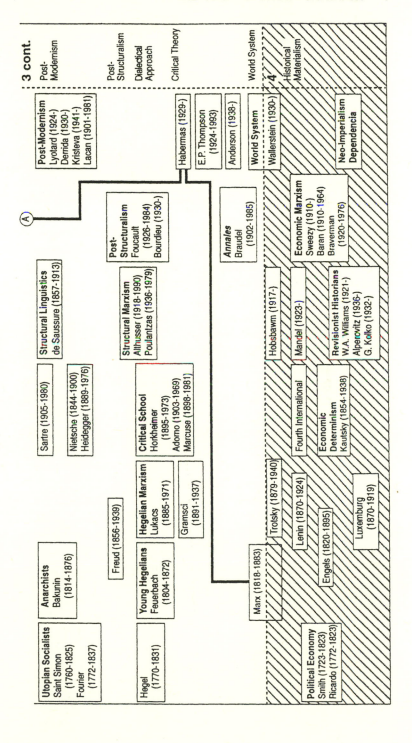

influence of Croce on Gramsci; of Weber on Lukacs; of Freud, Schopenhauer, Nietzsche, Dilthey, and Bergson on the Frankfurt School, of the French School of *Annales* on Wallerstein; and of the various structuralists on Marxist French structuralists and post-structuralists has been as potent an influence as has been the Marxian (Anderson Perry 1976).

Looking at Figure 2.1 from the bottom up, one notes, first of all, the shaded area of economic determinism (row 4). This is the familiar Marxist legacy. Many IR scholars are unaware of any other school of thought that might be derivative from Marxism other than "economic determinism." The "globalist" approach referred to in most IR textbooks originates from these sources. Among those listed in this row, there is the North American school of the *Monthly Review*, of Baran and Sweezy in particular, to whose contribution we owe to a large extent the renaissance of classical theories of imperialism and the impetus for the development of dependency theories. Wallerstein's more recent analysis of the world capitalist system has well-documented affinities with this school.

Second, there are the American "revisionist" historians associated with the University of Wisconsin and journals such as *Studies on the Left* (and later with *Socialist Revolution* and *Socialist Review*): W.A. Williams, G. Kolko, G. Alperovitz, and others. They are important for their persistent argument that the Cold War was constructed by the United States. Finally, there is the Trotskyist tradition as perpetuated in works of high scholarly value by such prominent Leftist writers as British historian E. Hobsbawm and Belgian economist Ernst Mandel. The Trotskyist tradition, as David MacLellan has pointed out, was extremely important until recently, since it was the dominant form of Marxism in English-speaking countries (MacLellan 1979, 308) and was an obvious influence on more authors than would admit to it, including I. Wallerstein.

Above the shaded band, there is row 3, which begins with historical sociologists who gave up or subdued the economic determinist inclinations under the influence of the French School of *Annales* or Max Weber. Generally speaking, above the shaded band we enter what to many international relations specialists have been until recently, areas that they never connected to Marxism: Referred to as Hegelian Marxism, this is a tradition that has held sway over continental (Western) Europe and that only recently has found its way to Britain and the United States, displacing there Trotskyist influences. As I mentioned in discussing the changes in emphasis of the contemporary Marxists, Hegelian Marxism is virtually freed from such concerns as economic substructure, political economy, and the historical materialist method. Here are the origins of a "nondeterministic" Marxism characteristic of this century. Hegelian Marxists still explore society as a complex network of social relations and material interests, and insist that none of these can be understood in isolation from the others, but that ideas play an increasingly important role.

The beginnings of the tradition of Hegelian Marxism in this century are associated with the work in particular of (Hungarian) Georg Lukacs, (German) Karl Korsch, and (Italian) Antonio Gramsci. Into the same Hegelian tradition falls the work of members of the German Frankfurt School, such as Horkheimer, Benjamin, Adorno, and Marcuse, and later the work of Jürgen Habermas. Their work is known as critical theory or sociology. The work of the late E.P. Thompson, the major figure of the British and European peace movement, has recognizable affinities with some of the themes of German critical theory.

I list Gadamer on behalf of hermeneutics as a significant influence on Habermas in particular. I list structural functionalism because of its influence on both French Marxism and "post-Marxism" as well as on the dependency theory. I list the work of French structuralists Althusser and Poulantzas only for the sake of completeness. With the tragic departure from the scene of the main protagonists of the approach (after Poulantzas's suicide and Althusser's death in a mental asylum) we are left mainly with many of their terminological innovations and terms that have become a part of scholarly language with no heed to their initial meaning, such as *problematique, conjecture,*[2] and many other terms. It is interesting that nobody has tried to explore the contribution of the exceptionally talented Nicos Poulantzas, who in fact wrote quite explicitly on international relations.

It is the post-structuralists such as Foucault and Bourdieu who appear to have attracted considerable attention. They are not only post-structuralist but also "post-Marxist." As I mentioned, the critical sociologist Jürgen Habermas maintains that post-structuralists and anyone beyond them, that is, post modernists, have nothing to do with Marxism. It has been noted, however, that, despite these protestations, Habermas and Foucault reach strikingly similar conclusions.

With the exception of Max Weber, the area into which we enter next (row 2 in Figure 2.1) will likely be as alien to IR scholars as the ones we have already explored. There are the late 1940s Oxford analytical philosophers H.A.L. Hart and J.L. Austin. The former played a major role in the transformation of the philosophy of law and the latter was a key influence on the later development of "linguistic philosophy." Ludwig Wittgenstein is the giant of philosophy in this century. He has a connection to the pedigree of the "old" IR discipline through his association with the Vienna circle (from which the IR discipline derives its version of positivism). Some of the ideas of Wittgenstein will be known to the students of the IR discipline through a slim book by Wittgenstein's student, Peter Winch (1958), which was widely read by students of IR. In it, Winch adapted some of Wittgenstein's ideas to social sciences. Hart, Austin, and Wittgenstein are all associated with what is called a "linguistic turn": a recognition of limitations imposed on philosophy by the imperfections and inadequacies of language, calling into question positivists' belief in objective knowledge. Anthony Giddens's prolific work has understandably changed its focus over the years: His earlier work should be listed in the historical materialist row. His later work is more influenced by Weber and particularly by Durkheim, and I list him close to the "old" IR discipline (row 1 in Figure 2.1) because of his idea of structuration that has been drawn upon by a range of IR scholars in their attempts to develop a constructivist approach.

The top row depicts the philosophical roots of the mainstream IR discipline as we used to know it, before the arrival of the "post" movement. Here in row 1, we can see the distinction between the utopian-idealist tradition and the "post-Carr" realists. I list Hempel, Popper, and Lakatos as philosophers of science whom IR students hear about in connection with the different mixes of logical positivism, logical empiricism, and falsificationism and their different modifications, as taught in most American IR programs.

If we look in today's IR literature for a continuation of Carr's realism-idealism distinction in terms of partners in a debate, it is obvious that the intellectual resources necessary to mount a meaningful dialogue and critique of the mainstream realist approach have been exhausted inside the discipline. What Figure 2.1 makes clear is just how important the opening up to the sources from outside the discipline in the last twenty years has been. Most of these approaches, idealist in the sense of dealing with ideas and their dominance or influence over the world, have all drawn on outside sources, particularly from the scholarship that can be found in row 3 in Figure 2.1. Many topics of IR publications, Ph.D. dissertations, and conference papers reflect influences coming from all strands depicted in Figure 2.1. It is not surprising that very few IR scholars care to examine the roots of the new approaches. However, whether anybody likes it or not, this is the intellectual pedigree of the IR discipline as it has been enlarged in the last twenty years.

First Stage: 1977–1986

In Table 2.1 I list chronologically the first important works. For lack of space, I do not go into detail of all the works that influenced the arrival of the new approaches: works of Galtung, Krippendorff, Brucan, and others. The presence of new influences in the IR field was first noted because of

Table 2.1

Selected Publications of the "Post" Movement, Stage 1: Until 1986

Cox, R.W. 1979. "Reflections of Some Recent Literature." *International Organization*.

McGowan, P., and Harmer, F. 1979. "Teaching International Political Economy: The Role of Values, History, and Theory." *Teaching Political Science*.

Ashley, R.K. 1980. *The Political Economy of War and Peace: The Sino-Soviet American Triangle and the Modern Security Problematique*.

Galtung, J. 1980. *The True Worlds*.

Alker, H.R. 1981. "Dialectical Foundation of Global Disparities." *International Studies Quarterly*.

Cox, R.W. 1981. "Social Forces, States and World Orders: Beyond International Relations Theory." *Millennium*. Reprinted in *Neorealism and its Critics*, ed. Keohane, 1986.

Cox, R.W. 1981. "In Search of International Political Economy: A Review Essay." *New Political Science*.

MacLean, J. 1981. "Marxist Epistemology, Explanations of 'Change' and the Study of International Relations." In *Change and the Study of International Relations*, ed. Barry Buzan and R.J.B. Jones.

MacLean, J. 1981. "Political Theory, International Theory, and Problems of Ideology." *Millennium*.

McGowan, P., and Walker, S.G. 1981. "Radical and Conventional Models of U.S. Foreign Economic Policy Making." *World Politics*.

Ashley, R.K. 1981. "Political Realism and Human Interests." *International Studies Quarterly*.

Alker, H.R. 1982. "Logic, Dialectics, Politics: Some recent controversies." In *Dialectical Logics for the Political Sciences*, ed. H.R. Alker. Poznan Studies in the Philosophy of the Sciences of Humanities.

Ashley, R.K. 1983. "The Eye of Power: the Politics of World Modeling." *International Organization*.

Ashley, R.K. 1983. "Three Modes of Economism." *International Studies Quarterly*.

Mittelman, J.H. 1983. "World Order Studies and International Political Economy." *Alternatives*.

Cox, R.W. 1983. "Gramsci, Hegemony and International Relations: An Essay in Method." *Millennium*.

Halliday, Fred. 1983. *The Making of the Second Cold War*.

Alker, H.R., and Biersteker, T.J. 1984. "The Dialectics of World Order: Notes for a Future Archaeologist of International Savior Faire." *International Studies Quarterly*.

Ashley, R.K. 1984. "The Poverty of Neorealism." International Organization. Reprinted in *Neorealism and Its Critics*, ed. Keohane, 1986.

MacLean, J. 1984. "Interdependence—an Ideological Intervention in International Relations?" In *Interdependence on Trial: Studies in the Theory and Reality of Contemporary Interdependence*, ed. R.J. Barry Jones and Peter Willetts.

Walker, R.B.J. 1984. ed. *Culture, Ideology and World Order*.

Cox, R.W. 1986. "Postscript 1985." In *Neorealism and Its Critics*, ed. Keohane.

rather unusual footnotes. Instead of Thucydides, Machiavelli, Hobbes, Grotius, Rousseau, or Kant and the IR exemplars such as Carr, Morgenthau, and regular academics citing each other, the footnotes of the international relations journals became populated by such new and unfamiliar names as Gramsci, Habermas, Bourdieu, and Foucault, with works dealing not with IR but rather with a decayed capitalist system, madness, prisons, psychiatry, social medicine, mental institutions, sexuality, architecture, and tribal rituals. Practically nobody and nothing in the IR discipline escaped attack, although structural realism or neorealism was the prime target. Significantly, the teaching of IR was criticized. On the basis of a survey of syllabi of IR courses offered at leading American universities, the authors found not only ordinary geographical parochial attitudes but also "paradigmatic" parochialism. Paradigmatic parochialism was defined as the exclusion from syllabi and students' reach of one or two of the three paradigms that the authors identified—including the radical dialectical paradigm—and that were found to be in a dialectical relationship to each other (Alker and Biersteker 1984). Alker and Biersteker's article was also the first attempt to present a full-fledged and comprehensive classification of the IR paradigms, as could be found not just in the IR discipline but across the world and time. The authors' own "radical dialectical approach" was proposed as a designation for all the new theoretical developments, what we call here the "post" movement.

In this first period, the main activities of the protagonists of the new approach consisted often of discovering and lifting concepts from those sources that might be applied to IR and trying to stretch them in various ways to make them fit. Though very small, the group was heterogeneous: virtually every Leftist thinker listed in the two bottom rows, and particularly in row 2, of Figure 2.1, has "auditioned" for an international relations role. What is noticeable is how underrepresented in its influence on this emerging group is the economic determinist "band"—confirming the developments of Leftist thought in other social sciences in this century. Indeed, if anything, the emerging group of writers, Ashley in particular, were critical of economic determinism, of economism, of dependency, and of the World Systems approach. Marx's ideas were directly extended to IR mainly through the work of McLean. Alker derives his concepts of dialectics from Lenin. The other influences included in Figure 2.1 tended to be drawn upon randomly and quite indiscriminately.

As I have already mentioned, R.W. Cox combines in his work the concept of critical theory, Gramsci's concept of hegemony, and civil society, which for the international context he redefines as being based on "hegemonic consensus, created by a variety of cultural and ideological instruments." (Cox 1981, 165ff.). Academics like ourselves are by no means excluded from the processes of creating such as "hegemonic consensus." Instrumental in fostering the hegemonic consensus is the "historical bloc" of bourgeois intellectuals, including academics. Gramsci's hegemony, as applied to the international level by Cox, refers to "an order within the world economy expressed in the dominant mode of production supporting universal norms, international institutions, and mechanisms for the behavior of states and other actors" (171–72). Most of this literature was introduced to IR through articles by Richard Ashley. Despite his denial of the fact, Ashley's intellectual path began with a Lenin-inspired dissertation, subsequently published as a book. He progressed soon after through more esoteric ideas ranging from critical to post-structuralist and then to postmodern. Ashley was obviously "learning on the job," often taking up a lot of space simply paraphrasing and explaining concepts to his IR colleagues, often not even getting far enough to show the relevance to international relations.

The Second Stage: 1987 On

Stage 2 marks a clear shift from the footnotes into the texts of IR studies. Table 2.2 lists again only samples of full-fledged literature of this kind. In the incredibly short period of one decade, the new generation of IR scholars, most of whom would still have been at graduate schools during the first period, have more than made up for the time lost by the chronic absence of Leftist thought from the IR discipline. Marxism made a fleeting appearance in the IR discipline and was fast replaced by its Hegelian or indeed post-Marxist versions. There is no longer any hesitation. The main approaches, as I have identified them in Figure 2.1 (right-hand column), have not just one or two, but a contingent of full supporters who have written book-length studies inspired by this or that source. There has been a continuous outpouring of work on historical sociology which challenges the IR discipline's neglect of theories of state and which, for lack of space, I do not include in Table 2.2. There is the historical materialist approach, initially clearly Trotskyist, of Fred Halliday. The critical school has new energetic supporters in many authors such as Linklater, in addition to Cox. Many post-structuralist authors have moved on to post-modernism, and both of these influences have been taken up by a large group of feminist authors, a new and rapidly growing section of the IR discipline. Walker and Der Derian lead the field of post-modernist treatises of IR. Walker's work in particular has been earmarked as a future classic. The main features of the sources when applied to IR are kept intact. Thus the distinguishing feature of critical theory and post-structuralism continues to be the stress of

Table 2.2

Selected Publications of the "Post" Movement, Stage 2: After 1986

DIALECTICAL

Alker, Hayward R. 1995. *Rediscoveries and Reformulations*.

CRITICAL THEORY

Cox, R.W. 1987. *Production, Power, and World Order: Social Forces in the Making of History*.
————. 1992. "Multilateralism and World Order." *Review of International Studies*.
————. 1995. *Approaches to World Order*.
Hoffman, M. 1987. "Critical Theory and Inter Paradigm Debate." *Millennium*.
————. 1988. "Conversations on Critical International Relations Theory." *Millennium*.
Linklater, Andrew. 1990. *Beyond Realism and Marxism: Critical Theory and International Relations*.
————. 1992. "The Question of the Next Stage in International Relations Theory: A Critical Theoretical Point of View." *Millenium*.
Neufeld, Mark. 1995. *The Restructuring of International Relations Theory*.

POST-STRUCTURALIST–POST-MODERN

Ashley, R.K. 1987. "The Geopolitics of Geopolitical Space: Toward a Critical Social Theory of International Politics." *Alternatives*.
————. 1988 "Untying the Sovereign State: A Double Reading of the Anarchy Problematique." *Millennium*.
————. 1989. "Living on the Border lines: Man, Post-Structuralism and War." In *International/Intertextual Relations*. Der Derian ed.
Ashley, R.K., and R.B.J. Walker. 1990. "Reading Dissidence/Writing the Discipline: Crisis and the Question of Sovereignty in International Studies." *International Studies Quarterly*.
————. 1990. "Speaking the Language of Exile: Dissident Thought in International Studies." *International Studies Quarterly*.
Bartelson. J. 1995. *A Genealogy of Sovereignty*.
Campbell, David. 1990 "Global Inscription: How Foreign Policy Constitutes the United States." *Alternatives*.
————. 1992. *Writing Security: United States Foreign Policy and the Politics of Identity*.
————. 1993. *Politics Without Principle: Sovereignty, Ethics, and the Narratives of the Gulf War*.
Der Derian, James. 1987. *On Diplomacy: A Genealogy of Western Estrangement*.
————. 1988. "Philosophical Traditions in International Relations." *Millennium*.
————. 1989. "Boundaries of Knowledge and Power." In *International/Intertextual Relations*. Der Derian and Shapiro, eds.
————. 1989. "Spy Versus Spy: The Intertextual Power and International Intrigue." In *International/Intertextual Relations*. Der Derian and Shapiro, eds.
————. 1990. "The (S)pace of International Relations: Simulation, Surveillance, and Speed." *International Studies Quarterly*.
————. 1992. *Antidiplomacy: Spies, Terror, Speed and War*.

———. ed. 1994. *International Theory: Critical Investigation.*

Der Derian, J., and M.J. Shapiro, eds. 1989. *International/Intertextual Relations: Postmodern Readings of World Politics.*

Dillon, Michael. 1996. *Politics of Security: Towards a Political Philosophy of the Continental Thought.*

George, Jim, and Campbell, David. 1990. "Patterns of Dissent and the Celebration of Difference: Critical Social Theory and International Relations." *International Studies Quarterly.*

George, Jim. 1994. *Discourses of Global Politics: A Critical (Re)Introduction to International Relations.*

Klein, Bradley S. 1987. *Strategic Discourse and Its Alternatives.*

———. 1987. "Hegemony and Strategic Culture: American Power Projection and Alliance Defence Politics." *Review of International Studies.*

———. 1988. "After Strategy: Toward a Postmodern Politics of Peace." *Alternatives.*

———. 1989. "The Textual Strategies of Military Strategy: Or, Have You Read Any Good Defence Manuals Lately?" In *International/Intertextual Relations.* Der Derian and Shapiro, eds.

Shapiro, Michael. 1989. "Textualizing Global Politics." In *International/Intertextual Relations.* Der Derian and Shapiro, eds.

Walker, R.B.J. 1987. "History and Structure in the Theory of International Relations." *Millennium.*

———. "Realism, Change and International Political Theory." *International Studies Quarterly.*

———. 1988. *One World, Many Worlds: Struggles for a Just World Peace.*

———. 1989. "The Prince and 'The Pauper': Tradition, Modernity, and Practice in the Theory of International Relations." In *International/Intertextual Relations.* Der Derian and Shapiro, eds.

———. 1993. *Inside/Outside: International Relations as Political Theory.*

FEMINIST POST-STRUCTURALIST–POST-MODERN

Enloe, Cynthia. 1989. *Bananas, Beaches and Bases: Making Feminist Sense Out of International Politics.*

Flax, Jane. 1990. *Thinking Fragments: Psychoanalysis, Feminism and Postmodernism in the Contemporary West.*

Grant, Rebecca, and Kathleen Lewland, eds. 1991. *Gender and International Relations.*

Peterson, V. Spike, ed. 1992. *Gendered States: Feminist (Re)Visions of International Relations Theory.*

———. 1992. "Transgressing Boundaries: Theories of Knowledge, Gender and International Relations." *Millennium.*

Peterson, V. Spike, and Runyan Anne Sisson. 1993. *Global Gender Issues.*

Sylvester, Christine, ed. 1993. "Feminists Write International Relations." *Alternatives.* Special Issue.

———. 1993. *Feminist Theory and International Relations in a Postmodern Era.*

HISTORICAL MATERIALISM

Halliday, Fred. 1994. *Rethinking International Relations.*

purpose or interest that creates knowledge, alleged by positivists to be objective and value-free. The critical school adds its important leitmotif—the possibility of emancipation. A number of IR scholars tried their hand at deconstructing a variety of IR traditional texts, reinterpreting IR as intertextual relations and deconstructing its main concepts, such as anarchy or sovereignty.

Constructivism

Throughout this chapter the verb *construct* has frequently appeared. If the use of the term alone is a qualification, then everybody I have referred to is a constructivist. There is no doubt about the importance of the active creation of societal structures and their purposeful manipulation in the "post" movement. The thrust of this approach derives from the notion of a perversion of the concept of praxis, the abuse of "power over opinion" so loosely termed by Carr, disguised and marketed as value-free objectivity. I now turn to constructivism as Onuf defined it in 1989 and as he himself introduces it in this volume in Chapter 3.

Here it will suffice to say that Onuf's constructivism is totally different from the other varieties and it is his approach alone which should continue using that designation. My discussion of the "post" movement would have shown how tenuous any similarities are if only we review the intellectual origins in Onuf's case, marked in Figure 2.1 by arrows: Onuf links together the old and the new IR pedigree, as the arrows in Figure 2.1 indicate. Through Habermas and the early Giddens, there is a distant connection to Marx, while his starting point is an attempt to overcome the impasse in the "old" IR. The other sources, which he alone in the IR discipline uses, provide him with tools totally different from any of those used in the extended IR discipline. Onuf's constructivism abandons obsessive critique of structural realism or Western society and simply offers an alternative ontology of what the social world is all about. Nor is Onuf's constructivism mainly an epistemological device providing a layer of unreal or surreal "construction" over reality to disguise the underpinning ontology. While for other constructivist approaches described in Chapter 3 in this volume, the act of the construction is restricted to "states," for Onuf constructivism is a universal experience. His constructivism is not only a contribution to the IR discipline; it is a full-fledged social theory as well. Onuf's constructivism is applicable not simply to the level of states, but to humans in any dimension of their social activity, international relations being merely one, albeit an extremely important one, among many.

Unfortunately, instead of welcoming this development as a positive trend, some of his IR colleagues express concern about his challenge to the central IR concept of anarchy, without which international studies fears losing its claim to having a distinct subject matter (Buzan, Jones, and Little 1994).

Onuf obviously does not share these fears. His constructivism makes it possible to see layers of mutually constructed relations operating along the same basic lines. The key point is that speech acts, rules, and norms, which are at the heart of his approach and at the heart of human existence as social beings, are generated from within people; that is to say, they are *endogenous* to real people as active, creative beings, and to their practice. They are not dictated by some outside, *exogenous* structure (as in Waltz or Wendt) which has taken a life and dynamism of its own. Onuf opens a broad theoretical avenue for incorporating into the IR discipline a host of phenomena of the post–Cold War world for which there is no apparent place in the traditional approaches. In contrast to these approaches, Onuf's framework makes it easy to understand concepts such as identity and culture, or the implications of the Information Age, concepts which are among the central issues of our time.

E.H. Carr, Realism, and Idealism

To return to E.H. Carr: An IR discipline that does not exclude Leftist influences and that allows for an interplay of a whole spectrum of ideas would seem to be something Carr called for. Onuf might be portrayed within Carr's terms as trying to integrate or transcend realist and idealist traditions as defined by Carr, although there are candidates for exactly the same role—Carr himself, at least in broad outline, or critical theory, as Linklater suggests (1997).

For those of us who are not dialecticians, Onuf's approach, as he describes it in Chapter 3, offers a constructive way forward, away from the unabating war waged in the IR discipline. One thing is for sure. The discipline of IR is now complete. It is no longer like an airplane trying desperately to lift off without its left wing. It can now fly. And out of the turmoil of the cathartic last twenty years a brand-new approach to IR, to which Chapter 3 and the rest of this volume are dedicated, has been born.

Whodunit?

There was no body, no villain; no crime was committed; no charges were pressed. We all did it in our characteristic academic way, shooting ourselves in the foot. Did I just use Carr to construct an argument, and did I misunderstand him or cite him out of context? Certainly no more than the IR discipline has done, over the last fifty years. Unpleasant though it might be, there exists the empirical evidence to prove it!

Notes

I would like to thank Nicholas Onuf and Henry Hamman for their suggestions: the idea that I write this chapter as a whodunit story was Henry Hamman's. Nick Onuf's general comments were invaluable.

1. It was the Frankfurt School's second director, Max Horkheimer, who in 1937 coined the term *critical theory*, taking his inspiration from the understanding of Marxism as a "critique of political economy," a phrase used by Marx. It is therefore surprising that Habermas, the main contemporary figure of the same Frankfurt School, is not named among the sources of Cox's inspiration for the "critical theory" that he defined and introduced to the IR discipline. In fact, a negative footnote reference to Habermas suggests that Cox's and Habermas's understanding of the same expression, "critical theory," is not in any way related.

2. These terms have been used so frequently that it is worth reminding ourselves of their original meaning. *Problematique* conveys an ipso facto antipositivist attitude. It refers to a "theoretical or ideological framework" whose "production" necessarily involves a value judgment as to what is important in the world, namely "the objective internal reference system of its particular themes, the system of questions commanding the answers given by the ideology" (Althusser 1969, 67, note 30). That is, the use of the term has antipositivist implications.

The term *conjecture* is the "central concept of the Marxist science of politics." It "denotes the exact balance of forces at any given moment to which political tactics must be applied" (Althusser 1969, 250). The term is used by Cox as "historical conjecture" and also by Halliday (1983).

Bibliography

Alker, Hayward R. 1981. "Dialectical Foundation of Global Disparities." *International Studies Quarterly* 25: 69–98.

——. 1982. "Logic, Dialectics, Politics: Some Recent Controversies." *Dialectical Logics for the Political Sciences*. Poznan Studies in the Philosophy of the Sciences of Humanities, ed. H.R. Alker, 7. Amsterdam: Rodopi.

—— and T.J. Biersteker, 1984. "The Dialectics of World Order: Notes for a Future Archaeologist of International Savoir Faire." *International Studies Quarterly* 28: 121–42.

Althusser, Louis. 1969. *For Marx*. New York: Pantheon.

Anderson, Perry. 1976. *Considerations on Western Marxism*. London: New Left Books.

——. 1983. *In the Tracks of Historical Materialism*. London: Verso.

Anderson, R.J., J.A. Hughes, and W.W. Sharrock. 1986. *Philosophy and the Human Sciences*. Totowa, NJ: Barnes & Noble Books.

Ashley, Richard. 1984. "The Poverty of Neorealism." *International Organization*. Spring 38(2): 225–61.

Banks, Michael. 1978. "Ways of Analyzing the World Society." In *International Relations Theory: A Bibliography*, ed. A.J.R. Groom and C.R. Mitchell. London: Frances Pinter, 195–215.

————. 1985. "The Inter-Paradigm Debate." In *International Relations: A Handbook of Current Theory*, ed. Margot Light and A.J.R. Groom, London: Frances Pinter, 195–215.

Beer, Francis A., and Robert Hariman. 1996. *Post-Realism: The Rhetorical Turn in International Relations*. East Lansing: Michigan State University Press.

Booth, Kenneth. 1991. "Security in Anarchy: Utopian Realism in Theory and Practice." *International Affairs* 67(3): 527–45.

Brown, Chris. 1992. *International Relations Theory: New Normative Approaches*. New York, Oxford: Columbia University Press.

Bull, Hedley. 1969. "Twenty Years' Crisis: Thirty Years On." *International Journal* 24: 625–38.

————. 1977. *The Anarchical Society*. London: Macmillan.

Burawoy, Michael. 1982. "Introduction: The Resurgence of Marxism." *American Sociology* 88. Supplement. S1–10.

Buzan, Barry, Charles Jones, and Richard Little. 1993. *The Logic of Anarchy: Neorealism to Structural Realism*. New York: Columbia University Press.

Callinicos, Alex. 1983. *Marxism and Philosophy*. Oxford: Clarendon Press.

Carr, Edward Hallett. (1939) 1962. *The Twenty Years' Crisis 1919–1939: An Introduction to the Study of International Relations*. London: Macmillan.

Cox, R.W. (1981) 1986. "Social Forces, States and World Orders: Beyond International Relations Theory." *Millenium: Journal of International Studies* 10(2): 126–55. Reprinted in *Neorealism and Its Critics*, ed. Keohane, 204–54.

Deutscher, Isaac. 1955. *Heretics and Renegades*. London: Hamish Hamilton.

Deutscher, Tamara. 1983. "E.H. Carr—A Personal Memoir." *New Left Review* 137: 78–86.

Dunn, Timothy. 1995. "The Social Construction of International Society." *European Journal of International Relations*. 1 (3, September).

Foucault, Michel. 1977. *Discipline and Punish*. Harmondsworth, London: Penguin.

Fox, William T.R. 1985. "E.H. Carr and Political Realism: Vision and Revision." *Review of International Studies* 11: 1–15.

Galtung, Johann. 1961. "A Structural Theory of Imperialism." *Journal of Peace Research* 8: 81–117.

George, Jim. 1994. *Discourses of Global Politics: A Critical (Re)Introduction to International Relations*. Boulder, CO: Lynne Rienner.

Halliday, F. 1983. *The Making of the Second Cold War*. London: Verso.

Hoffmann, Stanley. 1977. "An American Social Science: International Relations." *Daedalus* 106 (3): 40–59.

Holsti, K.J. 1985. *The Dividing Discipline: Hegemony and Diversity in International Theory*. Boston: Allen & Union.

Howe, Paul. 1994. "The Utopian Realism of E.H. Carr." *Review of International Studies* 20: 277–97.

Inkeles, Alex. 1975. "The Emerging Social Structure of the World." *World Politics* (4): 467–95.

Jones, Charles. 1996. "E.H. Carr: Ambivalent Realist." In *Post-Realism*, ed. Beer and Hariman, 95–119.

Keohane, Robert O., ed. 1986. *Neorealism and Its Critics*. New York: Columbia University Press.

————. 1988. "International Institutions: Two Approaches." *International Studies Quarterly* 32 (4): 379–91.

———— and Joseph S. Nye. 1977. *Power and Interdependence: World Politics in Transition*. Boston: Little, Brown.

Kratochwil, F., John Gerard, and Ruggie. 1986. "International Organization: A State of the Art on an Art of the State." *International Organization* 40 (4, Autumn): 763–66.

Krippendorff, E. (First published in German in 1975) 1982. *International Relations as a Social Science*. Sussex: Harvester Press.

Kubálková, Vendulka, and Albert A. Cruickshank. 1989a. *Marxism and International Relations*, rev. ed. Oxford Paperback: Oxford University Press.

————. 1989b. *Thinking New About Soviet "New Thinking."* Berkeley: Institute of International Studies, University of California, Berkeley.

Kuhn, Thomas S. 1970. *The Structure of Scientific Revolution*. Chicago: University of Chicago Press.

Lapid, Yosef. 1989. "The Third Debate: On the Prospects of International Theory in the Post-Positivist Era." *International Studies Quarterly* 33 (3): 235–54.

Legvold, Robert. 1997. "The Soviet Union and Eastern Europe." In "Significant Books of the Last 75 Years." *Foreign Affairs* (September–October): 214–38.

Light, Margot, and A.J.R. Groom, eds. 1985. *International Relations: A Handbook of Current Theory*. London: Frances Pinter.

Lijphart, Arendt. (1975) 1981. "Karl W. Deutsch and the New Paradigm in International Relations. In *From National Development to Global Community*, ed. R.L. Merritt and B.M. Russett. 233–51, London and Boston: Allen and Unwin.

Linklater, Andrew. 1990. *Beyond Realism and Marxism: Critical Theory and International Relations*. New York: St. Martin's Press.

————. 1992. "The Question of the Next Stage in International Relations Theory: A Critical Theoretical Point of View." *Millennium* 21 (1): 77–98.

————. 1997. "The Transformation of Political Community: E.H. Carr, Critical Theory and International Relations." *Review of International Studies* 23: 321–28.

MacLellan, David. 1979. *Marxism After Marx*. London: Macmillan Press.

Mitroff, I.I., and R.O. Mason. 1982. "On the Structure of Dialectical Reasoning in the Social and Policy Sciences." *Theory and Decision* 14.

Morgenthau, Hans. (1948) 1962. "The Political Science of E.H. Carr." *World Politics* 1. Cited in *The Restoration of American Politics*, ed. Hans Morgenthau. Chicago: University of Chicago Press.

Pettman, Ralph H. 1978. *State and Class: A Sociology of International Affairs*. London: Croom Helm.

————. 1981. Competing Paradigms in International Politics." *Review of International Studies* 7: 39–50

Phillips, W.R. 1974. "Where Have All the Theories Gone?" *World Politics* XXVI (2): 155–58.

Polsby, W. Nelson, and Fred I. Greenstein, eds. 1975. *Handbook of Political Science* VII. Reading, MA: Addison-Wesley

Rescher, N. 1977. *Dialectics: A Controversy-Oriented Approach to the Theory of Knowledge*. Albany: SUNY Press.

Ritzer, G. 1983. *Sociological Theory*. New York: Alfred Knopf.

Rosenau, N. James. 1979. "Muddling, Meddling and Modelling: Alternative Approaches to the Study of World Politics in an Era of Rapid Change." *Millennium: Journal of International Studies* 8: 130–44.

Smith, Michael. 1986. *Realist Thought from Weber to Kissinger*. Baton Rouge, LA: Louisiana State University Press.

Thompson, E.P. 1978. *The Poverty of Theory and Other Essays*. London: Merlin Press.

Thompson, K.W., et al. 1980. *Masters of International Thought: Major Twentieth-Century Theorists and the World Crisis*. Baton Rouge, LA: Louisiana State University Press.

Trevor-Roper, Hugh. (1962) 1963. "E.H. Carr's Success Story." *Encounter*. Quoted in

Fly and the Fly-Bottle: Encounters with British Intellectuals, ed. Ved Mehta. London: Weidenfeld and Nicolson.

Tucker, Robert W. 1977. *The Inequality of Nations*. New York: Basic Books.

Wallerstein, Immanuel. 1979. *The Capitalist World Economy*. Cambridge: Cambridge University Press.

Waltz, Kenneth N. 1979. *Theory of International Politics*. Reading, MA: Addison-Wesley.

———. 1986. "A Response to My Critics." In *Neorealism and Its Critics*, ed. Keohane.

Winch, Peter. 1958. *The Idea of a Social Science and Its Relation to Philosophy*. London: Routledge and Kegan Paul.

3

Constructivism: A User's Manual

Nicholas Onuf

Constructivism is a way of studying social relations—any kind of social relations. While it draws from a variety of other ways of studying such a broad and complex subject, it stands on its own as a system of concepts and propositions. Constructivism is not a theory as such. It does not offer general explanations for what people do, why societies differ, how the world changes. Instead, constructivism makes it feasible to theorize about matters that seem to be unrelated because the concepts and propositions normally used to talk about such matters are also unrelated.

As presented here, constructivism applies to all fields of social inquiry. In recent years, dissident scholars in many fields have selectively used the language of social construction to criticize existing social arrangements and scholarly practices. A great deal of discord has ensued. (Also see Part I, Introduction.) When constructivism is used systematically, it has the opposite effect. It finds value in diverse materials and forges links where none seemed possible.

Full of discordant voices, International Relations is the field to which this particular system of concepts and propositions was first applied. While this manual is intended for the use of anyone with methical habits of mind, its users are most likely to have an interest in the subject of international relations. They may have also had some exposure to the field's scholarly controversies. If this is indeed the case, they will soon discover that the subject is less distinctive, but more complex, than they have been led to believe.

Overview

Fundamental to constructivism is the proposition that human beings are social beings, and we would not be human but for our social relations. In other words, social relations *make* or *construct* people—*ourselves*—into the kind of beings that we are. Conversely, we *make* the world what it is, from the raw materials that nature provides, by doing what we do with each other and saying what we say to each other. Indeed, saying is doing: talking is undoubtedly the most important way that we go about making the world what it is.

Countries such as France, the United States, and Zimbabwe are among the social constructions, or societies, that people make through what we do. Countries are self-contained worlds because people talk about them that way and try to keep them that way. Yet they are only relatively self-contained. Relations among countries—international relations—constitutes a world in its own right. This is a self-contained world for the simple reason that it covers the earth, but it is still nothing more than a world of our making—a society of relatively self-contained societies.

Constructivism holds that people make society, and society makes people. This is a continuous, two-way process. In order to study it, we must start in the middle, so to speak, because people and society, always having made each other, are already there and just about to change. To make a virtue of necessity, we will start in the middle, between people and society, by introducing a third element, *rules*, that always links the other two elements together. Social rules (the term *rules* includes, but is not restricted to, legal rules) make the process by which people and society constitute each other continuous and reciprocal.

A rule is a statement that tells people *what* we *should* do. The "what" in question is a standard for people's conduct in situations that we can identify as being alike, and can expect to encounter. The "should" tells us to match our conduct to that standard. If we fail to do what the rule tells us to, then we can expect consequences that some other rule will bring into effect when other people follow the rule calling for such consequences. All the ways in which people deal with rules—whether we follow the rules or break them, whether we make the rules, change them, or get rid of them—may be called *practices*. Even when we do not know what a rule says, we can often guess what it is about by looking at people's practices.

Among much else, rules tell us who the active participants in a society are. Constructivists call these participants *agents*. People are agents, but only to the extent that society, through its rules, makes it possible for us to participate in the many situations for which there are rules. No one is an agent for all such situations.

Ordinarily, we think of agents as people who act on behalf of other people. Considering the matter more abstractly, we see that rules make it possible for us to act on behalf of social constructions, which may be ourselves, other human beings, or even collections of people, along with the rules, the practices, and the actual things that we make and use. Conversely, agents need not be individual human beings to be able to act on behalf of others (here I refer to agents in the third person to emphasize that the terms *people* and *agents* are not completely interchangeable). Agency is a social condition. Thus the government of a country is a collection of people and a social construction. According to the relevant rules, these people act, together and in various combinations, on behalf of that country as a much larger collection of people.

Rules give agents choices. As we have already seen, the most basic choice is to follow the rule—to do what the rule says the agent should do—or not. Only human beings can actually make choices, because we alone (and not all of us) have the mental equipment to consider the probable consequences of making the choices that are available to us. Nevertheless, we always make such choices on behalf of, and in the name of, social constructions, whether ourselves, other people or collections of other people, or practices and artifacts.

Agents act in society to achieve goals. These goals reflect people's needs and wishes in light of their material circumstances. Every society has rules telling agents which goals are the appropriate ones for them to pursue. Of course, there are situations in which people are perfectly aimless. For example, when we freeze up in fear or fall asleep from exhaustion, we are no longer agents or, for that matter, social beings.

When we, as human beings, act as agents, we have goals in mind, even if we are not fully aware of them when we act. If someone asks us to think about the matter, we can usually formulate these goals more or less in the order of their importance to whomever we are acting as agents for, starting with ourselves. Most of the time, agents have limited, inaccurate, or inconsistent information about the material and social conditions that affect the likelihood of reaching given goals. Nevertheless, agents do the best they can to achieve their goals with the means that nature and society (together—always together) make available to them. Acting to achieve goals is *rational* conduct, and agents faced with choices will act rationally. Viewed from outside, these choices may appear to be less than rational, but this is due to the complexities of agency and human fallibility.

Agents make choices in a variety of situations. Rules help to define every such situation from any agent's point of view. In many situations, rules are directly responsible for presenting agents with choices. Agents have made or acknowledged these rules in the belief that following rules generally helps them reach their intended goals.

In these situations, rules are related to agents' practices, and to each other, through the consequences that agents intend their acts to have. Whether by accident or by design, rules and related practices frequently form a stable (but never fixed) pattern suiting agents' intentions. These patterns are *institutions*. As recognizable patterns of rules and related practices, institutions make people into agents *and* constitute an environment within which agents conduct themselves rationally. While it is always possible, and often useful, to think of agents—all agents—as institutions in their own right, we more commonly think of agents as operating in an institutional context that gives them at least some opportunities for choice.

Exercising choices, agents act on, and not just in, the context within which they operate, collectively changing its institutional features, and themselves, in the process. Nevertheless, from any agent's point of view, society consists of diverse institutions that seem, for the most part, to be held in place by rules linking them to other institutions. Any stable pattern of institutions (including agents of all sorts) is also an institution. Agents are aware of the institutions populating their environments, and not simply because the rules forming these institutions directly bear on their conduct. To the extent that some agents make choices, and other agents are affected by these choices, institutions produce consequences for other agents that they cannot help but be aware of and respond to.

In a complex world, agents often make choices that have consequences, for themselves and others, that they had not anticipated or do not care very much about. Unintended consequences frequently form stable patterns with respect to their effect on agents. A perfect market provides a compelling illustration of this phenomenon. One by one, a large number of sellers and buyers are incapable of affecting the supply of, and demand for, a good. Collectively, their rational choices have the unintended consequence of setting a price for that good which they must individually accept as fixed.

Anyone may notice such stable patterns of unintended consequences. In the case of a market, no one could fail to notice it in the form of a good's price, over which no agent seems to have any control. Sometimes agents will choose to prevent changes in such patterns by adopting rules that are intended to have this effect. A rule fixing the price of a good under certain conditions is only the most obvious example.

Any stable pattern of rules, institutions, and unintended consequences gives society a *structure*, recognizable as such to any observer. Agents are always observers. Insofar as they observe consequences that they had not intended, and accept them, such consequences are no longer unintended in the usual sense of the word. If agents decide that these consequences are bad for them, they will act to change them, perhaps with other unforeseen consequences resulting.

Outside observers (agents from a different society) may recognize a more complex structure than agents do as observers. Outsiders can stand back, so to speak, and see patterns that insiders cannot see because they are too close to them. As agents on the inside become aware of what observers have to say, observers become agents, whatever their intentions. When agents in general take this new information into account in making their choices, an even greater complexity of structure results.

Scholars who think of themselves as constructivists have given a good deal of attention to the "agent-structure problem." (See Harry Gould's contribution to this volume in Chapter 4 for a thorough review of these discussions.) The term *structure* is the source of much confusion (an *ontological* confusion), because scholars cannot agree on whether structures exist in reality or only in their minds. The important point to remember is that structure is what observers see, while institutions are what agents act within. Nevertheless, structure can affect agents. We are often affected by phenomena, natural and social, that we do not or cannot see, but we then respond as agents by putting what has happened to us in an institutional context. When agents do this, they *institutionalize* structure by bringing rules to bear on their situations.

Generally speaking, scholars today tend to think that the structure of international relations is not institutionalized to any great degree. This is so even for some scholars who think of themselves as constructivists. They believe that countries are highly institutionalized as *states*, but that states, through their agents, conduct their relations in an anarchic world. The term *anarchy* points to a condition of *rule* among states in which no one state or group of states rules over the rest. It also implies that there is no institution above states ruling them. When we say that states are *sovereign*, we are saying the very same thing.

By calling international relations anarchic, scholars are not saying that there is an absence of rule. This would be chaos, not anarchy. Instead, they seem to be saying that structure—and especially a stable pattern of unintended consequences—rules the day. In the same sense, we might say that the market rules the behavior of sellers and buyers.

Starting with rules, as constructivists often do, leads quickly enough to patterns of relations that we can only describe as a condition of rule. Usually this condition is sufficiently institutionalized that we can recognize specific agents as rulers. Sometimes there is very little evidence of institutionalization, as in mob rule, but there is also little reason to think that this condition will persist as a stable pattern without institutions emerging. In other words, where there are rules (and thus institutions), there is rule—a condition in which some agents use rules to exercise control and obtain advantages over other agents. Rule is a stable pattern of relations, but not a symmetrical one.

Anarchy is a condition of rule in which rules are not directly responsible for the way agents conduct their relations. To be sure, there are rules in the background. They make sure that the unintended consequences of agents' many choices, and not rulers, do the job of ruling. If unintended consequences *seem* to rule, it is because some agents intend for them to do so.

Some agents want to be ruled in this indirect sort of way because it suits their goals more than any other arrangement would. Other agents have little or no choice in the matter. Perhaps patterns just happen, but agents make arrangements. Arranging for anarchy is just one possibility.

Constructivists should seriously consider dropping the word *structure* from their vocabularies. *Social arrangement* is a better choice. Appearances aside, international anarchy is a social arrangement—an institution—on a grand scale. Within its scope, many other institutions are recognizably connected. In every society, rules create conditions of rule. The society that states constitute through their relations is no exception.

Whether we, as constructivists, start with agents or with social arrangements, we come quickly enough to particular institutions and thus to rules. If we start with rules, we can move in either direction—toward agents and the choices that rules give them an opportunity to make, or toward the social arrangements that emerge from the choices that agents are making all the time. Whichever way we go, we ought to keep in mind that rules yield rule as a condition that agents (as institutions) can never escape.

The practical problem is that, as constructivists, we want to move in both directions at the same time. Yet if we try to do so, we come up against the staggering complexity of the social reality that we want to know about. It is impossible to do everything. The practical solution is to start with rules and show how rules make agents and institutions what they are in relation to each other. Then we can show how rules make rule, and being ruled, a universal social experience.

The remainder of this user's manual is dedicated to these two tasks. To make points as clear and understandable as possible, it repeats most of what the reader has now had a taste of. In the process, it introduces many additional concepts and propositions, expressed in the simplest terms that its author can think of. Used consistently and systematically related, these concepts and propositions constitute a comprehensive framework for understanding the world in constructivist terms.

Rules Make Agents, Agents Make Rules

Rules make agents out of individual human beings by giving them opportunities to act upon the world. These acts have material and social consequences, some of them intended and some not. Through these acts, agents *make* the material world a social reality for themselves as human beings. Because agents are human beings, acting singly or together on behalf of themselves or others, they act as they do for human purposes—they have goals reflecting human needs and wishes. The tangled connections between agency (who is acting on whose behalf?), goals (whose goals are affected by what acts?), and circumstances (which features of the world actually matter?) make it difficult for agents to explain fully and convincingly why they act as they do. Even if they seem confused, observers can often figure the reasons for their conduct from the evidence at hand.

Agents use whatever means are available to them to achieve their goals. These means include material features of the world. Because the world is a social place, at least for human beings, rules make the world's material features into *resources* available for agents' use. Some resources are not directly material—rules also constitute agents and institutions as resources. Whether agents are able to spell out their reasons for using the resources available to them, or observers figure them out from the evidence, recognizable patterns in the results constitute agents' *interests*.

Agents need not know what their interests are to act on them. Once they learn more from other agents (as observers) about their own interests, they may act differently. Indeed, human beings do not need to think about themselves as agents to be agents. While being an agent does not require the degree of self-consciousness that we associate with having an *identity*, agents are usually aware enough of their identities, singular and collective, to have an interest in fostering those identities.

As agents, people can make other people into agents by giving the latter the opportunity to act on the former's behalf for particular purposes. The former may do so individually or collectively, and the latter may be one or more individuals acting on the former's behalf. Agents acting collectively become a singular agent. By using resources, they acquire a material existence, and, as the previous paragraph suggests, they become objects of identification.

Agency is always limited. Agents are never free to act upon the world in all the ways that they might wish to. Many limits have a material component. We need air to breathe; we do not have wings to fly. No rule can readily make things otherwise, even though rules allow us, agents, to use resources to alter these limits, for example, by fashioning scuba gear and airplanes. Rules that give any agent an opportunity to act create limits for other agents. Rules in general limit the range of acts that other agents are free to take.

It follows from this proposition that no individual human being, as an agent, has full *autonomy*. By the same token, agents acting together never have full *independence*. As noted, agents are always limited by rules that give other agents opportunities to act. Agents acting together are additionally limited by the very rules that give them the opportunity to act collectively. Rules allowing other agents, individual and collective, to act on their behalf limit them even further.

When a very large number of people collectively operate as an agent, when they have agents acting for them, when they have some considerable measure of identity (including some place identified as theirs), and when they are free to act within very wide limits, these people constitute a country. For several centuries, agents have had a consistent interest in talking about countries as if they are independent of each other and any other social construction. This is made clearest by defining sovereignty as absolute independence and describing countries as sovereign states. As constructivists, however, we should always bear in mind that full independence is a useful fiction, and sovereignty is a matter of degree.

The freedom that agents do have depends on their ability to recognize the material and social limits that apply to them. They must also be able to evaluate the consequences of exceeding those limits. To be an agent requires the mental equipment that individual human beings normally develop over the course of their social lives. Agents exercise their freedom by choosing to act one way or another, in an unending series of situations that make choosing unavoidable. It hardly needs saying that *not* choosing is a choice, presumably taken, as all choices are, to advance agents' goals. Agents make choices in light of the skills that they possess and the resources that they have access to, for reasons that they are more or less able to articulate. In short, they make choices in pursuit of their interests.

Rules offer agents the simplest kind of choices. Agents may choose to follow a given rule, or to break it. Compared to most situations in which agents make choices, the choice of following a rule or not following it involves consequences that are easy to calculate. While unintended consequences are always possible, rules give agents the opportunity to make rational choices—choices dictated by reference to goals—with some assurance that they are making the best choices available to them.

A rule makes rational choice relatively easy by telling the agents to whom it refers what they should do in some sort of situation that they might find themselves in. These agents may act on the contents of the rule without realizing that the contents form a rule. In principle, however, any agent (including any observer with enough information) can formulate contents of a rule in the form of a rule. There is nothing tricky about this. Saying what a rule is—putting its contents in the right form—is exactly the same as speaking in a form that gets anyone who is listening to respond to whatever we are saying. The point of speaking in this way is to have something take place—to accomplish something with the assistance of someone else.

The act of speaking in a form that gets someone else to act is commonly called a speech act. The form that a speech act must have will be clear from the following examples: (1) You assert that duck season has begun (you might actually say, "Duck season has begun!"). (2) She demands that we all go duck hunting (she might actually say, "Let's go duck hunting!"). (3) I promise to roast duck for dinner (I might actually say, "I'll cook!"). The generic form for a speech act is: I (you, etc.) hereby assert (demand, promise) to anyone hearing me that some state of affairs exists or can be achieved. The three examples suggest that speech acts fall into three categories, here called assertive speech acts, directive speech acts, and commissive speech acts.

Whether speech acts accomplish anything depends on whether others respond to what they hear. The response to your assertion about duck season was obviously positive. I, at least, accepted her inclusive but imperative demand to go hunting when I promised to cook. We may surmise that both of you accepted my offer, and we all three went duck hunting, perhaps after we checked the newspaper to be sure that duck season had indeed begun.

Whatever category a particular speech act falls within, particular speech acts imply nothing about future situations. We start all over again when deer season begins. A speaker may assert the existence of some state of affairs and others may agree, or may request something and others may comply, or may make a commitment that others accept, without any necessary consequences in the long run.

If, however, speakers frequently repeat a particular speech act with the same general effect, everyone involved begins to think that the repetition becomes significant. We end up hunting with each other all the time because we go through the same cycle of speech acts whenever hunting season begins. Constantly repeated, the same old speech acts turn into *convention* as everyone comes to believe that the words themselves, and not the speakers mouthing them, are responsible for what happens. Hunting together is what we do at certain times, whether any of us even have to say anything much about it anymore.

Conventions come close to being rules. Recall that rules tell agents what they should do. A convention reminds agents what they have always done.

The borderline between knowing that we have always done something and probably will continue to do it, and believing that we should do it because we have always done it, is exceedingly fuzzy. If a convention prompts agents to think that they should do something that they have always done, then the convention is indeed a rule. We should consider the rule in question a weak rule because it is *normative*, which means that agents accept the "should" element, only to the extent that the regular pattern of conduct (such as hunting together) continues.

As agents begin to realize that they should act as they always have, and not just because they always have acted that way, the convention gains strength as a rule. Rules keep the form of a speech act by generalizing the relation between speaker and hearer. Within the general form of a speech act, given rules make hearers into agents to whom those rules apply. Finally, agents recognize that they should follow the rules in question because they are rules and for no other reason.

Rules can take the general form of speech acts in each of the three categories presented above: assertive speech acts, directive speech acts, and commissive speech acts. Rules in the form of assertive speech acts inform agents about the world—the way things are, the way it works—and inform them what consequences are likely to follow if they disregard this information. The information contained in such rules may be stated in very general terms, in which case we might call it a *principle*. The principle of sovereignty is a conspicuous example.

At the other end of the spectrum of possibilities, rules in the form of assertive speech acts may be stated in very specific terms. Instructions for operating appliances, filling committee seats, or presenting diplomatic credentials are useful examples. Wherever rules in this form fall on the spectrum, they are *instruction-rules*. Providing information is not normative, but telling agents what they should do with that information is. Agents always know what they should do because the rule tells them something useful about their relation to the world.

Directive speech acts are recognizable as imperatives. If the speaker says that you must do something, the speaker wants you to believe that you should do it. Rules in the form of directive speech acts, *directive-rules*, are emphatically normative. By telling agents what they must do (no hunting!), these rules leave no doubt as to what they should do. Directive-rules often provide information about the consequences for disregarding them. Having this information (sixty days in jail!) helps rational agents to make the right choice in deciding whether to follow these rules or not.

Commissive speech acts involve promises. Speakers make promises that hearers accept. Commissive speech acts give form to rules when hearers, as speakers, respond with promises of their own. Once these webs of promises become sufficiently generalized and normative in their own terms, they become *commitment-rules*. Agents are most likely to recognize these rules in their effects. These effects are the *rights* and *duties* that agents know they possess with respect to other agents. Any given agent's rights constitute duties for other agents (private property—no hunting!).

Rights may entitle the agents possessing them to specific benefits. Rights may also empower agents to act toward other agents in specific ways. Obviously, powers and limits on powers turn people into agents. More generally, right and duties turn people into agents by defining opportunities for them to act upon the world. Instruction-rules and directive-rules also turn people into agents for exactly the same reason.

Speech acts fall into three categories because they perform different *functions*—they get things done for speakers and hearers together in three, and only three, ways. The same three categories hold for rules because they work in the same three ways that speech acts do—they get things done by instructing, directing, and committing agents. As observers, we see rules in each category performing different functions for society. Quite a few scholars in such fields as law and sociology have worked out variations on this functional scheme, but they have never used all three of these categories, and just these categories, at the same time.

Philosophers have devised a different scheme for categorizing rules, and a number of constructivist scholars have adopted it. On functional grounds, there are two categories of rules: constitutive rules and regulative rules. Constitutive rules are the medium of social construction. Regulative rules are the medium of social control.

While this scheme might seem to be constructivist, it is actually a source of confusion. From a constructivist point of view, all rules are always constitutive *and* regulative at the same time. By definition, rules regulate the conduct of agents because rules are normative—they tell agents what they should do. Furthermore, the regulation of conduct constitutes the world within which such conduct takes place, whether agents intend this consequence or not. Acting in the world means acting on the world, often as an unintended consequence. Intentions might be a useful way to categorize acts, but they are never a decisive basis for categorizing rules.

Even when agents intend that a particular rule serve only to regulate conduct (an intention that other agents may thwart by choosing, for example, to disregard the rule), the conduct in question will have the effect of strengthening or (if agents choose to disregard it) weakening the rule. In the same way, a rule that agents intend to be constitutive will have to affect conduct if it is to succeed. Often agents intend rules to be simultaneously constitutive and regulative. To give an obvious example, when agents called players take turns in playing a game, the rule instructing them to do so constitutes the game as one in which players regularly take turns.

As we have seen, rules serve three possible functions. Agents make rules and use them for instruction, direction, and commitment. Within each of these three functional categories, rules differ in the extent to which they have been formalized. Rules are formal if agents encounter them as fixed and unavoidable features of their world. Rules also differ in the extent which they are linked to other rules. Agents often discover that particular rules are linked to other rules telling other agents what to do in the event that the relevant agents disregard the particular rules in question. Formal rules that are effectively backed up by other rules are *legal*.

Formality strengthens a rule by making its normative character clearer, in the process separating it from rules that are normatively more ambiguous (conventions, for example). A rule supporting another rule strengthens the latter by increasing the chances that agents will choose to follow the latter rule. The more frequently agents follow a rule, the stronger the rule will be, normatively (and the easier it will be to make it formal). For example, the principle of sovereignty is a highly formal instruction-rule constituting the society of states. It is supported by commitment-rules empowering states, as agents, to bring new members into this society. These supporting rules, which we know as rules of recognition, are supported by instruction-rules that spell out a number of social and the material conditions that must be satisfied before statehood is possible.

Agents are inclined to make rules legal and to follow them if they are legal because they know what the rules are, how much they matter to other agents, and what consequences they can expect from not following them. When agents find themselves in a legal environment, it is rational for them to follow rules as a general proposition. It costs them less than careless conduct will. International relations is a peculiar environment in this respect, but still a legal environment. While there are very few formal directive-rules to be found, there are large numbers of other, quite formal rules intricately linked in support of each other. Relevant agents are perfectly aware of the situation and proceed accordingly.

Rules Form Institutions, Institutions Form Societies

Rules are linked to each other in content as well as function—both by what they say and by what they do. Standing back, agents can easily identify the ways that rules reinforce each other in what they say and do. Speaking figuratively, we might say that rules come in families, and that some families of rules come with rules documenting the family pedigree. Other families of rules depend on observers to document family resemblances. These and many other practices help to give families of rules their distinguishing features. Rules and related practices are almost impossible to separate in practice, because every time agents respond to rules, whether by making choices or by observing the choices that other agents make, they have an effect on those rules and on their places in families of rules.

By recent convention, scholarly observers of international relations call these families of rules and related practices "regimes." At an earlier time, they called them "institutions," and this remains the usual term for most scholars who devote their attentions to social relations. In practice, the two terms are indistinguishable. International regimes are said to consist of principles, rules, norms, and procedures. By whatever name, these are all categories of rules. Principles and procedures anchor the two ends of a spectrum of possibilities distinguishable by how general they are in content. Rules and norms are distinguishable by how formal they are, norms being sufficiently informal that observers are not always sure that they are rules until they see how other agents respond to them.

International regimes differ in size. They have rules that work in different ways (assertive-, directive-, and commitment-rules) in different proportions. Additionally, regimes differ in the extent to which they have rules backing up other rules. Institutions differ in exactly the same ways. They are made up of rules that vary, not just in generality and formality but also in number and arrangement.

Some simple institutions consist of a small number of rules whose content makes them a family, even if the rules seem to give little support to each other, and to get little support from other institutions to which they are connected. In the world of international relations, the balance of power is an example of such an institution. Instruction-rules constitute, and regulate, the balance of power. These rules tell the great powers what to expect when they choose allies and go to war. Yet even the balance of power, as an institution, is not as simple as it seems. Treaties give allies rights and duties. Rules limiting the conduct of war help to keep the balance from being permanently upset.

In the context of international relations, spheres of influence are also simple institutions made up of informal directive-rules. These rules direct weak states within the sphere to carry out a much stronger state's wishes. When these rules are backed up by principles justifying such arrangements, the sphere of influence is no longer quite so simple an institution. As formal equals, states may also adopt treaties distributing rights and duties that have unequal consequences within the sphere. Treaties are themselves simple institutions minimally consisting of formal commitment-rules that apply only to the states adopting such treaties. The principle that treaties are binding, and therefore legal, automatically provides them with support from other, highly formal rules.

Institutions such as the balance of power, spheres of influence, and treaties are simple only because observers can easily pick them out of an institutional environment characterized by a large number of linked rules and related practices. Agents act as observers when they recognize any institution as such, no matter how complex it is. Scholars often think of international regimes as something that they alone can see, while agents can see only the simpler institutions making up the regime. Yet observers become agents, and regimes become institutions, when other agents learn what observers have to say.

International regimes are hard to see because the rules connecting the institutions that make them up tend to be informal. Agents take them for granted. Formal rules make things clearer, and agents need not stand back. For a long time in the context of international relations, agents have had access to a legal institution, conventionally known as the sources of international law, through which they can make legal rules and thus institutions whose existence no one can doubt. Treaties are one such institution, thanks to the legal principle that treaties are binding on the states adopting them.

Agents respond to rules with goals in mind; institutions serve their interests. As a general matter, simple institutions have a more straightforward relation to agents' interests than do more complex and more difficult to recognize institutions. We think of relatively simple institutions as performing distinct functions for agents and for other institutions. Depending on what these relatively simple institutions do, they give priority to rules in one of the functional categories that we have already identified.

When instruction-rules are most in evidence, agents are situated in *networks* of rules and related practices. The balance of power is an example. Its rules assign an elevated *status* to a few great powers (ideally five states) that must act as if they are roughly equal in the resources available to them. If states' agents act as instructed, the consequences are supposed to be an ever-shifting and relatively peaceful balance of alliances among the great powers, whatever the immediate intentions of their agents might be. Recognizing the balance of power as an institution whose function suits their interests, agents intentionally foster those same consequences in the name of the balance.

When directive-rules are most in evidence, agents are situated in a chain of command, a firm, or an *organization*. A sphere of influence is a rudimentary institution of this sort. Its very informal rules assign each agent to an *office*, as we would call it in a more formal organization. Officers report up the chain of command and carry out orders that come down the chain. By this logic, the top officer decides what the organization's function is. In practice, most organizations are more complex than this. Nevertheless, a sphere of influence is so rudimentary in organization that its function is nothing more than to fulfill the wishes of a leading power, as top officer, over the weaker states within the sphere.

Finally, when commitment-rules are most in evidence, agents end up in partnerships, or *associations*, with other agents. In the institutional context of international relations, the principle of sovereignty and the supporting rules of recognition make states into formal equals. When two or more states adopt a treaty, they act as members of an association giving them at least some rights in common, including the right to commit themselves to each other. Under the terms of the treaty, all parties take on additional rights and duties with respect to the others. In this situation, states are formally equal because they all have the same *role*. The function of any association is to distribute roles to agents through its commitment-rules.

Only states (and the associations that they have created by treaty) can adopt treaties, because there is a commitment-rule assigning this role to them exclusively. To return to an earlier example, markets function by assigning agents either of two roles—they are either sellers or buyers. Every seller is formally equal in possessing the right to buy, and so is every buyer. Note, however, that neither sellers nor buyers have a right to a fixed price. Formally speaking, agents in these roles are free to compete with each other, presumably for the good of every agent in the association. The function of this, or any, association is implied by the commitments that agents have made to a given distribution of roles.

It is important to note, however, that an association's roles are not generally equal in the rights and duties that they create. Think, for example, of the roles that members of most households have. For that matter, agents holding the same status (for example, white males) are equal to each other within the terms of that status, even if different statuses are unequal in relation to each other. This is no less true for agents holding the same or similar offices (for example, foreign ministers). Nevertheless, commitment-rules are especially useful for making large numbers of agents formally equal for limited purposes.

Agency consists of statuses, offices, and roles. Depending on the institutional context, every agent must have a status, an office, or a role. Most, perhaps all, agents have all three in some combination. This is because most people are agents in a variety of institutions, and many institutions combine features of networks, organizations, and associations.

Institutions such as these are complex in function and structure. Instruction-, directive-, and commitment-rules are all present, even if the proportions differ from institution to institution. Observers usually have no difficulty in picking out the pattern of rules, because institutions are social arrangements that always reflect agents' interests. From an observer's point of view, institutions have purposes. It seems this way even if the observer is an interested agent.

A complex institution will have general instruction-rules, or principles, telling agents what the purposes of that institution are. Detailed instruction-rules may provide support for these principles by spelling out all relevant statuses. Directive-rules may also repeat and elaborate on what these principles have to say and then support them by demanding that officers do what these rules say that they should. In situations where there are no conspicuous instruction-rules or directive-rules supporting principles, commitment-rules create roles for agents that have, from any one agent's point of view, the unintended effect of supporting the institution's principles.

Rules in all three categories often work together to support an institution's principles. Sometimes, however, institutions develop in such a way that rules from one or even two categories are scarce or not to be found at all. If we consider international relations as taking place within a single, overarching institution, its rules constitute a conspicuously lopsided arrangement. Thanks to the principle of sovereignty, there are few if any formal directive-rules. Observers will discover informal directive-rules in practice, even if some agents routinely deny that such rules exist.

Considered as a complex institution, international relations takes place in a context where agents and observers find a large number of formal commitment-rules (rules of international law), behind which there is an even larger number of instruction-rules. These latter rules differ enormously in formality (quite a few are legal rules), detail, and the degree to which they are linked to each other. They support the principle of sovereignty and a few other principles more or less directly and effectively. Thanks again to the principle of sovereignty, states are complex institutions within which formal directive-rules allow agents to act on behalf of states in their relations.

The context within which any institution functions as an agent is itself an institution. Society is a complex institution within which many other related institutions are to be found. Agents are likely to act as if their society's boundaries are clear and accepted, even if observers, including agents, have a hard time specifying those boundaries to anyone's satisfaction. States are societies that have exceptionally clear boundaries as well as highly developed institutions for conducting relations with other states.

The complex institution within which states function as relatively self-contained societies is itself a society. Within *international society*, states function as primary agents simply by conducting relations with each other. International society includes many other, more or less self-contained institutions. Some of them add secondary agents, such as officers of international organizations, to that society. The sum total of institutions and their relations add up to a society of staggering complexity and constant change, even though its large patterns seem at least to some observers to call for generalization.

Rules Yield Rule

We have seen that institutions consist of related rules and practices. It is possible to think of a single rule as an institution. As a practical matter, we never find a single rule standing by itself. Every rule gives the agents to whom it applies the choice of following the rule, or not, with more or less predictable consequences.

Most of the time, agents choose to follow the rule. The pattern of agents' choices has a general consequence, whether or not it is intended by particular agents—it has the effect of distributing material and social benefits among agents. An extremely important category of such benefits is control over resources and control over other agents and their activities. Some agents benefit more than other agents. Over time, institutions work to the advantage of some agents at the expense of other agents.

As rational beings, those agents who benefit the most from the rules that apply to them are the most inclined to follow those rules. Agents who benefit less are still inclined to follow the rules because doing so still benefits them more than not doing so. Nevertheless, agents may proceed to break any given rule after weighing the consequences of either choice for themselves. As a general consequence, rule breaking is likely to involve a loss of benefits to other agents.

Agents who are negatively affected by the breaking of a rule also have a choice. They may accept the consequences (including a weakened faith in the broken rule and a greater chance of its being broken again). Alternatively, they may choose to follow a rule that has the consequence of presenting the rule breaker with a loss of benefits, which the rule breaker is either prepared to accept or had thought would not be likely to occur. The second choice, which we think of as enforcing the rule, involves using resources that might otherwise have been put to beneficial use. This loss of benefits is still less than the loss that comes from not enforcing the rule.

Instead of breaking a given rule, agents who do not benefit from following it may choose to use whatever resources are needed to change that rule, and thus to change the distribution of benefits that results from the rule's existence. If some agents try to change the rule, other agents who would benefit less from the changes may choose to use the necessary resources to keep the rule from changing. Furthermore, those agents who benefit the most from a given rule will probably have to use fewer of the resources available to them to keep the rule from changing than will agents who want to change the rule. Clearly, rules say what they say, and institutions are slow to change, because agents make rational choices in circumstances that always give the advantage to some agents over others.

The general consequence of agents' responding to rules with the resources available to them is that some agents exercise greater control over the content of those rules, and over their success in being followed, than other agents do. In other words, rules yield rule. By making agents and society what they are, rules make rule inevitable. Rule is something that agents do to, and for, other agents, and they do it by following rules. Rule is something that happens to agents when they follow rules or when they suffer the consequences of not following rules.

Specific institutions may formalize rule by seeming to limit its exercise to a particular agent or set of agents—to rulers. Just because we can identify rulers, we should not conclude that they alone do the ruling. Wherever there are informal rules (which is everywhere), there is informal rule, either supporting or undercutting formal institutions of rule, or both (probably in a complex and hard to observe pattern). Even if the formalities of rule are nowhere to be found, rule remains a pervasive condition for that society. Loaded with rules but lacking rulers, international society is a case in point.

Rules in different functional categories yield different forms of rule. Where instruction-rules are paramount and status is a defining feature of society, ideas and beliefs seem to do the ruling. Despite appearances, agents actually do the ruling by getting other agents to accept their ideas and beliefs. They do so by example and by indoctrination. Rule in this form is *hegemony*.

Any society where principles get most of their support from detailed instruction-rules is hegemonically ruled. Caste societies are examples. Each hegemonically ruled caste has clear boundaries and a fixed position in the network of castes constituting the society. Membership in a caste gives agents so much of their identity, defined as a set of ideas about self and position in society, that caste identity seems to rule the society as a whole. Hegemonically ruled institutions exist in societies where other sorts of institutions and a mixed form of rule can be identified. The professions offer an example. Detailed instruction-rules, ordinarily learned through a long apprenticeship, support professional standards and rule agents to their advantage in their relations with clients needing their professional services.

In institutions where directive-rules are paramount and office is a defining feature of society, offices are vertically organized in a chain of command. Officers at each position in the chain use resources that their offices make available to them to carry out the rules that their offices require them to carry out. From top to bottom, such an arrangement of offices is called a *hierarchy*, and so might we call the form of rule that results when officers carry out directive-rules. The state as a legal order exemplifies hierarchical rule.

When directive-rules are legal, hierarchy is formal. Despite the minimal description of the state as a legal order, formal hierarchies rarely stand alone. Hegemonical ideas typically reinforce formal hierarchy. The result is *authority*, conventionally defined as legitimate control. Military officers possess authority according to their rank, which is their status and office formally joined together in mutual reinforcement. Finally, informal hierarchy may reinforce hegemony that has achieved a relatively high level of formality. After World War II, the so-called *pax Americana* may be thought of as a condition of rule in which the United States ruled, in the name of freedom and prosperity, by intervening whenever and wherever it chose. Proclaiming principles had the effect (perhaps initially unintended) of formalizing the status of the United States as leader of "the free world," while acting on those principles gave it an informal office.

Where commitment-rules are paramount and role is a defining feature of society, agents hold a variety of roles that are defined by reference to the roles that other agents hold. No one role, or institution, even comes close to making particular agents into rulers. On the contrary, formal commitment-rules mostly seem to reinforce formal hierarchy. They do so by granting officers well-defined powers to help them issue orders and carry them out, and by granting agents well-defined rights to help protect them from officers abusing their powers. The result is a constitutional state, in which the constitution formalizes commitment-rules that limit the government of the state and make it responsible.

Taken as a whole, roles may yield rule on their own, and not just because they reinforce other forms of rule. Agents in association are the rulers—all of them together—even if none of them have the status or office to make them rulers. Ruled by association, agents do not see rule in their roles. As agents, they are mostly concerned with their roles and what they are free to do within them. To return once more to the example of a market, agents participating in it generally have the sense that this is an institution free of rule. As sellers and buyers, they are nevertheless ruled as an unintended consequence of the exercise of their right to buy and sell. Adam Smith's invisible hand is a hand that rules, and it rules to the advantage of some agents over others.

As we saw, quite a few scholars describe international relations as anarchical. An anarchy is rule by no one in particular, and therefore by everyone in association, as an unintended consequence of their many, uncoordinated acts. Recall that agents who observe a general pattern of unintended consequences can no longer be said to act without intending consequences, even if they continue to act as they had been acting. They intend to be ruled for good reasons, and if they did not have good reasons, they would make other choices.

If anarchy is a condition of rule unrelated to any agent's intentions, then international relations is no anarchy. We need another term to indicate the form of rule in which agents intend that they be ruled by what seem to be unintended consequences of exercising their rights. *Heteronomy* is a better term. Autonomous agents act freely, while heteronomous agents cannot act freely. Both terms refer to agents, not society. From a constructivist perspective, however, agents are always autonomous, but their autonomy is always limited by the (limited) autonomy of other agents. The exercise of autonomy makes heteronomy a social condition, which agents accept as an apparently unintended consequence of their individual, autonomous choices.

International society is heteronomously ruled because states exercise their independence under the principle of sovereignty and under a number of commitment-rules granting them rights and duties with respect to each other. One state's independence is a limit on every other's, and all states' agents accept the unintended consequences that result from their many individual choices. Within this general condition of rule are to be found a large number of institutions contributing to rule in a variety of ways. Agents (and not just states' agents) constantly work on these institutions and work within them. Despite their number and variety, and the complexity of their relations, they are arranged as they are on purpose, by agents' intentions, to serve their interests—including their shared interest in being ruled.

Note

Kurt Burch, Harry Gould, and Vendulka Kubálková persuaded me to write a concise exposition of constructivism as I had developed it in *World of Our Making* (1989). The result is "A Constructivist Manifesto" (Onuf 1997), which I wrote in a telegraphic style for a scholarly audience, introducing some new material and leaving a great deal out. While I had planned my essay for this book as a sentence-by-sentence reconstruction of the "Manifesto" for a larger audience, I ended up making quite a few substantive additions and changes, and I deleted all of its relatively few citations. I am grateful to members of the Miami International Relations Group for their questions and suggestions.

Bibliography

Onuf, Nicholas Greenwood. 1989. *World of Our Making: Rules and Rule in Social Theory and International Relations*. Columbia: University of South Carolina Press.
———. 1997. "A Constructivist Manifesto." In *Constituting International Political Economy*, ed. Kurt Burch and Robert A. Denemark, 7–17. Boulder, CO: Lynne Rienner.

4

What *Is* at Stake in the Agent-Structure Debate?

Harry D. Gould

Introduction

As noted in the introductory chapter to this volume, the division of international relations (IR) into a series of debates has become a conventional device for making sense of the field. Beyond the "great debates," at least three and possibly five in number (Wæver 1997, 12–25), two debates are of interest here: the "levels of analysis" debate touched off by David Singer in 1961 and especially the "agent-structure" debate initiated by Alexander Wendt in 1987.

Simply put, the conceptual problem at the heart of the agent-structure debate is: How are agents and structures related? Over the course of the debate, this problem has disappeared from view, or, more to the point, the debate itself has become problematic. There are several problems: the positions held by some of the participants have changed over time, the terms of debate have changed, and the serial subdebates have become further removed both from the core issue and from IR's substantive concerns.

The purpose of this paper is to put Onuf's constructivism into the context of the agent-structure debate, expanding on his contribution to this book, his book *World of Our Making* (1989), and several articles which have also served to refine his position (Onuf 1994, 1995, 1996, 1997). This will entail a brief review of constructivism, as well as a detailed analysis in which I shall put constructivism into dialogue with the various positions staked out during the debate. The concluding discussion will look at the levels of analysis debate in IR, the relation of which to the agent-structure debate formed an important part of Wendt's several exchanges with Martin Hollis and Steve Smith.

Constructivism

At its barest, the constructivist position on the relation of agents to structures is that they each constitute the other. Simultaneously, agents and structure enable and constrain each other. In itself, this advances very little beyond Anthony Giddens's "structuration theory" (Giddens 1979, 1984), to which Onuf is obviously indebted. The relation of constructivism to structuration is complex. Constructivism's debt to structuration is plain enough, but the origin and nature of the differences are important. The most important difference lies in the indispensable role played by rules in Onuf's constructivism. A fuller account of structuration is to be found below; what is important to note at the present is that Giddens's concern was to answer the question, which dominates: structure (determinism) or agency (free will)? His answer, put in the most basic way, is that each shapes the other.

Both accounts take as their starting point the rejection of ontological individualism and pure ontological structuralism. As we shall see, this is true of all of the perspectives voiced in the debate. Both claim that agents and structures actively and continuously constitute and change each other. Structuration, however, lacks a fully developed mechanism capable of explaining the means by which agents and structures constitute one another.

Onuf found this mechanism in the concept of *rules*, as developed in legal and linguistic philosophy. In his words:

> The co-constitution of people as social beings and of society is a continuous process. Rules are central to this process because they make people active participants (or agents) in society, and they give any society its distinctive character (or structure). Rules define agents in terms of structures, and structures in terms of agents. . . . As rules change in number, kind, relation and content, they constantly redefine agents and structures, always in terms of each other. (1996, 6)

For Onuf, the solution to the structurationist dilemma of how to deal at the level of method with the continuous, dynamic process of co-constitution—where to cut into the process—is to "emphasize rules, but never rules considered in a vacuum. To begin with rules simultaneously leads in two directions—toward agents and their choices, and toward social arrangements that eventuate from agents choices" (Onuf 1997, 8).

Concomitant with the focus on rules, and by necessity presupposing it, is a focus on *deeds*. Deeds are responses to and constituents of the circumstances in which people find themselves. People use language both to represent their deeds and to perform them. *Speaking is doing*. Utterances through which people accomplish social ends directly—perform deeds—are *speech acts*. Furthermore, rules take form from speech acts.

Rules link agents and structures in a common process of constitution, but only if rules have an ontological standing appropriate to their dual function. Giddens did not see this; he saw rules as a property of structure, not as a material property (Onuf 1996, 8–9). Rules have properties of their own. Language gives rules an autonomous character suited to their function; through language rules exist in their own right. "Competence with rules is a defining feature of human cognition, and the presence of rules is a defining feature of the human condition" (9).

According to Onuf (9–10), rules describe some class of actions and indicate whether these actions constitute warranted conduct on the part of those to whom the rules are addressed. They can do this because, as stated above, rules come from performative speech. Speech acts convey propositional content and elicit an appropriate response. Because people respond to these (speech) acts with their own performances, the pattern of speech acts and their responses make human life intelligible. The pattern of speech acts endows practices with normativity, giving rise to rules. As we shall see below, this is part of the way in which we "construct" structure.

As far as Giddens and Onuf are concerned, all rules are simultaneously constitutive and regulative. Rules are regulative by definition. Regulation yields constitution as an effect. Even if a particular rule is strictly intended to regulate conduct, it will have an additional constitutive effect. The converse is also true: rules intended to be only constitutive will have regulative consequences.

Agents are, or consist of, individuals whose acts materially affect the world. Rules constituting a society define the conditions under which individuals may intervene in the world. Rules make individuals into agents by enabling them to act upon the world in which they find themselves. As shown above, these acts have material and social effects; they make the world what it is materially and socially. Once constituted as agents, individuals intervene in the world by responding to choices offered by rules.

Wendt situated the agent-structure problem in a debate few scholars in IR had encountered: the debate in philosophy of science between positivists and scientific realists over the ontological status of phenomena that cannot be directly observed. Pure positivists refuse to consider such phenomena, even if their effects are observable. Most scientists take unobservable phenomena, such as magnetism, for granted. For purposes of debate, scientific realists attribute so much importance to unobservables that someone dipping into the debate might be inclined to underestimate the practical significance of observable phenomena. We see this particularly in Wendt's scientific realist treatment of structuration, in which he not only ignores Giddens's sense of the importance of rules and resources, but rejects Giddens's account of structure for this very emphasis.[1]

Above we saw that rules have an ontological status. Rules constitute themselves in regular patterns that may or may not be observed, but are always observable in principle. We observe a world of regularities upon which the mind seeks to impose order. The regularities are not themselves structures. They are better called "institutions," which is an ontologically unambiguous term. It is through the cognitive functions of the mind that patterned regularities have order, or structure, imposed upon them. When agents "see" structures and act on them, rules and institutions are affected—structures are real, even if "structure" is not.

Agents act on observable regularities for the same reason that scientific realists attribute causal significance to unobservable structures—to make the world a more orderly place for instrumental reasons. Insofar as observers impose structures on the phenomenal world, or perhaps make the world phenomenal, observers also act as agents. This tends to give phenomenal properties to structures, which then creates the feedback loop which constructivists and structurationists emphasize, the pattern of *co-constitution*.

This synthetic structure imposed upon the world functions like a template. In imparting order it imputes function; parts are related to wholes. Beyond this implicit teleology, function is also ascribed to structures; we assign meaning to what structures do. These conjoined problems betray an Aristotelian, teleological bias implicit in structuralism—parts are functionally related to wholes—to which both structuration and constructivism can all too easily fall prey. To avoid this, it must be remembered that structures have only those functions ascribed to them by agents; there is nothing natural (necessary) about either structures or the functions they perform. For this reason, structures are perhaps better thought of as institutions, because this term more adequately conveys the constitutive role played by agents, thus avoiding the functionalist road to structural determinism.

Constructivism and the Agent-Structure Debate

It should by now be plain what the constructivist stance on issues of agency and structure is, but to clarify at the outset just how this stance relates to the debate over agency and structure in IR, I make the following claims:

1. The agent-structure problem raises issues of importance to IR's second debate, not (as most scholars seem to think) the third debate.
2. The issues central to the debate are primarily of method, and to an extent ontological; they are not epistemological.
3. Structuration theory cannot resolve the debate; it does not adequately delineate the means by which agents and structures constitute one another.
4. The scientific realist focus on efficacious unobservables does not add the needed corrective.
5. The constructivist focus on rules is what is needed.
6. Scientific realism is not necessary to explain the ontological status of rules.
7. Rules are necessary to agency. They make states into agents at the macro level in much the same fashion that they make individuals agents at the micro level.
8. Rules form institutions. They link agents and institutions, which must be accorded equal ontological status.
9. Structure is in the mind's eye. Structures exist because agents see patterns to which they *impute* structure.
10. Once structures are "produced," knowledge about them takes on phenomenal properties. They become a property of institutions, any of which may function as agents.

The agent-structure debate has been remarkably one-sided. In IR, no self-conscious advocate of methodological individualism has taken up the debate. The nature of agency is so neglected that it is misleading even to speak of an "agent-structure debate." By and large, what we shall see is a fight over the middle, in which each theorist makes the claim that his or her representation of the effects that agents and structures have on one another is the most accurate or useful.[2]

In what may be reasonably called the prehistory of the debate, Kenneth Waltz (1979) attacked the rampant reductionism in the field because the unintended consequences of state behavior produce irreducible structures that have consequences for behavior. This unequivocal claim provided Wendt an opportunity to introduce the issue of structure from a scientific realist point of view. If his discussion of world systems theory seems cursory by comparison, reductionist science got no attention at all.

Waltz's defense of structural realism as good science links the agent-structure debate to IR's second debate. On the face of it, the second debate is about method. Should IR continue to be historicist in orientation, as it had been in its first decades, or should it follow the other social sciences and adopt the model of positivist natural science? Many scholars believed that all the secrets of human behavior, from individual to social, political, and economic, could be fully understood by proper application of positivist methods of inquiry. The actual debate largely pitted the British "traditionalists," trained in diplomatic history and law, against "scientists" from the United States.

Among the latter we find a running subdebate, which has probably engaged more intellectual energy and filled more journal pages than the second debate proper, pitting behavioralists against systemicists. The behavioralists probably made a better claim to being "scientific" by the standards of the day—their orientation was more explicitly empiricist than that of the systemicists, who came from the largely discredited rationalist epistemological tradition.[3] Rather than construct models of the workings of unobservable structures, the behavioralists studied regularities of behavior. Their method was inductive, beginning with observation of the actions of parts, rather than deductively working out the relations of parts in a hypothetical whole. In articulating the concept of levels of analysis, Singer (1961) tried to give both sides legitimacy, which each side accepted for itself but denied to the other.

Waltz overturned the preeminence of the behavioralists. He placed systemicism on top. In effect, he rejected brute empiricism, which had been dominant in its various forms since Hume, and the notion that knowledge progressively accumulates in the absence of deductive theory. Waltz accomplished this by treating structure as the unintended consequence of the interactions (behavior) of self-interested actors (here, states; in the microeconomic theory he emulated, firms). Structure is observable, irreducible, efficacious.[4]

Wendt 1987

"The Agent-Structure Problem in International Relations Theory" (Wendt 1987) is noteworthy on several counts, not least of which is that it was written when Wendt was still a graduate student, and it was IR's first sustained exploration of questions of agency and structure. Wendt had two purposes in this piece, first to demonstrate the inadequacy of both Waltz's version of structuralism and that of Immanuel Wallerstein, and second to advocate structuration theory as a replacement for structuralism generally. Wendt made the startling claim that Waltz was, in fact, not at all the structuralist he claimed, but, to the contrary, an ontological individualist. Conversely, he found Wallerstein's world systems theory to be too holistic.

In the case of Waltz's implicit individualism, Wendt claimed that the system and its structure are the creations of the states; despite the influence exerted by the structure over the states, the states must, by Waltz's logic, predate (be ontologically prior to) the system and its structure. Therefore, the unit exhibits a controlling influence over the structure. The exact converse is true of Wallerstein: the system both predates and creates the states—this is pure holism, the units derive all meaning from the generative structure. The problem with each position, as Wendt quite correctly asserted, is that, in each case, the ontologically prior entity is taken to be given and unproblematic. In short, Waltz has no theory of the state, Wallerstein no theory of the system.

In contrast to these extremes, Wendt advocated application of Giddens's structuration theory. As used by Wendt, structuration theory incorporates the best of both individualism and structuralism. The philosophical foundations for structuration, Wendt claimed, are to be found in scientific realism. Realists can be rigorously scientific about "unobservable generative structures." They are treated *as if* they are real if their effects can be observed (Wendt 1987, 350).

The importance of scientific realism to structuration becomes evident when one considers the scientific realist claim that to make an explanatory claim, it is necessary to identify the underlying causal mechanisms that make an event a necessary occurrence. If we can explain the physical dispositions and causal powers of unobservable entities, we can make legitimate inferences about necessary causal relations (354).

Having established what he takes to be the scientific realist *bona fides* of structuration, Wendt proceeded to discuss structuration itself. His central claim on behalf of structuration is that the "capacities and even the existence of human agents are in some way *necessarily* related to a social structural context—that they are inseparable from human sociality" (355). For Wendt, structuration theory is analytical in nature, not substantive; it is what he would later call metatheory—a theory about theory. It addresses the types of entities to be found in the social world and their relations.

Wendt offered four core claims on behalf of structuration theory:

1. In opposition to individualists, structurationists accept the reality and explanatory importance of irreducible and potentially unobservable social structures that generate agents.

2. In opposition to structuralists, structurationists oppose functionalism and stress "the need for a theory of practical reason and consciousness that can account for human intentionality and motivation."

3. These oppositions are reconciled by joining agents and structures in a "dialectical synthesis" that overcomes the subordination of one to the other,

which is characteristic of both individualism and structuralism.

4. Finally, structurationists argue that social structures are inseparable from spatial and temporal structures, and that time and space must therefore be incorporated directly and explicitly into theoretical and concrete social research (Wendt 1987, 356).

Although *structuration* is Giddens's term, Wendt relied more heavily on the work of Roy Bhaskar (1979), undoubtedly because Bhaskar was more explicitly scientific realist in orientation than Giddens. This is reflected in their respective conceptions of social structure. For Giddens, structure is conceptualized in terms of rules and resources, while Bhaskar treated structure in realist terms, as unobservable but still causally efficacious (Wendt 1987, 357, note 57).

Following Bhaskar, Wendt defined structure in generative terms as a set of internally related elements (agents, units). Because these elements or agents are internally related, they cannot be defined or conceived independently of their position within the structure. This translates to a view of the state system wherein states are viewed in relational terms. They are constituted by the internal relations of individuation and penetration. States are thus not conceivable *as* states, apart from their position in a global structure of individuated and penetrated political authority. States, thus, are not conceivable as such outside of their position in the international system (357).

As a set of possible transformations, social structures are not reducible to the relations between the structure's elements. Structures make a given combination of elements possible, but they are not limited to the combinations that have already manifested themselves. Because social structures generate agents and their behavior, and because they have observable effects, we can claim that they are real entities despite being quite possibly unobservable (357).

Dessler 1989

Two years after Wendt's celebrated essay appeared, another young scholar, David Dessler, published "What's at Stake in the Agent-Structure Debate?" (1989) in the same journal. It is not clear what motivated Dessler to substitute the term *debate* for *problem*, which is the term Wendt used. There is little easily construed as "debate" before the Wendt, and Hollis, and Smith exchanges beginning in 1991. Dessler addressed Wendt only at one point, and then only parenthetically in a footnote, which will be discussed below. The change was, however, prescient.

For Dessler, the root of the agent-structure debate lies in the recognition of human agency as the only force behind actions, events, and outcomes of the social world; human agency can be realized, however, only within a structure. Thus, while the need exists to acknowledge the powers of agents, we must concurrently recognize the causal relevance of structural factors. In Dessler's conception, "all social action presupposes social structure, and vice versa. An actor can only act socially because there exists a social structure to draw on, and it is only through the actions of agents that structure is reproduced" (Dessler 1989, 452).

For reasons similar to Wendt's, Dessler was critical of Waltz's approach. Dessler called the ontology of Waltz's structural realism "positional" because the system's structure results from the positioning of ontologically prior units. The system is, as discussed above, the product of the unintended consequences of interacting units. Dessler countered this with his own transformational ontology. To do so, he too relied on scientific realism, which, on his reading, holds that a theory's explanatory power is derived from the richness of its ontology. Central to this transformational ontology are the following two claims. First, structure both enables and constrains the possibilities for agent actions, and, second, structure is both medium and outcome of agent action. In both claims, he is well in line with structurationist and constructivist thought.

For scientific realists, the structural approach to international relations starts with the recognition that state action is possible only if the instruments of action exist to carry it out. Dessler identified two such instruments: resources and rules. Resources are material capabilities. Rules he defined as "the media through which action become possible and which action itself reproduces and transforms" (1989, 467). Dessler further identifies two types of rules. Regulative rules prescribe and proscribe behavior in particular circumstances; constitutive rules create types of behavior. In practice, however, the regulative have constitutive implications, and vice versa (453–56).

It is interesting to note at this point that Dessler and Onuf concurrently made rules ontologically central to the agent-structure relation, although Onuf did so without embracing scientific realism. Furthermore, "What's at Stake in the Agent-Structure Debate?" and *World of Our Making* came out nearly simultaneously, although the authors were unaware of one another's efforts.

In Dessler's transformational ontology, rules are the material conditions of action, which agents appropriate and through which action reproduces or transforms. Structure is a medium of activity that in principle can be altered through activity. Any given action will reproduce or transform some part of the social structure. Social action is both a product and a by-product. This ontology grounds consideration of rules not only by making their existence explicit, but also by providing a useful model of how they exist in relation to agents and structures (458–66).

Dessler specifically addressed Wendt's paper only with respect to Wendt's interpretation of scientific realism.

> On this crucial conceptual point [the realist definition of structure as "the social forms that preexist action"], Wendt misinterprets the scientific realist understanding of structure. . . . Wendt tilts toward a structural determinism in his analysis of the relation between state and system, conceptualizing the state as an *effect* of the internally related elements comprising structure. . . . According to scientific realism, agents and structures are not "two moments of the same process" but "radically different kinds of thing." (Dessler 1989, 452, note 45, quoting Bhaskar 1979, 42)

Wendt 1991

Wendt's 1991 piece is an extended review essay of Onuf's book, *World of Our Making* (1989), and Hollis and Smith's book, *Explaining and Understanding International Relations* (1990). In the course of this essay, Wendt reiterated some aspects of the position he took in his 1987 paper. He was largely approving of Onuf for his reliance on Giddens, but more critical of Hollis and Smith.

Wendt's primary criticism of Hollis and Smith's work is that they conflate the levels of analysis problem with the agent-structure problem. Wendt went back to Singer for his formulation of the former: "Levels of analysis had to do with determining which level of social aggregation offers the most promise for building theories" (Wendt 1991, 387). What Wendt felt Hollis and Smith importantly overlook is that, regardless of the level, the same *unit* of analysis is utilized as the dependent variable: the foreign policy of states. As formulated by Hollis and Smith, the phenomenon to be explained changes with the level. First, it is the behavior of states, then the behavior of the system (387–88).

This is, for Wendt, an ontological problem with methodological implications. The question seems to be whether the properties or behavior of one unit at one level of analysis can be reduced to those of another. Nevertheless, Wendt thought that methodological arguments about individualism and holism are really about agency and structure, not about analytic practices. The efforts of Hollis and Smith to defend structural realism as an exemplar of holistic theory at the systemic level of analysis are surprising (or so Wendt thought), since they argue at several points that international society contains too few constitutive rules and collective forms of life to sustain a truly social or constitutive analysis of state action. While questioning whether international society is developed enough to support a holistic worldview, they continue to endorse structural realism's claim to do just that.

Hollis and Smith 1991

Hollis and Smith used their reply to Wendt's review article to critique his and Dessler's structurationist positions, the scientific realism underpinning them, and the radical ontological individualism associated with Jon Elster, not articulated elsewhere in this debate. This is done in the context of a warning about following "gurus"—here, Giddens, Bhaskar, and Elster.

Hollis and Smith were particularly suspicious of Wendt's version of structuration theory, which they likened to trying to find the correct proportions of agent and structure to blend. "Agents and structures do not blend easily in any proportions, and the solutions tend to be unstable" (Hollis and Smith 1991, 393). They contended that structuration complicates the problem by employing both structural relations between units which are not necessarily human, and hermeneutic concepts the referents of which *must* be human. For them, structuration is more an ambition than an established body of theoretical achievements (405–6).

In advocating clarity about the terms *epistemology*, *ontology*, and *methodology*, which they found lacking in Wendt and Dessler, Hollis and Smith identify three sets of questions: ontological, epistemological, and methodological. There are three ontological questions: Is there a real-world difference in what it is to which the systems-terms and the unit-terms refer? How do systems relate to units? Is the shared referent primarily that of systems-terms or unit-terms? They also identify a basic epistemological question: How are statements about international relations known to be true or false? The methodological issue questions what forms of explanation or understanding are to be attempted, and how they are to be achieved. There is no dispute among all parties to the debate that all three kinds of questions are involved in the debate. The dispute is over which question or questions are primary; as Hollis and Smith saw it, empiricists favor epistemology, and scientific realists favor ontology (1991, 394).

Hollis and Smith claimed that Wendt focused on theoretically interdependent entities without any self-evident way to conceptualize the entities or their relations, which yields the ontological problem of knowing how many entities there are and what their relations are. In response to Wendt's claim that Hollis and Smith conflate the levels of analysis and agent-structure problems, they asked whether analysis should proceed from system to unit, or vice versa, but pointed out that this is not automatically reducible to ontology. Foreshadowing their response to Walter Carlsnaes and their later exchange with Vivienne Jabri and Stephen Chan, Hollis and Smith claimed that the ontological justification of a theory is connected to its explanatory merits, which is an epistemological issue.

Wendt 1992

In a rejoinder, Wendt maintained that Hollis and Smith conflated two (presumably) distinct problems, and he disputed their interpretation of Waltz. It is this second point which defines this exchange. Hollis and Smith imply, he claimed, that there can be only one type of systemic theory, that of Waltz and microeconomics. All else is reductionism. Wendt refused the choice between reductionism and systemicism. He argued that the idea of systemic theory should be broadened to include a concern with the process of identity and interest formation which should not be treated as exogenous (as per Waltz). This led him to argue again for the distinctiveness of the levels of analysis problem and the agent-structure problem (Wendt 1992a, 181). The structural realist attitude toward causation at the systematic level was, in Wendt's opinion, too behavioralist. Waltz did not claim that the system shapes states, but rather that states are exogenously self-interested. What is affected by the system is their behavior.

For Wendt, the central issue dividing individualists and holists is whether it is the properties of actors or their behavior that can be reduced to structural determinants. Here Waltz seems to be a holist, but, because he treated the identity and interests of states as exogenous, rather than as a "socially constructed function of interaction," and did not therefore address how these interests are produced, he is, in fact, an individualist. It is this inconsistency in Waltz which allowed Hollis and Smith to reduce the question of systemic causation to the question of whether the international system conditions the behavior of states. They thus reduced the agent-structure problem to the levels of analysis problem (Wendt 1992a, 182–83).

Wendt saw two answers to the question of how to explain the actions of states if they cannot be reduced to the anarchical system. The holistic position is particularly interesting to Wendt. In such a view, identities and interests are constructed by a process of interaction within anarchy (1992b). If they were less wed to a behavioralist vocabulary, Waltz, as well as Hollis and Smith, would see this. The difference, according to Wendt, is that a world in which these variables are exogenous—or are not variable—is necessarily one where the patterns of interaction do not change. In Waltz's language, the ordering principle does not change; anarchy is therefore an inescapable feature of international life. If identity and interests are regarded as capable of change, then the nature of international life can similarly change (1992a, 183).

Hollis and Smith 1992

Answering Wendt, Hollis and Smith contended that a holist need concede nothing in recognizing states as self-interested. A holist would only need to add that these interests are shaped by the system, because a holist considers the system the source of what matters. However, such a top-down explanation does need some kind of mechanism to explain the means by which agents contribute to the process, even if only in ways limited by the system (Hollis and Smith 1992, 187).

Although Wendt thought he was speaking only about the levels-of-analysis problem, his argument presupposes a stance on the agent-structure problem. This is because both levels of analysis involve questions about agency—not just about how to explain behavior, but also about what it means to be an actor. The latter question is necessarily central to the agent-structure problem. Therefore, as Hollis and Smith reiterated, the two cannot be separated.

Carlsnaes 1992

In "The Agency-Structure Problem in Foreign Policy Analysis" (1992), Carlsnaes claimed that the problem can be *overcome*. He warned against solutions of the problem which make either agents or structures the sole ontological primitive, and then attempt to explain the other by reduction to it. On this point he, Wendt, Dessler, and Onuf are, at least in principle, in agreement. Reducing each one to the other tends to rule out the interplay identified by structuration and constructivism. Since neither structures nor actors remain constant over time, good social theory must be able to account for social change as a dynamic phenomenon, in respect of which, neither factor "determines" the other, but both are independent variables linked in a "temporal process." He felt that Giddens (and anyone following in his footsteps) had failed to capture the dynamic interplay between agents and structures. For Giddens, the two merely presuppose one another. Each is irreducible to the other, but they are still conflated.

To overcome the problem of conflation, Carlsnaes found a new "guru" in Margaret Archer. From Archer, Carlsnaes borrowed the term *morphogenesis*. As used by Archer and Carlsnaes, morphogenesis contrasts with structuration. According to Archer:

> The emergent properties which characterize socio-cultural systems imply discontinuity between interactions and their product, the complex system. In turn this invites *analytical dualism* when dealing with structure and action.

> Action of course is ceaseless and essential both to the continuation and further elaboration of the system, but subsequent interaction will be different from earlier action because conditioned by the structural consequences of that prior action. Hence the morphogenetic perspective is not only dualistic but sequential, dealing in endless cycles—of structural conditioning/social interaction/structural elaboration—thus unraveling the dialectical interplay between structure and action. (Carlsnaes 1992, 259, quoting Archer 1982, 458; emphasis in original)

The analytic strategy at work involves uncovering the morphogenetic cycles that can be analytically broken into intervals in order to penetrate relations between structure and action. This represents for Carlsnaes the core to the solution of the epistemological part of the problem (Carlsnaes 1992, 259). This solution is predicated, however, on two ontological assumptions. The first is that "structure logically pre-dates the action(s) which transform it," and the second is that "structural elaboration logically post-dates those actions." Such a position is strongly in contrast to the structurationist position, which views structure and structuration as process but not product (Carlsnaes 1992, 259, quoting Archer 1982, 468). The rationale behind morphogenesis is that structural factors logically predate and postdate any action affecting them; and that action logically predates and postdates the structural factors conditioning it. This encapsulates the ontological notion of a continuous cycle of action-structure interactions.

Hollis and Smith 1994

Returning to the debate, Hollis and Smith felt that Carlsnaes failed to overcome the agent-structure problem merely by allowing for time as a variable ("adding a dash of diachronics") (Hollis and Smith 1994, 244). For them, one cannot settle an ontological problem without worrying about the more fundamental epistemological one. They identified two presumptions at work in Carlsnaes's piece. First, Carlsnaes assumed that agents and structures can be placed on the same ontological footing, as if they were distinct objects in the social world. He then assumed that their relation is one of causal conditioning (Hollis and Smith 1994, 244). In effect, Carlsnaes claimed to solve the agent-structure problem by treating agents and structures as if they take turns affecting the social world.

For Hollis and Smith, morphogenesis is no solution. If Giddens is to be criticized for conflating agents and structures at any given time, how does adding time as a variable help? How does it help to judge rival accounts of agents and structures over time? (247–50).

Furthermore, Carlsnaes went too far in claiming that ontology is paramount; it does affect what can be accepted epistemologically, but importantly, the reverse is also true. "[E]pistemology can only be secondary if you are unpuzzled by what is a cause." If one is unclear as to what constitutes a cause, then one's position on epistemology is similarly unclear (250–51). Carlsnaes can only have claimed to have resolved the agent-structure problem because he is, in Hollis and Smith's terminology, a resolute "interpretivist," for whom issues of causality are distinctly secondary.

In 1994, Wendt published an article that is not directly relevant to the agent-structure debate, but, like his immensely influential "Anarchy Is What States Make of It" (Wendt 1992b), is professedly constructivist. Both pieces evince a drift toward structuralism, and an avoidance of the role of rules in the co-constitution of agents and structures. Wendt (1992b) turned instead to symbolic interactionism as an explanation for the construction of collective identity. Still wed to a realist philosophy of science, Wendt has yet to confront the fact that symbolic interactionism is rooted in an antithetical tradition, pragmatism.[5]

Jabri and Chan 1996; Hollis and Smith 1996

This latest phase of the debate is particularly unhelpful, especially the confused piece by Jabri and Chan, which takes the debate in new and unproductive epistemological directions.

Jabri and Chan felt that any critical post-positivist IR necessarily requires abandoning criteria for "universal epistemological legitimacy" in favor of focusing on ontological claims. Jabri and Chan claimed to follow Giddens in granting the primacy of ontology. They also claimed that "an assumed universalist epistemology negates *difference*" (1996, 107; emphasis in original). In their view, Giddens's "duality of structure" expresses not causality, but relations of mutual constitution. Structuration is an attempt to show how agents and structures are mutually constitutive. In this conception (as we have seen so many times before), action is meaningful only in terms of its relations to structure, just as structure is definitionally dependent upon agents and their actions.

With regard to Hollis and Smith's claim that epistemology must be regarded as being of equal importance to ontology, Jabri and Chan concluded that, for Hollis and Smith, there is only one correct epistemology. They also concluded that such a position does violence to difference (109–10). In response, Hollis and Smith accused Jabri and Chan of misconstruing the relationship between epistemology and ontology in their "discussion of what is a cause" (1996, 111). They never said that epistemology was *as* important as ontology, merely that, *contra* Giddens, Wendt, Dessler, and

Carlsnaes, it does matter. Any ontology that asserts itself without establishing what it holds as standards of epistemological warrant is, for them, mere dogma (111).

For Hollis and Smith, epistemology matters because ontological disputes can almost never be solved by "direct appeal to how the world is." Each side in a dispute must give reasons for believing what it does. To make sense of the world, they claim, we need an ontology, an epistemology, and a methodology. This has, however, nothing to do with questions of whether agents and structures are causally linked (112).

Appearing too late for the complete assessment it deserves in these pages is Roxanne Doty's highly critical review of the agent-structure debate from a post-structural perspective (1997). For Doty, the general problem is that scientific realism, "which either explicitly or implicitly underpins the various 'solutions' to the agent-structure problem, remains wedded to an essentialist notion of structure" (366). Attempts to make rules "the basic constitutive elements of structures" illustrate the problem because connecting rules to structure disconnects them from "the intersubjective understandings of agents in their immediate and local practices" (371).

Doty's critique makes no mention of Onuf's constructivist emphasis on rules as having an independent ontological basis. If indeed scientific realism is the problem, Onuf's version of constructivism offers a solution that Doty should find appealing, because it affirms (as she does) the importance of practice. It also insists that practice always takes place in a ruled context (a reality that her emphasis on the "play" of practice neglects). While Doty's conception of practice would seem to deny agents an ontological status in their own right, at least she has brought agency back into the debate.

If individualists and post-structuralists were capable of talking to each other, at least they would agree that scientific realism's preoccupation with structural properties is the problem with the agent-structure debate. Instead, participants in the debate toss around philosophical terms that bounce off their targets like defective grenades. Hollis and Smith seem generally to have meant "methodology" when they talked about "epistemology," and the "interpretivism" they see about them is merely a methodological response to the difficulties in observing complex relations of causality. If Jabri and Chan are right about the epistemological consensus underlying the debate (they are, as Doty more successfully demonstrates), then the ontological issues they pursue are beside the point. From a post-structural point of view, there is literally nothing to debate.

Levels of Analysis

The relationship of the levels-of-analysis debate to the agent-structure debate has been a running theme in this chapter. While never directly entering the agent-structure fray, Onuf's 1995 article, "Levels," may be considered an oblique entry. As we have seen, when behavioralists and systemicists took sides on levels of analysis, they placed the issue squarely within IR's second debate—the ontological debate between positivists and historicists. The positivist focus on units as positivities brings the discussion of levels back to its ontological core, an effort well served by analyzing the relation between levels and social constructions as an ontological issue.

It is essential to note at the outset that all positivities are always simultaneously parts and wholes. A level is the imputed demarcation at which a whole ceases to be relevant as such, and becomes a part. By necessity, the converse must be true. Before exploring the means by which this comes about, let us look more closely at the assertion that parts are wholes, and vice versa.

Any given positivity, any *thing*, a *whole*, is composed of *parts*, each of which is further composed of smaller parts. In this respect, we see that these (initial) parts are also wholes. This regression can hypothetically continue *ad infinitum*. Returning to the original positivity, which we had initially treated as a whole, we see that it too is a part of a larger whole, which is part of a yet larger whole, again conceivably *ad infinitum*. Any object can thus be seen as part or whole, as well as being seen as part and whole.

Even the individual as a social being is reducible, although the relations of parts are no longer social nor the being herself. Every whole is composed of many parts, which are the units of analysis of one discipline, while the aggregation is the unit of interest to the first. Further, there will be yet another discipline for which the initial aggregation/whole is the unit/part. This is the great insight of Comtean positivism: wholes are systematically stratified into levels, and discrete fields of study occupy the spaces between levels.

As has been said of structures, levels are methodological contrivances, templates imposed by the observer to order the world for instrumental purposes. As such, they have no phenomenal existence until they are contrived. Onuf identified two means by which levels are constructed, identified respectively with Comtean positivism and Kantian historicism, and linked to the Aristotelian conception of parts and wholes. "[W]holes have like attributes defining them as parts; parts have continuous and limited relations defining them as a whole" (1995, 50).

The positivist method (which is linked to the first part of Aristotle's conception) revolves around the stipulation of a criterion for membership in one level that clearly sets it apart from that of adjacent levels. The focus is on *attributes*. "All positivities possessing that attribute are deemed alike; they and only they qualify as parts in the whole; the whole and the space thus created are effectively the same" (50).

Onuf's second method focuses on *relations* rather than attributes. Immanuel Kant distinguished relations of causality and relations of community; in this Kantian schema, relations of causality are unidirectional, while those of community are reciprocal. For Kant, causal relations take place between wholes, while relations of community take place between parts (51).

However, as explained above, all wholes are also parts of greater wholes. This causes an apparent paradox, since as both parts and wholes, they should engage in relations both causal and communal, which is (stipulatively) nonallowable. The operational question is to determine where communal relations end and causal relations begin. In the instance of social relations, a constructivist sees these boundaries as created by rules. "Rules work to make some relations more consistently causal in pattern than would otherwise be the case" (52).

At the level of the social, rules empower individuals to act—to become agents. Such rules are responsible for demarcating levels in the social realm. "Each level contains sets of rules and arrangements that include as parts all of those sets of rules and arrangements in the level beneath" (52). Whether one chooses the Comtean positivist formulation or the Kantian historicist formulation, it is important to note that both are appropriate ways to study social construction.

With regard to the distinctness of the levels of analysis and the agent-structure problems, it should by now be clear that for a constructivist, in agreement with Hollis and Smith's assertions, the question of the primacy of agents and structures is repeated at each unit. The agent is the part. The structure is the whole. At the next level of analysis, the original structure/whole is now the agent/part, while at the next level down, the original agent/part is now the relevant structure/whole. Bearing this in mind, however, the determination of the degree of structural constraint imposed upon the agent is still left to be determined, or, in line with constructivist thought, the co-constitution of agents and structures is still there to be observed.

Conclusion

From a constructivist point of view, agents and structures make each other *real*. They do so through rules that are real because agents make those rules, know what they are, and generally choose to follow them. The agent-structure debate arose because structure is not observable as such, and especially because the idea that the unintended consequences of agents' conscious choices can have an efficacious structure seems doubly removed from reality. In this context, Onuf's increasing aversion to the term *structure* and his effort to show that agents, as status holders, officers, and role occupants, always act in institutional settings, may be construed as an effort to keep things real.

Are rules real enough? Can social science do without the concept of structure? What are we to make of the "institutional turn" now so much in evidence in several disciplines? These are questions that might bring the agent-structure debate back to earth.

Notes

I thank Nick Onuf for patiently reading multiple drafts, and Archie Arghyrou, John Clark, Lourdes Cue, Heidi Hobbs, Vendulka Kubálková, Dario Moreno, Ellie Schemenauer, and John Woolridge for support and criticism.
    1. "Giddens indicates that he also accepts a realist conception of science, but his realism is generally less explicit and thus more attenuated than Bhaskar's. A more important reason for relying on Bhaskar rather than Giddens, however, is the latter's weaker conception of social structure as rules and resources rather than as a set of real but unobservable internal relations" (Wendt 1987, 357, note 57).
    2. I am grateful to Paul Kowert for this astute observation.
    3. On this matter, Hollis (1995, chaps. 2–3) is particularly useful.
    4. On the matter of unintended consequences, cf. Waltz (1979, chaps. 3, 5) with Hollis (1987, 47–58).
    5. For discussion of the tensions between scientific realism and pragmatism, see Bhaskar (1991). These tensions are further discussed in Hollis (1994).

Bibliography

Archer, Margaret. 1982. "Structuration versus Morphogenesis: On Combining Structure and Action." *British Journal of Sociology* 33 (December): 455–83.
Bhaskar, Roy. 1979. *The Possibility of Naturalism.* Brighton: Harvester.
———. 1991. *Philosophy and the Idea of Freedom.* Oxford: Basil Blackwell.
Carlsnaes, Walter. 1992. "The Agency-Structure Problem in Foreign Policy Analysis." *International Studies Quarterly* 36 (September): 245–70.
Dessler, David. 1989. "What's at Stake in the Agent-Structure Debate?" *International Organization* 43 (Summer): 441–73.
Doty, Roxanne Lynn. 1997. "Aporia: A Critical Exploration of the Agent-Structure Problematique in International Relations Theory." *European Journal of International Relations* 3 (September): 365–92.
Giddens, Anthony. 1979. *The Central Problems in Social Theory: Action, Structure and Contradiction in Social Analysis.* Berkeley and Los Angeles: University of California Press.

————. 1984. *The Constitution of Society: Outline of the Theory of Structuration*. Berkeley and Los Angeles: University of California Press.

Hollis, Martin. 1987. *The Cunning of Reason*. Cambridge: Cambridge University Press.

————. 1994. *The Philosophy of Social Science: An Introduction*. Cambridge: Cambridge University Press.

————. 1995. *Reason in Action: Essays in the Philosophy of Social Science*. Cambridge: Cambridge University Press.

————, and Steve Smith. 1990. *Explaining and Understanding International Relations*. Oxford: Clarendon Press.

———— and ————. 1991. "Beware of Gurus: Structure and Action in International Relations." *Review of International Studies* 17 (October): 393–410.

———— and ————. 1992. "Structure and Action: Further Comment." *Review of International Studies* 18 (April): 187–88.

———— and ————. 1994. "Two Stories About Structure and Agency." *Review of International Studies* 20 (July): 241–51.

———— and ————. 1996. "A Response: Why Epistemology Matters in International Theory." *Review of International Studies* 22 (January): 111–16.

Jabri, Vivienne, and Stephen Chan. 1996. "The Ontologist Always Rings Twice: Two More Stories About Structure and Agency in Reply to Hollis and Smith." *Review of International Studies* 22 (January): 107–10.

Onuf, Nicholas Greenwood. 1989. *World of Our Making: Rules and Rule in Social Theory and International Relations*. Columbia: University of South Carolina Press.

————. 1994. "The Constitution of International Society." *European Journal of International Law* 5: 1–19.

————. 1995. "Levels." *European Journal of International Relations* 1 (March): 35–58.

————. 1996. "Rules, Agents, Institutions: A Constructivist Account." *Working Papers on International Society and Institutions* 96–92. Global Peace and Conflict Studies at University of California, Irvine.

————. 1997. "A Constructivist Manifesto." In *Constituting International Political Economy*, ed. Kurt Burch and Robert A. Denemark, 7–17. Boulder, CO: Lynne Rienner.

Singer, J. David. 1961. "The Level-of-Analysis Problem in International Relations." *World Politics* 14 (October): 77–92.

Wæver, Ole. 1997. "Figures of International Thought: Introducing Persons Instead of Paradigms." In *The Future of International Relations: Masters in the Making*, ed. Iver B. Neumann and Ole Wæver, 1–37. London: Routledge.

————. 1979. *Theory of International Politics*. Reading, MA: Addison-Wesley.

Waltz, Kenneth N. 1979. *Theory of International Politics*. Reading, MA: Addison-Wesley.

Wendt, Alexander. 1987. "The Agent-Structure Problem in International Relations Theory." *International Organization* 41 (Summer): 335–70.

————. 1991. "Bridging the Theory/Meta-Theory Gap in International Relations." *Review of International Studies* 17 (October): 383–92.

————. 1992a. "Levels of Analysis vs. Agents and Structures: Part III." *Review of International Studies* 18 (April): 181–85.

————. 1992b. "Anarchy Is What States Make of It: The Social Construction of Power Politics." *International Organization* 46 (Spring): 391–425.

————. 1994. "Collective Identity Formation and the International State." *American Political Science Review* 88 (June): 384–96.

Part III

International Relations
Under Construction

5

Agent versus Structure in the Construction of National Identity

Paul Kowert

But how will each single individual succeed in incorporating himself into the collective man, and how will educative pressure be applied to single individuals so as to obtain their consent and their collaboration, turning necessity and coercion into "freedom"?

Antonio Gramsci (1971, 242)

How can nation-states made up of citizens whose interests might diverge sharply choose foreign (or any other) policies to serve the *public* good? This problem of collective action, and the related problem of how states themselves can cooperate, dominates international relations. It animates debates over whether war can serve a general interest or only particular interests (munitions producers, for example), or whether lower barriers to trade are good for the whole country or only for some groups within it (perhaps favoring importers over domestic producers and laborers).

The collective action problem also lies at the heart of disagreements over whether or not international relations can be a positive sum game (Grieco 1988). As Alexander Wendt argues, many of the contortions to which both neorealist and neoliberal theories are forced to subject themselves as they address this problem are made necessary by their failure to offer an account of national (or other actor) identity and interests. Instead, "they either bracket the formation of interests, treating them *as if* they were exogenous, or explain interests by reference to domestic politics, on the assumption that they are exogenous" (Wendt 1994, 384). Because these approaches incorporate no theory of national identity or collective interest formation, they cannot explain collective behavior by referring to collective goals. They must focus, instead, on the mechanisms that allow rationally egoistic agents to integrate their goals. To explain international cooperation, neorealists might look to hegemony or coercion for incentives that restrain the ambitions of particular nations. Neoliberals look instead either to the "shadow" of future interaction or to the coordinating role of institutions such as international regimes that reduce transaction costs. Neither approach envisions collective ambitions grounded in a common political identity (although neoliberalism's positive-sum view of international relations at least admits to the possibility).

In opposition to the individualism and rationalism of such approaches (which either deny collective identities or treat their formation as exogenous and usually imposed), Wendt offers the rival claim that state identity is endogenous to structured interaction among states. Drawing on integration theory and some versions of interpretivist scholarship (see Chapter 1), Wendt proposes that the structural context of state interaction, systemic factors such as interdependence and the transnational convergence of domestic values, and even the manipulation of symbols in the strategic practice of rational agents all contribute to the formation of collective identities. To put this more plainly, Wendt points out that: (1) states often share interpretations of their environment (e.g., as "Cold War," "détente," or "new world order"); (2) states depend on each other, at least in part, for some of these interpretations (e.g., a common fate might encourage a common identity); and (3) the strategic interaction of states further contributes to shared understandings (1994, 389–91). Each of these relationships between states not only shapes behavior but also shapes the self-understanding of the agents involved. Thus, Wendt concludes, neorealists and neoliberals are not constrained—as they have themselves generally assumed—to treat collective identity and interests as exogenous. Many of the processes on which they already focus shape identity.

Yet one need not make the dualistic assumption that identity must either be given intrinsically (and determined exogenously) as an actor property or else be determined by the social structures of the environment that actors inhabit. The first approach is broadly rationalist (assuming intrinsic preferences and constant identities) and ontologically naturalist (ignoring collective interpretation). The second approach is dynamic (because it permits identity to change) and ontologically interpretivist (insisting that material and social reality are always the product of collective interpretation). But what these two approaches share is structuralism (for discussions of structuralism in international relations, see Ashley 1984; Dessler 1989; and Wendt 1987). The first approach assumes that the structures of international politics constrain state behavior; the second argues that international structures affect both behavior *and* identity.

Neorealist and neoliberal theories ordinarily focus on the material determinants of structure such as the distribution of physical, technological, geographical, or other material determinants of power. Even when discussing such intangibles as political ideology and identity, neorealists and neoliberals take care to trace ideas to an underlying physical reality (see, for example, Goldstein and Keohane 1993). The intersubjective structures to which Wendt refers, on the other hand, are more broadly defined. They leave "room for the emergent effects of material capabilities" but consist themselves "of the shared understandings, expectations, and social knowledge embedded in international institutions and threat complexes" (Wendt 1994, 389). In both cases, however, identity is shaped (to the extent it is malleable) by structural constraints and incentives. Such arguments de-emphasize the ways the behavior of agents *within* structures shapes identity (although Wendt's description of strategic interaction among states is a partial exception; 1994, 390–91). While Wendt's critique of material rationalism is a valuable ontological corrective, it pays less attention than it might to the active role people and nations play in the fabrication of their own political identities.

This chapter will offer no defense of the proposition that theories of political identity are a useful things to have (see Katzenstein 1996; Lapid and Kratochwil 1996; and Legro 1996). That much, it assumes, is evident in light of the way competition to define identity currently plays (and has always played) a prominent role in both domestic and international conflicts. The next section will examine the contribution constructivism and psychological theories of social identification can together make to an account of national identity. It argues that, in concert, they yield an account of national identity that explains changing interests and foreign policy behavior and that more fully appreciates the role national leaders play in forging national identities. The remainder of this chapter illustrates this synthetic approach to national identity by examining the evolution of British attitudes toward Egypt prior to and during the Suez crisis.

From Agency to Identity

Constructivism (see Chapter 3 and Onuf 1989) holds that social structure, by itself, cannot serve as the basis for a complete account of identity. Agents and their behavior must also be considered. Speaking *is* doing, and constructivists maintain that social meanings, institutions, and structures (all, in a sense, the same thing) are constructed out of practical linguistic rules. The instruction-, directive-, and commitment-rules that are the foundation of Onuf's approach, for example, are all instances of behavior as well as social acts (see Searle 1969). They occur at the nexus of biology, psychology, and sociology. But constructivists take biological, psychological, or social performance one step further. They argue that people strive not only to make sense out of their world and to act within it, but also to communicate their understandings to others. At the same time, the process of communication *is* a process of making sense. This extends the syllogism offered above: speaking *is* doing *is* knowing. As communication is a social act, so is knowledge. This is precisely the bridge that constructivism offers between *ontology* (the socially constructed world) and *epistemology* (our ability to know something about it).

Although the "semantic dimensions of the language" permit some social constructions, they render other constructions unintelligible (see Giddens 1984; Kratochwil 1989). Johan Galtung (1990) describes U.S. foreign policy as a theological system in which certain constructions make sense (such as order versus disorder or hierarchy versus anarchy) and other alternatives do not (see also Campbell 1992). While American presidents might occasionally denounce other states as "evil empires," for example, they engage in no sustained discussion of the morality of foreign policy. The language of realism offers little purchase to those, such as President Jimmy Carter, who might wish to do so. For Galtung, language is pivotal. Once discussions of international politics are framed in certain terms, interests and identities become obvious: "With anarchy sufficiently decried this option is rejected; what is left is hierarchy. In hierarchy the strongest have to be on top. . . . The rest becomes almost a tautology" (Galtung 1990, 138). In such a discussion, one's own identity—presumably—should be "on top" (e.g., that of the "hegemon"). Kratochwil's (1996) analysis of "belonging" and "citizenship" explores another set of linguistic polarities with similar consequences for identification. Here, too, language is structured to promote identity. Who would not wish to "belong"?

Feminist international relations theorists have also devoted special attention to the role of language in identity formation, arguing that traditional and androcentric metaphors of international politics not only ignore but in fact prevent consideration of alternative politics and identities (Enloe 1989; Peterson 1992; Sylvester 1994; Tickner 1992). According to Tickner (1992, 36), the language in which most (traditional) discussions of international politics are conducted "comes out of a Western-centered historical worldview that . . . privileges a view of security that is constructed out of values associated with hegemonic masculinity." She argues, moreover, that the masculine discourse of international politics directly informs national identities and "has all but eliminated the experiences of women from our collective national memories" (138).

The intensification of concern with language has led some to proclaim a "linguistic turn" in international relations.[1] Although some scholars view the linguistic turn as emancipatory (George and Campbell 1990; Lapid 1989; Neufeld 1995; Sylvester 1994), in that it permits alternative conceptions of international politics, they must also reckon with the problems posed by this very malleability. Language is not just a social mechanism that creates and reinforces meaning and identity; it can be manipulated by speakers (especially those with power). Soviet officials who spoke of "new thinking," to take one example, not only challenged a conception of history that had not admitted the possibility of *perestroika* but also served their own political interests. These liberal reformers especially benefited from the vagueness of the category they created. Because many people with very different political agendas could all see themselves as "new thinkers," *perestroika* was a useful idea around which to mobilize (see Herman 1996). Thus language is not simply the repository of what exists. It is also the means through which things are brought into and out of existence. Political leaders are able to manipulate this process, but they are also constrained by it.[2] Scholars, who have their own ambitions, also participate in this process, certainly complicating their own efforts to study it. The incentives of academia encourage a bias toward novel constructions. Perhaps it is no accident that Soviet reformers were also influenced by academic exchanges that brought Soviet and American physicists, social scientists, and other scholars together (Herman 1996; Mendelson 1993; Zisk 1993).

Recognizing the way people and nations manipulate language to "construct" themselves challenges common assumptions about the fixity of the main characters in the drama of international relations. But the purpose of this chapter is to show what constructivism contributes to research on national identity, not to play with language. It is easy to show how linguistic rules and procedures are implicated in the formation of social identities. This is unsurprising. All language consists of distinctions. Instruction-rules distinguish one thing from another. Directive-rules and and commitment-rules distinguish one state of affairs (desired) from another (actual) and, in so doing, also specify who (the listener or the speaker, respectively) is expected to reconcile the two states. At a very basic level, language and identity thus depend on each other. Identity exists through the "distinguishing" function of language. But language—directives and commissives in particular—also depends on the identities of self and other. As Onuf (1989, 109) puts it, "constituting practices in categories (even perception takes practice) is not just universal, it is fundamental." And yet, "if categorization is fundamental, no set of categories is" (109). This is as far as constructivism can proceed toward a theory of identity. It does not prescribe any particular set of categories or identities. It simply acknowledges that language functions, in part, to constrain uncategorized experience and transform it into categorized meaning. For language to function, there must be categories. But it is up to agents to determine which categories.

Cognitive psychology picks up where constructivism leaves off in its discussion of identity: with the claim that the ordinary functioning of human cognition cleaves the social world into "self" and "other" categories of agency.[3] Psychologists have shown that, even when no obvious grounds for categorizing exist, people will invent them. Muzafer Sherif (1961, 1966) argued that two groups given competing (interdependent) goals will form negative attitudes about each other—even in the total absence of information about the personal qualities of out-group members—as well as more positive and cohesive attitudes about themselves (the in-group). Placing people in situations of objective conflict, he reasoned, would promote distinct identities, while providing superordinate goals for the groups would erode these identities and reduce out-group bias.[4] Later research showed that the presence of objective conflict or competition was not necessary to produce distinct identities, leading to a "minimal group paradigm." Henri Tajfel (1978, 1981) found that whenever social divisions are salient, people will invent correspondingly divergent identities. In other words, one need do little more than divide people into groups for distinct identities to begin to emerge. And when groups *are* in competition, their identities and biases will become even more distinct (Cartwright and Zander 1968).

The minimal group paradigm (MGP) suggests that distinct group identities will quickly and inevitably emerge in social interactions. A variety of explanations for this phenomenon are consistent with the MGP. One interpretation, appealing in its simplicity, is that social identity emerges from individual cognitive "miserliness." According to John Turner, "[t]he first question determining group-belongingness is not 'Do I like these other individuals?', but 'Who am I?'" (1982, 16). Individuals are continually confronted with the problem of locating themselves, and others, in a web of social categories that periodically confront them as salient. They have limited cognitive resources to devote to this task and, as a result, must make use of certain simplifying and memory-enhancing strategies (see also Turner 1991). In constructivist terms, "rules" present agents with simpler ways to interpret the world and to make choices.

Psychological experiments indicate that the earlier and the more frequently individuals are exposed to information about the attributes of others, the more extreme will be their ratings of the others on these attributes (Oakes and Turner 1986; Tajfel 1981, 62–89, 110–14). Put succinctly, people tend to exaggerate their perceptions of others in order to make memory and categorization easier. And they particularly exaggerate attributes that, perhaps because of priority (early exposure) or frequency, are more salient. One implication of this finding is that distinctions between members of different social groups are often exaggerated. This tendency to perceive intergroup distinctions is matched by a corresponding tendency to perceive intragroup homogeneity. Members of one group are consistently perceived as more similar to one another than to members of other groups (McGarty and Penny 1988; Tajfel 1969). Again, the cognitive advantages of such a simplifying assumption are apparent. Gordon Allport (1954) made a similar point in his classic work on prejudice, arguing that the classification of others into distinct social groups (with group-related identities) facilitates processes of identification and adjustment in new social situations. Fine distinctions require that one remember more information, and this in turn increases the difficulty of recalling the information.

Consistent with the cognitive biases described so far—toward intergroup differentiation and intragroup homogeneity—is another bias in causal attribution. Because out-groups are perceived as homogeneous, their behavior can more easily be explained as the result of positive intent (see Deschamps 1977; Hewstone and Jaspars 1982). This attributional bias is, in effect, a social identity version of what cognitive psychologists have called the "fundamental attribution error"—the attribution of other people's behavior to their intent or dispositional qualities rather than to some situational constraint.[5] In this case, the behavior of other groups is more readily explained by attributes of group members (presumably shared homogeneously by members) than by external constraints on their behavior. A particularly interesting variation of this argument is Jean-Claude Deschamps's suggestion that when out-groups are perceived as powerful, then the attributional error will be enhanced (1982). Powerful groups, even if they face situational constraints, could presumably use their power to overcome these constraints. This bias leads to the tautological perception that all behavior of powerful out-groups is intentional ("since they are powerful, they can do whatever they want").

Much of the literature on self-categorization suggests that in-groups will also be seen as homogeneous (although this effect is not as robust as with out-groups; see Mullen and Hu 1989; Park and Judd 1990). For several reasons, however, this homogeneity does not necessarily impede a self-serving (in-group-serving) bias. First, even though one's own group may seem homogeneous relative to others—thereby establishing its identity—

some differences between group members will nevertheless be apparent (Judd, Ryan, and Park 1991; Park, Ryan, and Judd 1992). The behavior of one's own group can thus readily be explained not only as the product of situational constraints but also as the result of negotiations within the group (Bendor and Hammond 1992; Welch 1992). Moreover, information about situational constraints on the behavior of one's own group may be much more readily available than similar information for out-groups (Hewstone and Jaspars 1982). Thus, while a cognitive intragroup homogeneity bias may exist for all social categories, the process of behavioral attribution might be very different (and more forgiving) for in-groups than for out-groups.

It is one thing for psychologists to explain how cognitive bias affects the way we view ourselves and others. It is a much bolder step to suggest that the same process works at the level of nation-states. Mercer (1995) takes just this step, arguing that even if constructivists are correct in assuming that the world can be constructed in different ways, the MGP nevertheless predicts that international relations will be constructed in the highly competitive and egocentric mold of neorealism. There are two problems with this daring analytic leap: first, the MGP is not so deterministic that it predicts only one form of national identity (egoistic) or international relations (anarchical); and second, the linkage between individual biases and images (or identities) ascribed to nation-states deserves closer attention.

Just as people are not highly suspicious of every other person they encounter, so states are not equally threatened by (or suspicious of) every other state they "encounter." Democracies may find, for example, that they belong to a common in-group (Chafetz 1995; Doyle 1986). Some states seem more trustworthy than others, and it is precisely such differences that a theory of national identity must explain. To apply the insights of social identity theory and the MGP to international relations, then, narrower hypotheses must be considered.

Many different hypotheses about the creation, maintenance, and impact of social identity might be derived from the complex body of research on the MGP, self-categorization, prejudice, stereotyping, cognitive balancing, and social attribution. For present purposes, however, three fairly simple lessons will suffice:

1. Whenever distinctive categories for political groups are salient, group members will perceive strengthened group identities (ordinarily evaluatively positive for in-groups and negative for out-groups). Conflict between groups will strengthen these identities and encourage exaggeration of group attributes.

2. People will also tend to exaggerate differences between political

groups and to underestimate differences within these groups. Again, conflict will strengthen this tendency.

3. Finally, people will tend to attribute the behavior of political out-groups to the intent or desires of those groups; in-group behavior, however, will more often be attributed to the influence of environmental constraints. Perceived increases in the power of out-groups will strengthen the tendency to assume intent (attributional bias).

These lessons seem plausible given the extensive body of research supporting the MGP. At the level of individuals, they are well tested. But the problem of the leap to international relations remains.

Constructivism makes this leap possible by insisting that people construct larger social realities—including national identity. To make this leap reasonable, however, we must once again turn to the relationship between language and psychology. The MGP predicts a linguistic bias in the relationship between instruction-rules and directives or commissives. In short, people should not be equally willing to commit themselves to action on behalf of all groups. Once instruction-rules categorize the social world, demands will be made of out-groups, while commitment will occur primarily on behalf of in-groups. Constructivism thus provides an important link across levels of analysis. Cognitive bias not only shapes the identities of other people (as they are meaningful to oneself); it biases the functioning of language to create (biased) identities at every level of human relations. Language translates individual bias even into international relations. Agents at all levels are made meaningful, then, because individuals confer identity on themselves and on the institutions that represent them (such as the nation-state). Serious students of diplomatic history might decry the tendency of novices to reify states and to treat them as pseudo-individuals with coherent objectives. But doing so is not merely an error to be corrected in the graduate training of historians. It is, in fact, a widespread and unavoidable tendency—with some negative consequences—on which ordinary usage of the term *national identity* depends. Constructivism and psychology together predict that national identity is rarely (if ever) neutral with respect to self.

An Illustration: National Identity in the Suez Crisis

The 1956 crisis provoked by Egyptian president Nasser's decision to nationalize the Suez Canal brought questions of identity to the fore in dramatic fashion. At the time, both Egypt and Israel confronted wrenching dilemmas as they attempted to carve out new sovereign, national identities for themselves. Similarly, the United States and the Soviet Union both faced the problem of accommodating themselves to their new roles as superpowers in a competitive bipolar world. France and Britain, meanwhile, were playing out the last act of their rapidly eroding colonial identities. The remainder of this chapter will focus exclusively on the evolution of Britain's perceptions of identity (both its own and Egypt's), first taking up the origins of these perceptions and then briefly considering their impact on British policy.

It may be helpful, at the outset, to restate the above hypotheses in the context of this case. First, as political categories become more salient, participants in the crisis will exaggerate both their opponent's and their own identities. We might therefore expect the British prime minister, Anthony Eden, to regard the Egyptian prime minister (later, president), Gamal Abdel Nasser, as more and more "typically Egyptian" as the crisis wears on, and himself as more "typically British." Second, we might expect Eden to exaggerate the distinctions between these two identities, assigning negative attributes to the outgroup. Nasser will be seen, therefore, not only as increasingly Egyptian, but as increasingly different from—and somehow inferior or opposed to—the British. Finally, as the exaggerated in-group and out-group identities develop, they will encourage in turn a series of attribution errors. We might expect Eden to view Nasser's (or Egyptian) behavior as purely intentional while readily perceiving the constraints on British options and behavior.

Long before the crisis, both Eden and his predecessor, Winston Churchill, were well aware of Egyptian discontent with the British presence in Egypt. For this very reason, and because the lone British base along the Suez Canal was of comparatively little strategic value in any case, English policy favored a gradual withdrawal from the region. Earlier, these troops had served the important function (from London's perspective) of securing easy British access to India via the Suez Canal and then, in the early twentieth century, to Middle East oil deposits as well. Yet, although the access to oil reserves remained important, its value was increasingly overshadowed by the negative consequences of Egyptian hostility toward the foreign troops. By the early 1950s, Churchill confided to an associate that "not even a single soldier is in favor of staying there" (Neff 1981, 56). As Britain prepared to withdraw from the Middle East at the conclusion of World War II, therefore, it hoped to fill the resultant political and military vacuum by promoting an alternative security arrangement: the Baghdad Pact.

The Baghdad Pact was actually one part of a two-part British strategy for the Middle East. The Pact itself sought to organize "northern tier" Arab states (Turkey, Iraq, Iran, and Pakistan) into a defensive alliance against the Soviet Union. To this end, Britain joined an existing alliance between Turkey and Iraq, hoping that other Arab countries and the United States would follow its lead.[6] The other part of British Middle East strategy, "Operation ALPHA," was a joint effort with the United States to resolve the Arab-Israeli problem. Operation ALPHA sought rapprochement between Egypt and Israel and, in consultation with Jordan, a negotiated territorial settlement for Palestinian refugees. Unfortunately, the two objectives of British policy worked against each other. As Sir Evelyn Shuckburgh (one of the chief architects of ALPHA) later reminisced, "We did not face up soon enough to this basic contradiction in our strategy" (Shamir 1989, 90).

Nasser and other Egyptian nationalists certainly approved of British withdrawal from the region. But Nasser recognized the Pact for what it clearly was: an attempt to maintain some European influence over the region and, as such, a direct affront to the pan-Arab collective security arrangement he favored. Nasser's blunt appraisal of the Pact was that it represented an attempt by the West "to get [the Arabs] to unite to fight *your* enemy [Russia] while they know that if they show any intention of fighting *their* enemy [Israel] you would quickly stop all aid" (Neff 1981, 76). Despite these strong reservations, however, Nasser remained willing for a time to work with the British, hoping thereby to secure the first complete withdrawal of British troops from Egyptian soil since 1882. And despite Nasser's clear opposition to the Baghdad Pact, the British government remained convinced until early 1955 that it could work with Nasser. In fact, after his only face-to-face meeting with Nasser in February 1955, Eden reported to Churchill that he was "impressed by Nasser, who seemed forthright and friendly" (Kyle 1991, 39). Roger Allen, the British assistant undersecretary for the Middle East, similarly concluded that England should attempt "to consolidate his (Nasser's) position . . . it looks as though he is our best bet" (Louis 1989, 48). One way of achieving this, clearly, would be to withdraw from Egypt—something Britain had long promised. The irony of the Suez crisis, therefore, is that Nasser simply pushed Britain further in a direction it was already moving.

In the year after Eden met with Nasser, a series of events dramatically changed the relationship between them. The first of these events occurred only eight days after their meeting: on the night of February 28, a special detachment of Israeli commandos led by Ariel Sharon attacked an Egyptian military base at Gaza, ostensibly in response to a series of border incursions by Palestinians from the Gaza Strip. In this attack, thirty-eight Egyptians were killed, and "from this moment on Nasser's . . . overriding need was to ensure Egyptian rearmament from whatever sources it could be obtained" (Kyle 1991, 65). Nasser quickly appealed to the American ambassador in Cairo, Henry Byroade, for arms. But, despite a barrage of telegrams from

Byroade to Washington requesting these arms, President Dwight Eisenhower and Secretary of State John Foster Dulles moved ahead cautiously, faced with opposition to an arms sale both from abroad (Israel) and at home (in Congress). Inevitably, Nasser sought assistance elsewhere, and on September 27, he announced a sizable contract to buy Soviet armaments from Czechoslovakia.

From this point onward, British perceptions of Nasser began to change inexorably for the worse. Even before the arms deal became public, Eden's impression of Nasser had soured. When Egypt backed Saudi Arabia in a dispute over Buraimi (an oasis in the Saudi desert), Eden reacted strongly: "This kind of thing is really intolerable. Egyptians get steadily worse. . . . They should surely be told firmly no more arms deliveries while this goes on" (Lucas 1991, 49). The arms deal was the first overt confirmation of Eden's fears, indicating that Nasser might not only challenge Britain but perhaps even side with the Soviets. Yet Britain had nowhere else to turn. As Shuckburgh concluded at the time, "the plain fact is that, however disappointed we may be in the attitude of Colonel Nasser and his colleagues, we can see no alternative Egyptian Government in sight which would be any better" (Lucas 1991, 49). The absence of a clear alternative to Nasser made it even easier for Eden to view Egyptian leadership as monolithic—and increasingly threatening.

If Nasser's stance on Buraimi and his acceptance of the Czechoslovakian arms deal had begun to call his "identity" into question, a series of intelligence reports received beginning in November from a British agent in Nasser's entourage swiftly pushed Eden and his cabinet toward an even more pessimistic reassessment of this "emerging enemy." The agent, codenamed "Lucky Break," raised the disturbing prospect that Nasser planned once again to turn to the Soviets for assistance, this time for funding to build the Aswan High Dam. Eden himself had pushed hard for a $200 million Western aid package to help finance the dam, but Britain lacked the resources and the United States (especially the American public) lacked the will for such a massive loan program. Despite their awareness that Nasser believed the situation to be pressing, Eden and his advisors were shocked by the news that Nasser was actually considering a Soviet aid package. The specter of communist Egypt loomed even larger.

Ironically, the final straw for Eden was an event for which Nasser bore no direct responsibility—the removal of General John Bagot "Pasha" Glubb from his post commanding the Arab Legion in Jordan. In fact, Pasha Glubb's ouster was, indirectly, a product of the British decision to seek Jordanian membership in the Baghdad Pact. After Britain's clumsy efforts to woo Jordan destabilized the Jordanian government, Glubb was forced to step in and restore order. This action, in turn, convinced King Hussein that Glubb himself had become a threat. The Pasha was ordered to leave the country on short notice, and British officials leapt to the conclusion that Nasser had somehow orchestrated the whole affair. The British foreign minister, Selwyn Lloyd, was in Cairo at the time. In a meeting with Nasser the morning after Glubb's dismissal, Lloyd mused that the Egyptian leader "had deteriorated since their first meeting. . . . 'He smiled a great deal more, for no apparent reason. He had lost the simplicity I rather liked in 1953' " (Kyle 1991, 94). Eden's reaction was far stronger.

> The news of Glubb's removal convulsed Eden with fury. Anthony Nutting was with the Prime Minister until 5 A.M. trying to calm him: "[Eden] put all the blame on Nasser and brushed aside every argument that mere personal considerations had in fact influenced Hussein's arbitrary decision. . . . He decided that the world was not big enough to hold both him and Nasser." (Lucas 1991, 95)

In fact, when Nutting did try to reason with Eden, the Prime Minister could not contain himself. " 'You love Nasser,' he burst out, 'but I say he is our enemy and he shall be treated as such' " (Nutting 1967, 29). After this incident, Eden began to compare Nasser to Mussolini. In the prime minister's view, there no longer remained any room for compromise: "It is either him or us" (Kyle 1991, 96).

By this time, Nasser's identity (and Egypt's to a lesser extent) had clearly become very salient to Eden and his cabinet. They made frequent reference to his untrustworthiness and his sympathy to communism. Their opposition to him thus came more from who he was and what he represented—a communist, or possibly a fascist, and clearly an enemy of Britain—than from what he had actually done. Nutting's (1967, 28) observation that it "was almost as if No. 10 itself had been attacked and a howling mob of Arabs were laying siege to Downing Street" is a vivid illustration of the new identity the British had conferred on Nasser. But more than Nasser was at issue. The new "out-group," Egypt, would thereafter be treated as a homogeneous entity—a "howling mob of Arabs"—with just one more of the "mob" at the helm. And Eden's response to Nutting's ill-considered attempt to defend Nasser—that Nutting must "love Nasser"—shows the strength and extent of this new social categorization. By this point, Eden could conceive of only two camps: those who "loved" Arabs and those who did not.[7] Not only was this social categorization increasingly salient but, with the frequent (if inconsistent) references to Hitler, Mussolini, and communists, it was greatly exaggerated.

As one might expect, this negative redefinition and exaggeration of

Nasser's identity also encouraged attribution bias within the British government. Eden's strong reaction to the Lucky Break intelligence suggests a failure to appreciate the constraints the Egyptian leader faced. After the Czechoslovakian arms deal, the British ambassador to Egypt reported that he "saw no reason that [Nasser] would not have preferred to get arms from the West and [he] only decided to accept the Soviet offer when he felt he could wait no longer in the face of increased tension on the Gaza frontier and internal pressure" (Lucas 1991, 65). But while Eden was well aware that Washington was once again dragging its heels and, in the end, unlikely to provide financing—and although Nasser took steps to minimize Western criticism, emphasizing that "it was a once-for-all deal" and that "there would be no Soviet technicians"—Eden could not help but jump to the conclusion that the Soviet financing represented a fundamental shift toward communism on Nasser's part (Kyle 1989, 107). In other words, Eden found it easier to attribute the Soviet offer to Nasser's own (changing) desires and identity than to the constraints that the Egyptian leader faced. This attribution bias is set in further relief by the fact that the Americans interpreted the *same* intelligence much differently. From the CIA's perspective, there "was a sweeping and absolute quality about [the British] analysis that grated on the American agents and was not borne out by their own sources" (Kyle 1991, 102). And if Eden's reaction to Lucky Break exhibited attribution bias, his response to Glubb's dismissal is an even better example of serious attribution error. In this case, without any supporting evidence at all, Eden blamed Nasser for the behavior of the king of Jordan. The apparent rise of Nasser's power and prestige in the region, after he assumed the Egyptian presidency and then successfully negotiated the Czechoslovakian arms deal, may have further contributed to Eden's biases. Nasser's increasing power made it that much easier to blame him for British setbacks.

By the summer of 1956, the prospect of Western support for the Aswan High Dam had become remote. Dulles formally withdrew American support for the loan package on July 19. Seven days later—perhaps in retaliation and perhaps in an effort to secure a new source of funds—Nasser announced the nationalization of the Suez Canal. By this time, little further damage could be done to Eden's exceedingly low estimation of Nasser. Nationalization merely served to confirm what Eden already believed and to intensify his already-strong tendency to view Middle East politics through the singular lens of Anglo-Egyptian conflict. From this point onward, Eden "was out of sync with his old cautious, compromising self. He was obsessed, a driven man, his vast experience and intellect reduced to tunnel vision. At the end of the tunnel was Nasser" (Neff 1981, 278). Of course, after the seizure of the Canal, Eden was hardly alone. The general consensus in the British cabinet, according to Andrew Foster (the U.S. chargé d'affaires in London), was that "Nasser must not be allowed to get away with it" (Lucas 1991, 142). And the British press thereafter "maintained a steady drumbeat of shrill criticism against Nasser," ranking him among the worst threats to freedom and democracy (Neff 1981, 204). Even Winston Churchill, who up this point had been concerned about Eden's newly aggressive attitude toward Egypt, swung quickly into line with the prevailing national mood. "We can't have that malicious swine sitting across our communications," he proclaimed (277).

What is particularly notable about these expressions of British outrage is their emphasis on Nasser's personal character (that is, his identity) as the explanation for his behavior and as sufficient reason for British reprisals. The problem was not the nationalization per se, which British lawyers quickly agreed was legal since the Suez Canal Company was registered as an Egyptian company and since its shareholders were all to be compensated. The problem was that Hitler had been reincarnated in the Middle East. And, as social identity theory predicts, Nasser's behavior was assumed to reflect on all Egyptians. Consistent with this form of social stereotyping, the British ministers concluded in a cabinet meeting on July 27 that "[t]he Egyptians . . . did not possess the technical ability to manage the Canal effectively" (Kyle 1991, 138). As the London *Times* put it, "An international waterway of this kind cannot be worked by a nation with low technical and managerial skills such as the Egyptians" (Neff 1981, 277). The crisis was not simply a personal matter between British and Egyptian leaders. Their mutual animosity was writ large in the way they viewed their antagonist's national identity and in their diplomatic practice.

Once the crisis was truly under way, the leaders' own national identities came into play as well. When out-group identity becomes salient, a corresponding transformation should occur in definitions of the in-group. The available documentary evidence on the Suez crisis provides less evidence for this than for exaggerated attributions to out-groups. Nevertheless, there is at least some evidence to support the claim that in-group identity also became increasingly salient during the course of the crisis. The principal manifestation of this transformation in Britain was an increased emphasis on the potential damage to British reputation (thus, identity) as a major power if Nasser were allowed to succeed. Indeed, Harold "Macmillan flatly declared to Dulles that Britain would be finished as a world power if Nasser won: 'This is Munich all over again'" (Neff 1981, 290). And Sir Ivone Kirkpatrick (the permanent undersecretary at the Foreign Office) managed to take, if possible, an even more alarmist position:

> [I]f we sit back while Nasser consolidates his position and gradually acquires control of the oil-bearing countries, he can, and is, according to our information, resolved to wreck us. If Middle East oil is denied to us for a year or two our gold reserves will disappear. If our gold reserves disappear the sterling area disintegrates. If the sterling area disintegrates and we have no reserves we shall not be able to maintain a force in Germany or, indeed, anywhere else. I doubt whether we shall be able to pay for the bare minimum necessary for our defence. And a country that cannot provide for its defence is finished. (Kyle 1989, 123)

Although Kirkpatrick strikes an alarmist tone, his point was essentially correct: Britain faced a test of its survival as a great power.

The importance of both British and Egyptian national identity in this case was far-reaching. One obvious effect of the changing British views of Egyptian identity, as already noted, was the tendency toward attribution error that these changes encouraged. In the year following Eden's meeting with Nasser, English officials tended more and more often to blame Nasser for setbacks to Britain's Middle East policy. This became a self-fulfilling prophecy. The more the British focused on Nasser, the more they attributed every failure to him, and thus the larger he loomed. The increasingly negative British view of Nasser contributed in turn to the collapse of project ALPHA, undermined financing for the Aswan Dam, and made Nasser's eventual retaliation all the more likely. And when Nasser did nationalize the Suez Canal Company, the British conception of him left only one conceivable response. To simply accept nationalization had, for Eden, become synonymous with appeasing a new Hitler. In short, British leaders constructed the very threat to which they were ultimately compelled to respond.

Ironically, the British tendency to demonize Nasser had the unintended effect of *enhancing* the Egyptian leader's popularity. Egyptians might well conclude that "if the West hated Nasser so much then surely he must be powerful" (Neff 1981, 205). The strong emotions evoked among British leaders by defining Nasser as another Hitler had the further effect of blinding Eden and his colleagues to the likely American response to their invasion plan. Even after Eisenhower sent a letter explicitly warning against the use of force, Eden simply refused to comprehend the line the Americans had just drawn. "Eden's passion so clouded his reason that after reading Ike's forceful letter he concluded that 'the President did not rule out the use of force.' True, but there were so many qualifiers in the letter that only Eden in his blind hatred of Nasser could have missed the point" (Neff 1981, 291). And, as Eden soon discovered, Britain was no longer in a position to undertake such a project without American support. After this crisis, the British "habit of using the language and assumptions of a Great Power had been smothered" (Kyle 1989, 130).

Conclusion

The elaborate edifice of constructivism in not required simply to observe that, in British eyes, the image of Egypt and its leader changed dramatically in the year leading up to the Suez crisis. But cognitive theories of social stereotyping do not address the problem of how in-group bias is inscribed in higher levels of collective behavior. One might thus dismiss the cognitive account of Egypt's changing identity, viewed from London, as so many individual perceptions with no particular relevance to international relations. Or, at best, these perceptions might be deemed relevant only insofar as they affected the beliefs and policies of Britain's prime minister. Morgenthau (1948) warned long ago that rationalizations and justifications should not be allowed to conceal the true nature of foreign policy—that it is dangerous to take states at their "word" and that perceptions are often misleading. Yet, misleading or not, rationalizations and justifications *are* foreign policy. The contribution of constructivism is to make it clear that these perceptions *were* international relations in this case. They were the instruction-rules that formed the reality to which Eden responded.

A constructivist approach would be unnecessary if this reality were uncontested. A simpler alternative to the account offered here is that Nasser's actions represented a genuine threat and that Britain's response was dictated by considerations of power politics and national security. Indeed, the frequent references by British leaders to Nasser's resultant control over Europe's oil lifeline evoke a straightforward concern with material issues (and a concern not too different from the concerns voiced about Iraq during the Persian Gulf War).

But Britain's reaction remains difficult to explain on these grounds alone. As Nasser himself pointed out during the crisis, Egypt was already eligible to purchase the Suez Canal Company beginning in 1968. "Why should Britain say that this nationalization will affect shipping in the canal?" he complained. "Would it have affected shipping twelve years hence?" (Neff 1981, 283). Moreover, the threat that Britain apparently perceived to its oil supply could well have been mitigated by less drastic means than a military invasion of the canal zone. One approach, advocated by the United States during the crisis as a way of dissuading Britain from more bellicose action, was the creation of an international board to oversee canal operation. Britain's response seems too hasty and too disproportionate to the actual threat posed by nationalization, therefore, to explain on material grounds alone. Indeed, the fact that Britain finished withdrawing its troops from Suez little more than a month before Nasser announced nationalization indicates the limited practical importance of British control of the canal. Not surprisingly, "when Anthony Nutting pointed out to Eden that Britain might not actually have any worry about the canal staying open since it was now in Egypt's best interests to collect as many tolls as possible, the prime minister 'merely replied that I should know that the capacity of the Arabs to cut off their noses to spite their face was infinite' " (284). Apart from being a striking example of negative out-group identification, Eden's remark suggests that he found it impossible, by this point, to believe that Nasser was remotely capable of rational action—despite Nasser's considerable effort to assure the smooth functioning of the canal and to carry out the nationalization plan in accordance with Egyptian and international law.

Eden's response makes it plain that his attention focused not on what Nasser had done (or could reasonably be expected to do) but on what he thought Nasser had become. The act of nationalization itself was not the problem. It was what the act said about what Nasser and Egypt had become (a growing nationalist and possibly communist threat) and about what Britain was in danger of becoming (a declining power). Nationalization warranted to Eden that Egypt was no longer competent to deal with a complex environment of international directive-rules and commitment-rules, no matter the care that Nasser actually took to obey these rules. The British interpretation of Egyptian behavior hinged not on the behavior itself but on the ascribed identity of Egyptian agents. Moreover, Eden and his cabinet not only redefined Egyptian identity but increasingly exaggerated both the identity itself and the distinction between this identity and their own (the Egyptians would not respect the rules; the English were honorable and law-abiding). Finally, with these exaggerations of political identity came attribution errors, generally ascribing to Nasser malicious intent regardless of the constraints he may have faced.

Not only were these transformations of identity endogenous to the interaction between Britain and Egypt, but they depended heavily on the behavior of political agents. No international structures (not even those of the Cold War) completely determined the pattern of interaction between Eden and Nasser. Even if the West might eventually have found Nasser's nationalism intolerable for other reasons, greater cooperation on the Aswan Dam might well have forestalled that conflict long enough to prevent the Suez crisis. The crisis occurred because of "who" it involved, not because of what it involved. And long before the crisis, the character of the states involved in it was conceived and reconceived in the minds of a small group of individuals.

Notes

The author is grateful for support in the form of a National Science Foundation grant (DIR-9113599) to the Ohio State University's Mershon Center Research Training Group (RTG) on the role of cognition in collective political decision making. Deborah Avant, Martha Finnemore, Richard Herrmann, Peter Katzenstein, Jeffrey Legro, Nicholas Onuf, participants in three Social Science Research Council/MacArthur Foundation workshops on "Norms and National Security," members of the Mershon Center RTG, and members of the Miami International Relations Group at Florida International University and the University of Miami have all offered helpful comments and advice that enriched this paper. This chapter also draws on ideas developed, in part, in Kowert and Legro (1996).

1. Actually, appreciation of the relationship between language and identity is nothing new. In his classic study of European nationalism, for example, Karl Deutsch (1953) recognized that communication was a key to social identity. See also Kubálková's "The Twenty Years' Catharsis," Chapter 2 in this volume.

2. In a superb illustration of the way political leaders are affected by their own manipulations, Jack Snyder (1991) shows that not only may domestic interest groups benefiting from national expansion be very successful at promoting imperialist ideologies, but also their leaders may come to believe passionately in these ideologies, blinding them to the dangers of overexpansion. Snyder calls this process "blowback."

3. For a psychological approach different from the one developed in this chapter, see Kratochwil's brief discussion of social norms, *eros*, and *thanatos* in Freudian psychology (1989, 126–29). Also see Brewer's theory of social distinctions that relies on motivational psychology (1991).

4. In an experiment notable perhaps as much for the ethical issues it raised as for its results, Sherif (1961) tested his hypothesis by dividing children attending a summer camp into two groups and giving them first competing and then superordinate goals. Not only did Sherif find that the competing goals produced considerable hostility toward out-group members, but it was much harder to restore collective identity with superordinate goals than to fracture it. See also Blake and Mouton (1961).

5. A natural complement to the fundamental attribution error is the attribution of one's own behavior to situational constraints ("I had to do it") rather than to personal desires ("I didn't want to"). For an excellent discussion of this and other related attributional biases, see Fiske and Taylor (1984, 72–99).

6. Unfortunately for Eden, once Britain had joined Turkey and Iraq to form the core of the Baghdad Pact, the United States had little incentive to follow. Britain's presence alone would serve as a deterrent to Soviet expansion, and joining the Pact would only alienate Egypt—the opposite of what Eisenhower and Dulles hoped to achieve (see Louis 1989, 44–46).

7. Ironically, Eden had studied Arabic and was himself on many earlier occasions a strong advocate of Arab positions, often in the face of a French foreign policy that was generally more supportive of Israel. In 1941, Eden admitted to his private secretary that "if we must have preference, let me murmur in your ear that I prefer Arabs to Jews" (Neff 1981, 206).

Eden's interest in Arab culture does not, of course, necessarily imply a positive image of the "other"; see Said's discussion of "orientalism" (1979). The dramatic reversal of Eden's views toward Nasser may also have been hastened by the prime minister's physical ailments. Eden's health deteriorated markedly prior to and during this crisis as a result of a damaged bile duct and chronic infections. To compensate, he routinely took both antibiotics and amphetamines. This condition may account for much of Eden's irritability and perhaps even his emotional response to Nasser's behavior. See Neff (1981, 182–83).

Bibliography

Allport, Gordon. 1954. *The Nature of Prejudice*. Reading, MA: Addison-Wesley.

Ashley, Richard K. 1984. "The Poverty of Neorealism." *International Organization* 38: 225–86.

Bendor, Jonathan, and Thomas Hammond. 1992. "Rethinking Allison's Models." *American Political Science Review* 86: 301–21.

Brewer, Marilyn. 1991. "The Social Self: On Being the Same and Different at the Same Time." *Personality and Social Psychology Bulletin* 17: 475–82.

Blake, Robert R., and Jane S. Mouton. 1961. "Reactions to Intergroup Competition Under Win-Lose Conditions." *Management Science* 7: 420–35.

Campbell, David. 1992. *Writing Security: United States Foreign Policy and the Politics of Identity*. Minneapolis: University of Minnesota Press.

Cartwright, Dorwin, and Alvin Zander. 1968. *Group Dynamics*. London: Tavistock.

Chafetz, Glenn. 1995. "The Political Psychology of the Nuclear Nonproliferation Regime." *Journal of Politics* 57: 743–75.

Deschamps, Jean-Claude. 1977. *L'Attribution et la Catégorisation Sociale*. Berne: Peter Lang.

———. 1982. "Social Identity and Relations of Power Between Groups." In *Social Identity and Intergroup Relations*, ed. Henri Tajfel, 85–98. Cambridge: Cambridge University Press.

Dessler, David. 1989. "What's at Stake in the Agent-Structure Debate." *International Organization* 43: 441–74.

Deutsch, Karl W. 1953. *Nationalism and Social Communication: An Inquiry into the Foundations of Nationality*. Cambridge: M.I.T. Press.

Doyle, Michael. 1986. "Liberalism and World Politics." *American Political Science Review* 80: 1151–69.

Enloe, Cynthia. 1989. *Bananas, Beaches, and Bases: Making Feminist Sense of International Politics*. Berkeley: University of California Press.

Fiske, Susan, and Shelley Taylor. 1984. *Social Cognition*. New York: Random House.

Galtung, Johan. 1990. "U.S. Foreign Policy as Manifest Theology." In *Culture and International Relations*, ed. Jongsuk Chay, 119–40. New York: Praeger.

George, Jim, and David Campbell. 1990. "Patterns of Dissent and the Celebration of Difference." *International Studies Quarterly* 34: 269–93.

Giddens, Anthony. 1984. *The Constitution of Society: Outline of the Theory of Structuration*. Cambridge: Cambridge University Press.

Goldstein, Judith, and Robert O. Keohane, eds. 1993. *Ideas and Foreign Policy: Beliefs, Institutions, and Political Change*. Ithaca: Cornell University Press.

Gramsci, Antonio. 1971. *Selections from the Prison Notebooks*, ed. and trans. Quintin Hoare and Geoffrey Nowell Smith. New York: International Publishers.

Grieco, Joseph. 1988. "Anarchy and the Limits of Cooperation: A Realist Critique of the Newest Liberal Institutionalism." *International Organization* 42: 483–508.

Herman, Robert. 1996. "Identity, Norms, and National Security: The Soviet Foreign Policy Revolution and the End of the Cold War." In *The Culture of National Security: Norms and Identity in World Politics*, ed. Peter Katzenstein, 271–316. Ithaca: Cornell University Press.

Hewstone, Miles, and J.M.F. Jaspars. 1982. "Intergroup Relations and Attribution Processes." In *Social Identity and Intergroup Relations*, ed. Henri Tajfel, 99–133. Cambridge: Cambridge University Press.

Judd, Charles M., Carey S. Ryan, and Bernadette Park. 1991. "Accuracy in the Judgment of In-Group and Out-Group Variability." *Journal of Personality and Social Psychology* 61: 366–79.

Katzenstein, Peter, ed. 1996. *The Culture of National Security: Norms and Identity in World Politics*. Ithaca: Cornell University Press.

Kowert, Paul, and Jeffrey Legro. 1996. "Norms, Identity, and Their Limits: A Theoretical Reprise." In *The Culture of National Security: Norms and Identity in World Politics*, ed. Peter Katzenstein, 451–97. Ithaca: Cornell University Press.

Kratochwil, Friedrich. 1989. *Rules, Norms, and Decisions: On the Conditions of Practical and Legal Reasoning in International Relations and Domestic Affairs*. Cambridge: Cambridge University Press.

———. 1996. "Citizenship: On the Border of Order." In *The Return of Culture and Identity in IR Theory*, ed. Yosef Lapid and Friedrich Kratochwil, 181–97. Boulder, CO: Lynne Rienner.

Kyle, Keith. 1989. "Britain and the Crisis, 1955–1956." In *Suez 1956: The Crisis and its Consequences*, ed. W. Roger Louis and Roger Owen. Oxford: Clarendon, 103–30.

———. 1991. *Suez*. New York: St. Martin's Press.

Lapid, Yosef. 1989. "The Third Debate: On the Prospects of International Theory in a Post-Positivist Era." *International Studies Quarterly* 33: 235–54.

——— and Friedrich Kratochwil, eds. 1996. *The Return of Culture and Identity in IR Theory*. Boulder, CO: Lynne Rienner.

Legro, Jeffrey. 1996. "Culture and Preferences in the International Cooperation Two-Step." *American Political Science Review* 90: 118–37.

Louis, W. Roger. 1989. "The Tragedy of the Anglo-Egyptian Settlement of 1954." In *Suez 1956: The Crisis and Its Consequences*, ed. W. Roger Louis and Roger Owen, 43–72. Oxford: Clarendon.

Lucas, W. Scott. 1991. *Divided We Stand: Britain, the US and the Suez Crisis*. London: Hodder and Stoughton.

McGarty, C., and R.E.C. Penny. 1988. "Categorization, Accentuation and Social Judgement." *British Journal of Social Psychology* 22: 147–57.

Mendelson, Sara. 1993. "Internal Battles and External Wars: Politics, Learning, and the Soviet Withdrawal from Afghanistan." *World Politics* 45: 327–60.

Mercer, Jonathan. 1995. "Anarchy and Identity." *International Organization* 49: 229–52.

Morgenthau, Hans J. 1948. *Politics Among Nations*. New York: Knopf.

Mullen, Brian, and Li-tze Hu. 1989. "Perceptions of Ingroup and Outgroup Variability: A Meta-Analytic Integration." *Basic and Applied Psychology* 10: 233–52.

Neff, Donald. 1981. *Warriors at Suez*. New York: Linden Press.

Neufeld, Mark. 1995. *The Restructuring of International Relations Theory*. Cambridge: Cambridge University Press.

Nutting, Anthony. 1967. *No End of a Lesson: The Story of Suez*. New York: Clarkson N. Potter.

Oakes, Penelope, and John Turner. 1986. "Distinctiveness and the Salience of Social Category Memberships: Is There an Automatic Perceptual Bias Towards Novelty?" *European Journal of Social Psychology* 16: 325–44.

Onuf, Nicholas. 1989. *World of Our Making: Rules and Rule in Social Theory and International Relations*. Columbia, SC: University of South Carolina Press.

Park, Bernadette, and Charles M. Judd. 1990. "Measures and Models of Perceived Group Variability." *Journal of Personality and Social Psychology* 59: 173–91.

———, Carey S. Ryan, and Charles M. Judd. 1992. "The Role of Meaningful Sub-groups in Explaining Differences in Perceived Variability for In-Groups and Out-Groups." *Journal of Personality and Social Psychology* 63: 553–67.

Peterson, V. Spike, ed. 1992. *Gendered States: Feminist (Re)Visions of International Relations Theory.* Boulder, CO: Lynne Rienner.

Said, Edward. 1979. *Orientalism.* New York: Vintage.

Searle, John R. 1969. *Speech Acts: An Essay in the Philosophy of Language.* Cambridge: Cambridge University Press.

Shamir, Shimon. 1989. "The Collapse of Project Alpha." In *Suez 1956: The Crisis and its Consequences,* ed. W. Roger Louis and Roger Owen, 73–100. Oxford: Clarendon.

Sherif, Muzafer. 1961. *Intergroup Conflict and Cooperation: The Robbers Cave Experiment.* Norman: University of Oklahoma Book Exchange.

———. 1966. *In Common Predicament: Social Psychology of Intergroup Conflict and Cooperation.* Boston: Houghton Mifflin.

Snyder, Jack. 1991. *Myths of Empire: Domestic Politics and International Ambition.* Ithaca: Cornell University Press.

Sylvester, Christine. 1994. *Feminist Theory and International Relations in a Postmodern Era.* Cambridge: Cambridge University Press.

Tajfel, Henri. 1969. "Cognitive Aspects of Prejudice." *Journal of Social Issues* 25: 79–97.

———, ed. 1978. *Differentiation Between Social Groups: Studies in the Social Psychology of Intergroup Relations.* London: Academic Press.

———. 1981. *Human Groups and Social Categories: Studies in Social Psychology.* Cambridge: Cambridge University Press.

Tickner, J. Ann. 1992. *Gender in International Relations: Feminist Perspectives on Achieving Global Security.* New York: Columbia University Press.

Turner, John C. 1982. "Towards a Cognitive Redefinition of the Social Group." In *Social Identity and Intergroup Relations,* ed. Henri Tajfel, 15–40. Cambridge: Cambridge University Press.

———. 1991. *Social Influence.* Buckingham, UK: Open University Press.

Welch, David. 1992. "The Organizational Process and Bureaucratic Politics Paradigms: Retrospect and Prospect." *International Security* 17: 112–46.

Wendt, Alexander. 1987. "The Agent-Structure Problem in International Relations Theory." *International Organization* 41: 335–70.

———. 1994. "Collective Identity Formation and the International State." *American Political Science Review* 88: 384–96.

Zisk, Kimberly. 1993. *Engaging the Enemy: Organization Theory and Soviet Military Innovation, 1955–1991.* Princeton: Princeton University Press.

6

Feminist Struggle as Social Construction: Changing the Gendered Rules of Home-Based Work

Elisabeth Prügl

"Those who were marginal are now entering the mainstream" was the hopeful conclusion of Ela Bhatt, secretary general of the Self-Employed Women's Association (SEWA) of India, at the Meeting of Experts convened by the International Labor Organization (ILO) in Geneva in the fall of 1990. The meeting explored the situation of homeworkers (i.e., those who work at home for pay), their conditions of work, government policies toward them, and the possible role of the ILO in improving their lives. Ubiquitous in urban and rural areas around the world, home-based workers sew garments; embroider; make lace; roll cigarettes; weave carpets; peel shrimp; prepare food; polish plastic; process insurance claims; edit manuscripts; and assemble artificial flowers, umbrellas, and jewelry. Some subcontract with factories, large firms, intermediaries, or merchants; others are quasi-independent and sell their goods and services—often in a highly dependent fashion. Some work by themselves; others are embedded within family enterprises. Virtually all receive low wages and work under adverse conditions. While the meeting in Geneva was divisive, Bhatt's sentiment proved visionary: in June of 1996 the International Labor Conference (ILC), the policy-making assembly of the ILO, passed an international convention (multilateral treaty) committing ratifying states to develop national policies on home-based workers, which recognized them as employees and secured them basic worker rights and protections.

The fight for an international convention on homework provides a case for the study of gendered rules in global politics and for the central role that social movements play in the reconstruction of such rules. A network of women in nongovernmental organizations from Asia, Europe, and South Africa lobbied for the homework convention. Their efforts built on those of the global women's movement, which had long argued that female workers were no different from male workers and that women's home-based work, both paid and unpaid, was as valuable as work outside the home. Employing a constructivist framework allows me to interpret events that led to the convention as a process of changing, institutionalizing, and codifying different categories of rules.

A disproportionate number of home-based workers are married women with children. Their work is embedded in a number of overlapping institutions, and both conforms to and clashes with the rules of these institutions. As members of households, home-based workers occupy the roles of wives, mothers, daughters, or sisters, and are expected to fill these roles according to culturally diverse expectations. As agents in a polity, women workers gain rights and duties of citizenship which carry strongly gendered overtones. As participants in a labor market, women workers are subject to the rules of sex-typing and the unequal distribution of rewards this engenders. Frequently, gender rules in households, the economy, and states have functioned to disempower women. The disadvantaged status of home-based workers is one result, and has spawned the movement to rectify this situation. Changing rules about home-based work thus implies a wider change of rules in households, the economy, and the state.

The focus of my investigation is the practices of the "homeworker movement," embedded within the global feminist movement and the labor movement. Social movements constitute a counterpart to the globalization of production and the accompanying internationalization of states which increasingly orient their economic and social policies to the systemic imperatives of global capitalism. In finding alliances across borders and focusing their activities "above and below the state" (Wapner 1995), social movements question the reality of states as the containers of legitimate politics and open up space for the democratization of global politics. They do so by seeking to influence international treaties, conventions, and other commitments. They do so as well by establishing the legitimacy of new claims to rights (e.g., human rights), and by creating commitments on the part of those in power to honor these rights. But they exercise democracy perhaps most importantly by changing the rules of identity. Arguably the main accomplishment of the global women's movement has been to fundamentally challenge understandings of proper womanhood and manhood, which have long served to subordinate women.

Feminism and Constructivism

Although feminism is not a monolithic body of thought, and although it thrives on disagreements and multiple perspectives, most contemporary feminists agree on one issue: gender is a social construct. The rejection of biological determinism was at the base of early feminist critiques in the second wave of the women's movement. Today many feminists have shifted from talking about sex and women to talking about gender in order to focus attention from the biological to the social. This is reflected in Sandra Harding's characterization of gender as "a systematic social construction of masculinity and femininity that is little, if at all, constrained by biology" (1987, 8). As a social construct, gender has history and is an integral part of politics. Joan Scott's definition complements Harding's in framing gender politically as "a constitutive element of social relationships based on perceived differences between the sexes, and . . . a primary way of signifying relationships of power" (Scott 1986, 1067). As a constitutive element of social relations, gender involves symbols, norms, organizations, institutions, and subjective identities. As a way of signifying relationships of power, gender divides the world in a binary fashion which provides the means for the articulation and legitimation of power.

Feminist writers on international relations have long argued that gender is a useful category for understanding global politics and have insisted that gender constructions are pervasive. Unfortunately, feminist international relations (IR) literature typically does not connect the term *social construction* to a body of theory. This usage papers over considerable differences in approach of authors steeped in different theoretical traditions. At the risk of oversimplification, it is possible to suggest theoretical influences in recent texts. Michel Foucault's concerns with the formation of identities and Jacques Derrida's method of deconstruction resonate in Christine Sylvester's usage of the term. Sylvester describes men and women as "socially constructed" in the sense "that men and women are the *stories* that have been told about 'men' and 'women' and the constraints and opportunities that have thereby arisen as we take to our proper places" (1994, 4). Foucaultian and Marxist themes appear in Cynthia Enloe's emphasis on the *practices* of various global actors to describe manipulations of and contests over definitions of masculinity and femininity (Enloe 1989, 1993). Similar frameworks may underlie Jan Jindy Pettman's recent book in which social constructions emerge as the *manipulations* of states which, she argues, construct the public/private divide, "manufacture" citizens, and construct "'deviant' forms of sexuality" (Pettman 1996). Spike Peterson and Anne Sisson Runyan draw on sociological and Marxist concepts to suggest that social construction involves the socialization and social reproduction of *stereotypes* and *ideologies* (1993, 19–26). Sandra Whitworth and Deborah Stienstra, in Coxian/neo-Gramscian fashion, conceptualize social construction as an *interaction* of material conditions, institutions, and ideas or discourses (Whitworth 1994, 4; Stienstra 1994).

These texts use *social construction* to convey two ideas. First, the term signals a concern with "the social" as opposed to material capabilities, static structures, unquestioned positivities, or "pre-given" identities. The social becomes real in discourses, stories, practices, and ideas. Second, the term is meant to indicate impermanence, historicity, and malleability. Stories can be rewritten; discourses can be deconstructed; practices can change; stereotypes can alter; ideologies can be revealed; and material conditions, institutions, and ideas can change. The texts thus do capture basic insights of social constructivism, especially those which are useful to an understanding of feminist struggle and in this way to informing feminist practice. Yet, what is lacking is an understanding of the processes of institutionalization, of the way in which agency and structure are co-constituted in the social. This gives rise to both theoretical and practical problems. Closer looks at two exemplary authors, Whitworth as an advocate of the materialist framework and Sylvester as a protagonist of post-structural ideas, show the difficulty.

I see two weaknesses in Whitworth's approach, which result from not following through on social constructivism. First, Cox's materialist foundations trap her in modernist dualisms inimical to some of the most consequential feminist theorizing which insists that the biological and bodies are as much part of the social as other expressions of gender. Whitworth (and Cox) insist that the relationship between ideas, institutions, and material conditions is reciprocal and that no one determines the other. Yet, material conditions appear to have a reality of their own, not outside history but outside politics and social construction. This leads to problematic conclusions when Whitworth grafts nonclass categories onto Cox's class-based framework. "Age, race, sex, sexual orientation, etc." emerge as prepolitical givens, material realities which may be politicized in particular contexts but, like class, exist as categories in themselves (Whitworth 1994, 69). However, human sexuality and sexual orientation are not prediscursive. Social orders create biological conceptions that perpetuate unequal distributions of power. Gender discourse requires that there be a coherence between sex and gender, and this coherence is built on a compulsory heterosexual matrix (Harding 1986, 126–30; Butler 1990). From a social constructivist perspective, the distinction between the material and the ideal is not tenable; ideas contaminate material reality. From the perspective of many feminists, the distinction is at a minimum problematic; at a maximum it participates in the naturalization of sex and gender.

A second problem with Cox's approach arises from its failure to adequately address the agent-structure problem. While Whitworth discusses extensively the need for an approach that accounts for both individual purpose and the social constraints of history, Cox does not provide her with the analytical tools to follow through on this insight. To be sure, her analysis explores the interests, intentions, and agitations of activists, states, and the ILO, together with material conditions in various phases of history. But aside from stating correspondences, Whitworth is not able to connect ideas, institutions, and material conditions. Ideas and material conditions appear ontologically separate, and institutions emerge as *reflections* of ideas and material conditions. One is left to wonder how these reflections are generated and how ideas, institutions, and material conditions relate to agency and structure. Cox and Whitworth miss an opportunity in not taking seriously Cox's own definition of institutions as social constructs, as "the broadly understood and accepted ways of organizing particular spheres of social action" (Cox 1996, 149).

Sylvester's *Feminist Theory and International Relations in a Postmodern Era* tackles a major debate among contemporary feminist theorists, which pits "post-structuralists," who destabilize and question the unity of subjects, against "humanists," who argue that such practice has pernicious effects. Critical of the implications of modernist logocentrism, of its concern with origins and foundations, and of its silencing of "Others" through the naturalization of identities, post-structuralist feminists reject an understanding of "women" as subjects of politics and insist that "women" need to be analyzed as an outcome of discursive practices. Humanist feminists reply that this understanding delegitimizes emancipatory claims on behalf of women as a group and does away with historical agents. As subjects disappear, so do notions of intentionality, accountability, self-reflexivity, and autonomy, ideas which they claim are central to feminist critique and practice (Benhabib et al. 1995).

Sylvester joins a growing number of feminist thinkers who seek to combine the insights of post-structuralists and humanists to make the case for "a position of negotiation between standpoint feminism [which privileges women's experiences as constituted subjects] . . . and postmodern skepticism [which questions the constitution of these subjects]" (Sylvester 1994, 12; see also Alcoff 1988; Ferguson 1993). Thus, Sylvester rescues humanist values by merging the standpoint approach's insistence on a fusion of being and knowing with post-modern understandings of the variability and multiplicity of identities. She insists that subjects can find temporary "homesteads" from which they can speak. Such homesteads enable a politics of emancipation. In this way "people called women" do not need to have a unitary, immobile, and monolithic identity. They speak from ever-shifting and different standpoints.

Sylvester's formulation is appealing. It foregrounds feminist practice while cautioning about the totalizing implications of fixing a unitary feminine identity. However, Sylvester's post-structuralist point of departure prevents her from developing a theory of agency, in which not only are men and women the "stories that have been told about 'men' and 'women'" (Sylvester 1994, 4), but also discourses are continuous with everyday communication and subjects actively construct each other through communicative practices. Sylvester remains caught in an ultimately static methodology that puts congealed texts at the center of its analysis. We learn that women at Greenham Commons and in the cooperatives of Zimbabwe challenge meanings and interpretations, but we do not learn how these challenges enter the stories about these women. What is lacking is a theory of agency that illustrates the institutionalization of narratives. Constructivism provides such a theory. Indeed, there is a significant strand of feminist constructivist theorizing in the social sciences (e.g., Connell 1987; Kessler and McKenna 1978; Lorber 1994).

Constructivism in International Relations:
A Method for Gender Analysis

Constructivism has emerged as one of the major strands of the "third debate" in international relations. The central tenet of constructivism is that people and societies, agents and structures, construct, or constitute, each other. Constructivists argue that international life is social, that is, that it follows norms and rules which make up social structures. These structures reproduce only through the practices of knowledgeable agents. Structures and agents cannot exist without each other: they are mutually constitutive. Actors draw on the rules that make up structures in their everyday routines, and in doing so they reproduce these rules. They have the capacity to understand what they are doing and why they are doing it, which allows them to "reflexively monitor" the social practices they engage in. Structures make possible similar social practices across time and space, thus ensuring the relative stability of social life.

Like the post-structuralists who influenced Sylvester, constructivists put language in the center of their understanding of the social. But unlike post-structuralists, constructivists focus on processes that produce the social, not on the social as an effect of relatively static discourses. They approach language as social practice, not as a textual artifact or discursive formation. They are interested not only in identities signified in narratives, stories, and discourses, but in the intersection of signifying and doing. The fluidity of the social is well captured in Jürgen Habermas's theory of communicative action, which roots social practice in communication and argumentation and which forms the basis of Nicholas Onuf's constructivist discussion of rules. Onuf's reformulation makes possible an understanding of the multiple ways in which gender forms, perpetuates, and mutates through communicative action.

According to Habermas, all communicative statements entail validity claims; that is, a speaker claims that a statement is factually correct, normatively right, and nondeceptive. If the hearer accepts these claims, understanding is accomplished and speech acquires a binding force. Communicative agents renew their interpersonal relationship and affirm their agreement about objective facts of the world and about subjective experiences (Habermas 1984, 295–305). Onuf argues that the speech act agreements that underlie communicative action produce and reproduce social structures. *Rules* provide the "missing link" between social structures and temporary agreements resulting from understanding. The normative force of a speech act agreement becomes a convention when others join in the agreement and repeat propositions with complementary content. Conventions become rules once people follow conventions as a matter of routine and once they recede from conscious deliberations (Onuf 1989, 78–95).

Various authors in the field recently have thrown light on the importance of studying norms and rules in international politics from a sociological perspective. Onuf criticizes this work, together with post-positivist literature, for treating norms as context. He argues instead that rules (a term he prefers to norms) are positivities and as such are capable of empirical investigation and classification (Onuf 1997). His classification of rules into instruction-rules, directive-rules, and commitment-rules provides a heuristic tool for investigating the interlacing ways in which gender is constructed. Instruction-rules define, describe identities, and state beliefs about the way things are. They make claims about facts, elicit agreement about these facts on the part of others, and thereby bring about conformity. Directive-rules imply commands, requests, demands, permissions, and warnings. They elicit compliance, obeisance, submission. Commitment-rules imply promises and offers that oblige individuals to act accordingly. All three types of rules are both regulative and constitutive. In other words, all three elicit action on the part of others while also establishing social facts (Onuf 1989, 78–95).

Constructivism provides a promising method for studying the struggle of homeworker advocates. First, constructivism allows for a specification of gender as a constellation of rules and in this way provides a tool for investigating a social fact which, as many feminists have correctly argued, is both historical and fluid. Second, the focus on rules uniquely puts activism in the center and allows for an understanding of the ways it effects changes. Rather than depicting a singular oppressive structure, reflections of material or ideological changes, or the economics of a static text, a constructivist approach allows for a specification of the types of rule changes which different forms of activism accomplish. Third, constructivism provides for an understanding of how rule changes effect new realities within institutions, themselves sets of rules. Such institutions may be individuals or other agents, such as households or states (see Onuf's essay in Chapter 3 of this volume). In addition, gender itself constitutes an institution, one that cuts across other institutions and supports the constellations of rule and power they constitute. Altering rules of gender thus inevitably affects the rules of other institutions as well. A focus on institutions allows me to trace such interlocking changes.

The Gendered Rules of Home-Based Work

Home-based work carries very different meanings in different contexts. For some women it means an extension of their domestic activities to provide an additional "service" to their families, for some it is an opportunity to save in a honorable way for their dowries, for some it is a tradition, and for some it is the equivalent of factory jobs in the absence of a factory. For example, in Rio de Janeiro, Brazil, cultural ideas about proper womanhood and religious identifications merge with exploitative practices of employers to construct home-based seamstresses as housewives. In Lahore, Pakistan, understandings of honor, respectability, and family status, together with the need to save money for their dowries, encourage young women to engage in home-based work. For rural, home-based Turkish carpet weavers, weaving is part of a girl's socialization, and is integral to farming households where female household members share their labor power and weaving subsidizes agricultural investments. In Thailand, rural homeworkers fall into two groups: a group of older women and men for whom homework is a supplementary activity that easily integrates into the agricultural cycle, and a group of younger women who produce for export-oriented firms and for whom home-based piecework is the main source of income.

Despite the differences in contexts and the divergent meanings they spawn, understandings of home-based work have one thing in common: they invariably define such work as secondary. On the one hand, home-based work emerges as subsidiary to either male income or agricultural income. On the other hand, it appears as transitional for those moving toward marriage or for those who think of themselves as unemployed. Instruction-rules that associate home-based work with women are grafted onto a basic principle that identifies women as subordinate to men; in this way instruction-rules facilitate a construction of home-based work as supplementary. This goes along with an identification of men as primary income earners and of women's work as "not real work." The gendered rules of households, labor markets, and states powerfully conspire to effect a construction of home-based work as secondary.

Rules of the Household

Households are institutions defined largely by commitment-rules. These rules pervasively commit women to take on the duties of motherhood and housework, duties that come with marriage. There is considerable variation, as expectations about women's roles within households respond to local rules of custom and religion. A woman in Pakistan may have to commit herself to live in one of various degrees of seclusion, while custom tells a woman in Ghana to work the fields and grow food for the family, or a working-class woman in the United States may be expected to make an economic contribution to the household in addition to performing her domestic duties. Despite these differences, married women in particular tend to share a tie to the home, which limits their work options. In the Western context it is appropriate to describe this limitation as implied in a "marriage contract" through which women in effect give up part of the property in their own person, including full control over their labor power (Pateman 1988). The language of contracts may be inappropriate for describing the situations of women in other cultures, but for them marital status and motherhood equally are defined through a series of commitment-rules which often function to tie their labor power to the needs of the household. Not surprisingly, statistics confirm that a disproportionate number of home-based workers in countries all over the world are not only female but married with small children. Home-based work allows such women to combine their household and mothering duties with earning an income (Prügl 1992).

From those in the garment industry in Delhi to those in white-collar jobs in Great Britain and Silicon Valley, many home-based workers see themselves primarily as housewives, mothers, or dutiful daughters and only secondarily as income-earners; they consciously subordinate their paid work to family commitments (Rao and Husain 1987, 62–63; Hakim 1987, 98; Lozano 1989, 122). Women who participated in the clerical homeworker program of the Wisconsin Physicians Services Insurance Corporation believed that a woman's place was in the home with her family and that she should not take away a male breadwinner's job (Costello 1989, 201). In Rio, 50 percent of the seamstresses who said they preferred to work at home did so because of family or domestic reasons. They perceived being a seamstress not as a profession but as a service to themselves and their families (Sorj 1991, 7f.). Garment homeworkers in Central Java were often their families' main income earners in a context of high levels of male unemployment. Yet they insisted that they were only "working for salt," and that the men were the true breadwinners. They maintained that their domestic work came first, even though they had no time to cook during the peak sewing season and frequently bought food from local vendors (Susilastuti 1990, 9).

Despite this primary commitment to the family, home-based income earning often conflicts with household duties, and home-based workers draw negative consequences from violating their promises to be good mothers and housewives. Husbands of home-based workers rarely reduce their expectations about domestic work. For example, a homeworker from the U.K. complained that "if I haven't managed to get some housework done because I've been too busy doing homework then I'm asked—'What do you do all day long[?]' as if I just sit around all day long" (Trivedi 1985, 18). The attitude of men in Pakistan was that home-based work was something which women indulged in and which therefore should not cut into their time for housework: "Well, we did not ask them to work. If she wants to work it's her responsibility to make sure she can handle her house work first, which is her first duty as mother and wife" (Shaheed and Mumtaz, n.d., 53–54).

Women's home-based work affected gender roles in the household by questioning who was the breadwinner. Husbands used various techniques to deny this challenge and to uphold the notion that they were breadwinners and their wives were nonworking housewives. In Narsapur, husbands did not produce lace but created a myth that they invested money in their wives' work and portrayed themselves as entrepreneurs. In Turkey and Afghanistan, men sold the carpets that women in their household made, and kept the money. In this way they retained control over household spending decisions and appeared to be the true breadwinners (Mies 1982, 95; Berik 1987, 72).

The rules of households are one element in definitions of gender and the privileges they distribute. They are a central element in a set of interlocking institutions that keeps home-based workers subordinate. The commitment-rules of marriage and the household thus emerge as a crucial challenge for homeworker advocates.

Rules of the State

Many states today are built on liberal understandings that divide a society into a public and a private sphere. The line that divides the two spheres is a matter of social agreement, but liberal states typically have treated households as private and out of the reach of the state. Since the industrial revolution moved most manufacturing into factories, and with the creation of welfare states, work outside the home has become a target of state intervention effected by law, or formal directive-rules. In parallel, the home increasingly has been defined as the sphere of women and has been constructed ideologically as outside the regulatory reach of the state. In an effort to reduce the unfair competition home-based workers posed to factory workers, legislators in Europe, the Americas, and Australia regulated home-based work in the first half of the twentieth century. But in most countries today legislation on home-based work is severely lacking. Out of 150 countries the ILO surveyed in the early 1990s, only 18 (mostly European) countries had specific homework legislation; another 22 (mostly Latin American) countries addressed the matter in their labor codes. With the exception of Japan, India, and the Philippines, no country in Africa or Asia regulated home-based work. The definition of households as homes, supposedly out of the reach of the state and ruled by private convention under the authority of male heads of households, prevented regulation (International Labor Office 1994, 28).

In most cases if home-based workers want to qualify for legal protection, they have to claim that they are not only members of households but also employees of a firm. But legal tests of employment status typically address the situation of office and factory workers. Under a number of common law legal criteria, home-based workers often emerge as self-employed. Such criteria test whether work is carried out on the employer's premises, whether the worker owns any of the tools, whether the worker works for more than one employer, or whether the worker has been engaged for a continuous period of time. Many home-based workers would fail to qualify on all these criteria. Furthermore, home-based workers often are preempted from benefits because benefits are frequently conditional upon the length of service or upon the number of hours worked.

It is therefore not surprising that lawyers, legislators, and other officers of the state have argued that home-based workers are not real employees. For example, the Indian Supreme Court, in a 1961 ruling, interpreted the Indian Factories Act to apply only when "workers were working on the premises of the employer, had no liberty to work at home and the employer could exercise the power of control by rejecting the sub standard [products]" (Mahajan 1985, 8). And while the Indian Bidi and Cigar Workers Act of 1966 clearly defined home-based bidi (cigarette) rollers as employees, the chief labor inspector in Gujarat "insisted on questioning as to how somebody working in a private house could ever be an employee" (31). When based on an instruction-rule that defined home-based workers as nonworkers, directives geared toward improving the status of workers failed home-based workers. The Japanese Industrial Homework Law of 1970 is one of the few homework laws which explicitly excludes home-based workers from protection under various labor laws and from social security protection. As a result, they do not receive benefits in cases of injuries or sickness, maternity benefits, unemployment benefits, or retirement benefits (Kamio 1991, 25–26). In other countries, laws do not exclude home-based workers explicitly, but confusion about their status often functions to exclude them *de facto*. In parallel to instruction-rules that define public and private, work and home, as separate, home-based workers are confirmed not to be real workers and are excluded from directives that gain employees benefits and protection.

Statistical practices reinforce these instruction-rules. National surveys routinely undercount home-based workers because such surveys typically take place at one point in time and miss seasonal or intermittent home-based work, because home-based work sometimes resembles production for domestic use, because male heads of households who respond to surveys consider the women's work a leisure-time activity or would like to hide this work for reasons of family honor, because surveys rarely ask about "secondary" employment, because census takers may not speak the language of home-based workers who—especially in England, the United States, Canada, and Australia—are often immigrants, because home-based workers themselves may not want to reveal their work and alert tax authorities and enforcers of labor law, and because surveys of business establishments do not cover these types of activities (Dixon 1982, 543–46). The practice of undercounting women's home-based work produces startling outcomes. For example, in Narsapur, India, the 1971 census showed 6,449 persons involved in household industries. But the main industry in town, with 8 million to 9 million rupees a year in turnover, was home-based lace making, employing an estimated 100,000 women. Because lace making was considered a leisure activity of housewives, lace makers did not appear as workers in the census (Mies 1982, 49, 54). In Turkey, carpet weaving was similarly deemed a pastime suitable for women and national employment statistics did not count weavers, although they earned about half the household income of poor families (Berik 1987, 2, 15, 61).

In changing the practices of states, homeworker advocates need to combine changes in instruction-rules with laws that direct employers to define homeworkers as employees and with administrative regulations that ensure the proper implementation of such laws, as well as making sure that home-based work is counted in censuses. Such directives are likely to strengthen changed images of what home-based workers are and also are likely to facilitate a sense that home-based workers are entitled to workers' rights.

Rules of the Labor Market

Labor market practices reinforce rules that construct home-based workers as nonworkers and their work as secondary and subordinate. On the face of it, the rules of supply and demand are systemic and outside social control, and gender biases are an unintended consequence resulting from constraints external to the labor market. But feminist critique has denaturalized the rules of the market, pointing out that employers draw on instruction-rules of gender in making employment decisions. Gendered notions of skill (women's skills, such as sewing, are usually defined as natural) and the sex-typing of jobs form the labor market counterpart to the rules of the household. They conspire with the understanding that home-based workers are housewives who earn merely supplemental income and whose work is not important for family survival, to provide a powerful legitimation for denying such workers basic rights. Most perniciously, these rules legitimate the puny wages of home-based workers. There is overwhelming evidence that home-based workers almost invariably earn less than minimum wages and less than their factory counterparts, lending credence to the assertion that these workers are "superexploited" (Mies 1982, 172–78; Prügl 1992, 226–39, 323–32).

Because home-based workers are defined as nonworkers, by the rules of the labor market they often become self-employed (even though they may actually qualify for employee status under national law). The self-employed constitute a default category, comprising all those who do not have employee status. In practice, the self-employed have considerably fewer rights and protections than employees. Their role in the labor market is defined through a "contract for services" in which they appear as individual sellers, not of their labor power, but of a service. They negotiate the price of that service, are not covered under minimum wage laws, and fall outside the umbrella of collective bargaining. They set their own hours, do not earn income when sick or on vacation, and are responsible for their own training. They lack any type of job security.

The rules of the market encourage self-employment status for all workers. From the perspective of employers, self-employed workers are desirable because they reduce labor costs: Employers can circumvent statutory minimum wages and collective bargaining agreements, and they do not have to provide a workplace and pay the overhead costs associated with maintaining a workplace. Furthermore, self-employed workers allow employers flexibility: Employers do not have to keep workers on the payroll when no work is available and thus effectively transfer part of the risk of doing business to the workers. By resorting to self-employed workers rather than employees, employers increase their chances of successfully competing in the market.

Conditions of surplus labor encourage situations in which workers will make themselves attractive to employers by assuming the status of self-employment. As a result, most home-based workers in Africa, Asia, and Latin America are *de facto* self-employed. The market functions as a heteronomous institution in which workers become complicit in their own exploitation. For women in addition, the rules of the household and the state encourage self-employment. Because labor laws have been written largely for male workers who have full control over their own labor power, they make no allowance for flexibility. Women workers need such flexibility because they need to integrate family and household duties with earning an income. Despite the considerable potential for exploitation, rigid labor laws leave self-employment as a desirable option.

Thus the seemingly innocuous rules of supply and demand conspire to keep home-based workers in a subordinate position in the labor market. The challenge for homeworker advocates is to shape the rules of employment contracts so that employers take on the obligations of ensuring basic worker rights while maintaining the flexibility of home-based work.

HomeNet International and the Struggle for Home-based Workers

In March 1994, a group of homework activists, representatives of international union federations, and ILO officers met in Brussels to launch HomeNet International, a loose network of individuals and organizations with the shared aim of improving the lot of home-based workers around the world. HomeNet's purpose would be to facilitate the exchange and dissemination of information about home-based workers and their organizations and to coordinate an international campaign to improve the living and working conditions of these workers. It was the Self-Employed Women's Association (see p. 123), a nongovernmental group from India, that called the meeting. SEWA had worked with home-based workers for many years and had actively lobbied the ILO to draft an international labor standard for such workers. SEWA was concerned that homeworker advocates mobilize support for such a standard in their countries because the 1995 International Labor Conference had placed homework on its agenda. Among those attending the founding meeting were representatives of SEWA, the National Homeworking Group in the United Kingdom, the Association for the Establishment of a Self-Employed Women's Union in South Africa, and the International Ladies' Garment Workers' Union in Canada; officers of Homework Support Centers and the Clean Clothes Campaign in the Netherlands; and delegates from international union federations and the International Labor Office (Ramirez 1995, 29–30). An all-female gathering, the meeting constituted a section of the organizational face of the global women's movement. Feminists in nongovernmental organizations joined forces with those in the ILO to push the case for an international convention on homework.

The homeworker advocates' success in realizing the formalization of rules to regulate homework was built on long-standing efforts within the global women's movement to change understandings of what it means to be a home-based worker. The "women in development" (WID) movement provided a devastating critique of technical assistance efforts and economic policies formulated under the presumption that all women were nonworking housewives. Such policies had a detrimental effect on women's status and frequently derailed development projects. The WID critique initiated a change in instruction-rules, creating awareness that home-based women contributed to national wealth. Increasingly, planners and policy makers understood that these women were workers. Homeworker advocates participated in this redefinition through research and public advocacy as well as through consciousness raising among home-based workers.

The fight for an ILO convention on homework drew strength from the degree to which changed understandings of women workers had become accepted. Homeworker advocates hoped that the convention would lead states to issue directive-rules about the way in which employers and officers of the state were to treat home-based workers. Indian, British, and Canadian advocates especially found national legislation to be insufficient. Neither country had homeworking laws, and all had encountered the damaging effects of neoliberal economic restructuring for unprotected workers. In Britain, the Thatcher administration abolished the "trades boards," which since the beginning of the century had established minimum wages in "low-pay industries." While many advocates found the boards problematic, doing away with them left British homeworkers without any legal recourse. In the Canadian garment industry, the effects of the North American Free Trade Agreement (NAFTA) showed in the form of jobs moving south and in increased subcontracting to home-based workers, many of them immigrants. Intensive lobbying yielded a few changes in regulations but no substantive reform of the law. In India, SEWA had managed to get introduced to the Indian parliament a homeworker protection bill, but the bill never reached the floor. In the context of talk about opening the economy to foreign investment and making the country internationally competitive, home-based workers and new regulations carried low priority for Indian lawmakers. Having encountered less than sympathetic governments, Indian and British advocates in particular turned to the international level.

While advocates expended a considerable amount of energy in lobbying for an ILO convention on homework, they retained a realistic view of its potential effects. Advocates knew that legislation was useless in the absence of strong organizations to stand guard over its implementation. To make the laws a reality—to turn government orders into workers' rights—would require the interventions of strong workers' organizations. But in India, the Bidi and Cigar Workers Act had taught advocates that having a law was in itself a powerful organizing tool. SEWA activists used the act to gather workers in the tobacco industry into their union while gaining them their legal rights. Knowing that the Indian government took very seriously any ILO action, SEWA's aim was to use the convention to lobby for a law for all home-based workers and to make these rights a reality for all.

Changing Instruction-Rules

At the 1995 ILC, conflict arose over a photo exhibit, organized by HomeNet, which was displayed at the entrance to the meeting room of the Committee on Homework. Australian union representatives criticized the exhibit as "too pretty," because it showed British homeworkers in tidy homes, Indian homeworkers in colorful saris working together in front of their houses, and Philippine homeworkers collaborating on decorative crafts items. The Australians added their own images of homeworkers: black-and-white photos showing tired immigrants at sewing machines in dilapidated houses. HomeNet representatives defended their pictures, insisting that it was necessary to get away from the image of homeworkers as victimized dupes who have no power to change their own situation.

The photo exhibit constituted an attack on instruction-rules about home-based workers prevalent in union circles. These rules define such workers as outside the working class, unable to act in concert on their own behalf. The advocates' attacks on instruction-rules about home-based workers also target the image that they are nonworking housewives. Research and media projects have provided two of the most salient tools in this effort.

Many homeworker advocacy groups have a close relationship with researchers and carry out considerable research themselves. The Leicester Outwork Campaign, one of the most successful homeworker advocacy groups in Britain, has coordinated research with academics and provided them with data (Allen and Wolkowitz 1987). In turn, the British homeworking campaigns gained support from research conducted by the Low Pay Unit, a nongovernmental organization which advocates for workers in low-pay industries. During the 1970s, its national survey on homework in Britain had a strong impact in the media and fueled a national debate about introducing a law on homework (Tate 1995, 84). In South Asia, several studies, some sponsored by the ILO's Employment and Development Branch, have given visibility to homework and prepared the ground for ILO action (Singh and Kelles-Viitanen 1987; Bhatty 1981; Mies 1982). In Southeast Asia, an ILO project on improving the protection of home-based workers sponsored and published research findings from Indonesia, the Philippines, and Thailand, which laid the ground for organizing efforts and raised interest within governmental bureaucracies, including social security agencies, which began to look for ways to cover these workers (Homeworkers of Southeast Asia 1992).

Typically, these studies unveil as a myth the image that home-based workers are housewives. They document the long hours these workers put into their work; the significant contribution they make to family income; and the importance of their work in the local, national, and global economy. They also document the variety of activities home-based workers engage in, to counteract understandings that homework is marginal and limited to the garment industry. In doing so, they instruct their readers that homework is not just a hobby for housewives, but central to the functioning of the economy. Therefore homeworkers must be considered workers just like those in factories and offices.

Those who organize home-based workers extensively use research as a tool to effect change of consciousness and as an entry to organizing. Through interviews, they educate home-based workers about their rights and about ways to improve their situation. Research also helps them identify potential leaders among home-based workers. Often organizers draw on home-based workers themselves to become researchers of their own situation, and such involvement has given workers a chance to participate in the attack on unwarranted instruction-rules in the process of defining their own alternatives. For example, when students started the Leicester Outwork Campaign in the early 1980s, they believed that homeworkers would be interested in struggling for better child care, which would allow them to go out and find better work. Action research taught the students that most home-based workers preferred to stay home with their young children. Rather than wanting to agitate for better child care, they were more interested in struggling for better and more flexible work arrangements. Home-based workers in effect disagreed with the students' implicit view that home-based work was undesirable—that good work and real work was that which took place outside the home. Action research fostered an identification of these home-based workers as workers—although in a nontraditional workplace. By changing self-identifications, action research weakens instruction-rules that define home-based workers as not real workers.

In addition to research, advocates use audiovisual materials to publicize the notion that home-based producers are workers. British campaigns have contributed to several video productions which have been made available to national and international television. For example, "A-Z Homework" is a short, professionally made film that shows the different kinds of products homeworkers make, interspersed with demands for just wages and working conditions. Its messages are: first, homework is pervasive and homeworkers make many everyday items; and second; homeworkers are real workers who deserve to be treated as such. The British campaigns also participated in an ILO documentary made for and distributed on the occasion of the 1995 ILC. Similarly, SEWA has been the object of at least one documentary shown on U.S. public television, and it runs its own video project, through which its members document their situation and demand their rights as workers.

Through these diverse interventions, homeworker advocates effect changes in an instruction-rule that is pervasive throughout society. The message that it is a myth to consider home-based workers housewives needs to reach everyone from husbands and neighbors to employers and governments. Defining home-based workers as workers is a first step toward changing their inferior status in society. Adding directive-rules to instruction-rules can support this change.

Changing Directive-Rules

The establishment of HomeNet International signals a step toward greater coordination and organization among homeworker advocates. HomeNet builds on the strength of SEWA in particular, an accomplished organization with tens of thousands of members, its own bank, social insurance schemes, several cooperatives, and a good track record of using technical assistance funds from international donors. When SEWA leaders decided to push for an ILO convention on homework, they established links with and membership in international trade union federations and won their support for the convention. This organizational strengthening, of which the formation of HomeNet was a part, positioned the movement well to begin formulating directive-rules and to demand that states write these directive-rules into laws. HomeNet members' most important demand was that home-based workers should be considered workers and gain the same protection as other types of workers.

The ILO convention on homework achieves precisely that. It directs ratifying states to "adopt, implement and periodically review a national policy on home work," and sets as the guiding principle for such a policy "equality of treatment between homeworkers and other wage earners." It then lists the areas where equality of treatment should apply: "(a) the homeworkers' right to establish and join organizations of their own choosing . . . ; (b) protection against discrimination in employment and occupation; (c) protection in the field of occupational safety and health; (d) remuneration; (e) statutory social security protection; (f) access to training; (g) minimum age for admission to employment or work; and (h) maternity protection" (International Labor Conference 1996, 3). In legislative and administrative practice this list will translate into directive-rules demanding that employers and agencies of the state ensure equal treatment.

A home-based worker who subcontracts from an intermediary or from an employer clearly belongs to a hierarchical organization in which the provider of work rules by giving directives. Indeed, the common definition of a dependent employee as "under the direction" of a work giver signals precisely this situation. Much of the discussion in formulating the convention on homework centered around Article 1, which defined homeworkers: Should they be considered part of the work giver's organization, or did they run their own enterprise? Were they in a dependent relationship, or were they self-employed? Employers insisted that it was impossible to decide which home-based worker was an independent contractor and which was an employee. Workers, on the other hand, insisted that a combination of criteria, most importantly gauging economic independence, allowed for such a decision. In defining a broad group of home-based workers as dependent, the convention not only changed an instruction-rule that identified home-based workers as nonworkers but acknowledged that they were part of an employer-defined organizational setting and were guided by the directives of this setting.

The task homeworker advocates have set for themselves at this point is not to change these directives but to gain a broad acceptance of the principle that home-based workers are indeed part of an employer's organization. At the same time, they seek to combine home-based workers into organizations that will provide them the opportunity to more effectively negotiate their interests vis-à-vis firms and organized employers' interests. Changing directives is the bread and butter of such organizations. While a loose network may be sufficient to support global aspirations and efforts to change instruction-rules, networks cannot substitute for organizations as actual vehicles effecting changes in the pay and treatment of workers.

Changing Commitment-Rules

In most industrialized countries, employees can expect employers to pay minimum wages and to abide by certain regulations of working hours. There is also a broad expectation that workers will be allowed to organize in unions and other associations representing their interests. The rules of a "contract for services" are quite different. They commit the worker to produce an item by the time agreed upon and they commit the employer to do no more than pay a price upon delivery. Self-employed workers may, in most democratic societies, have the right to join various groups, but their right to organize in unions may be severely circumscribed. For example, when SEWA tried to register as a union, its request was denied because, according to the registrar, self-employed workers could not organize into unions. Only after two years of argument and after the intercession of powerful union leaders could SEWA register legally as a union.

The ILO convention on homework signals a change of these rules by setting, as a standard for home-based workers, the rules of the employment contract. The challenges for homeworker advocates will be to turn the directive-rules implied in the convention and in laws that may result from the convention into employer commitments, and to create among home-based workers a sense of entitlement to employment rights and protections. Unions and homeworker advocacy groups play a crucial role in effecting such commitment-rules by acting as watchdogs over the implementation of laws. Some are doing so already. In Australia, the garment union has included homeworkers in collective bargaining agreements; in India, SEWA watches over violations of the Bidi and Cigar Workers' Act and has taken employers to court to gain workers their rights; in England, homework campaigns advise homeworkers about their rights under existing law and publicize violations. For most homeworkers the problem is still that the laws are lacking, but the homework convention provides a significant step toward writing better laws nationally and toward realizing basic worker rights for home-based producers.

Conclusion

The purpose of this chapter is to illustrate the value of a constructivist approach for studying gender in global politics: that which is meant by "womanhood" or "manhood," that which is demanded from women and men, and the different roles women and men play in contractually defined situations. It uses the case of home-based workers to trace definitions of gender through the mutually supportive rules of households, states, and labor markets, and it shows how feminist activism unfolds as a challenge to instruction-, directive-, and commitment-rules. In attacking rules, feminist activists change institutions. Households in which men no longer are the undisputed breadwinners can no longer uphold men's authority on the presumption that they ensure household survival. States in which supposedly feminine preoccupations such as child care and the distribution of power in households move into the public realm can no longer legitimize the notion that men are better at ruling and administering the affairs of states. And in labor markets where supposedly feminine skills and notions of women's pay as supplemental are denaturalized, discriminatory treatment is no longer justified. Activism changes rules, and rules change institutions.

Yet structures and institutions also circumscribe the activism of advocates. Employee status and union organizing surface as the logical methods of improving the wages and working conditions of home-based workers, because employee status and unions exist as well-established institutions with supporting rules codified in national and international labor laws and laws of association. Lobbying governments (and by extension the ILO) for changes in laws presents itself as an effective approach, because the rules of democratic government prescribe this venue. In contrast, advocates abstain from demanding changes to rules of supply and demand that have assumed the status of a systemic imperative under a capitalist mode of flexible accumulation, and have been defined as outside history, no longer amenable to change.

Gender statuses appear as bundles of social rules anchored in institutions that reach from the local to the global. Gender crucially defines these institutions by "engendering" distributions of power within them (rules create rule), and complementary rules in different institutions effect a global subordination of women. Feminist struggle has targeted all types of rules in all types of institutions, from the local to the global, and has destabilized a form of subordination based on the fiction that women are housewives. For home-based workers as well, instruction-rules that define them as true workers are becoming institutionalized; achieving pervasive directives and commitments from governments and employers to gain equal rights for home-workers remains a task to be accomplished.

Note

I would like to thank Nick Onuf for his thorough readings of this paper and for his constructive suggestions.

Bibliography

Alcoff, Linda. 1988. "Cultural Feminism versus Post-Structuralism: The Identity Crisis in Feminist Theory." *Signs: Journal of Women in Culture and Society* 13 (Spring): 405–38.
Allen, Sheila, and Carol Wolkowitz. 1987. *Homeworking: Myths and Realities*. London: Macmillan.
Benhabib, Seyla, Judith Butler, Drucilla Cornell, and Nancy Fraser. 1995. *Feminist Contentions: A Philosophical Exchange*. New York: Routledge.
Berik, Günseli. 1987. *Women Carpet Weavers in Rural Turkey: Patterns of Employment, Earnings and Status*. Geneva: International Labor Office.
Bhatty, Zarina. 1981. *The Economic Role and Status of Women in the Beedi Industry in Allahabad, India*. Saarbrücken: Verlag Breitenbach.
Butler, Judith. 1990. *Gender Trouble: Feminism and the Subversions of Identity*. New York: Routledge.
Connell, R.W. 1987. *Gender and Power: Society, the Person and Sexual Politics*. Stanford: Stanford University Press.
Costello, Cynthia. 1989. "The Clerical Homework Program at the Wisconsin Physicians Services Insurance Corporation." In *Homework: Historical and Contemporary Perspectives on Paid Labor at Home*, ed. Eileen Boris and Cynthia Daniels, 198–214. Urbana: University of Illinois Press.
Cox, Robert W. 1996. "Towards a Posthegemonic Conceptualization of World Order: Reflections on the Relevancy of Ibn Khaldun." In *Approaches to World Order* by Robert W. Cox with Timothy Sinclair, 144–73. Cambridge: Cambridge University Press.
Dixon, Ruth B. 1982. "Women in Agriculture: Counting the Labor Force in Developing Countries." *Population and Development Review* 8 (September): 539–69.
Enloe, Cynthia. 1989. *Bananas, Beaches, and Bases: Making Feminist Sense of International Politics*. Berkeley and Los Angeles: University of California Press.
———. 1993. *The Morning After: Sexual Politics at the End of the Cold War*. Berkeley and Los Angeles: University of California Press.
Ferguson, Kathy E. 1993. *The Man Question: Visions of Subjectivity in Feminist Theory*. Berkeley and Los Angeles: University of California Press.
Habermas, Jürgen. 1984. *The Theory of Communicative Action*, Volume 1: *Reason and the Rationalization of Society*, trans. Thomas McCarthy. Boston: Beacon Press.
Hakim, Catherine. 1987. "Homeworking in Britain: Key Findings from the National Survey of Home-Based Workers." *Employment Gazette* 95 (February): 92–104.
Harding, Sandra. 1986. *The Science Question in Feminism*. Ithaca: Cornell University Press.
———. 1987. "Introduction: Is there a Feminist Methodology?" In *Feminism and Methodology*, ed. Sandra Harding, 1–14. Bloomington: Indiana University Press.
Homeworkers of Southeast Asia. 3 volumes. 1992. Bangkok, Thailand: International Labor Office.
International Labor Conference. 1996. 83rd Session. "Authentic Texts: Convention Concerning Home Work." In *Record of Proceedings* (Geneva: International Labor Office).

International Labor Office. 1994. *Home Work.* Report V(1) to the 82d Session of the International Labor Conference, 1995.

Kamio, Kyoko. 1991. "Homeworkers in Japan." *Yorkshire and Humberside Low Pay Unit Newsletter*, no. 12 (March): 25–26.

Kessler, Suzanne J., and Wendy McKenna. 1978. *Gender: An Ethnomethodological Approach.* New York: John Wiley and Sons.

Lorber, Judith. 1994. *Paradoxes of Gender.* New Haven: Yale University Press.

Lozano, Beverly. 1989. *The Invisible Workforce: Transforming American Business with Outside and Home-based Workers.* New York: The Free Press.

Mahajan, Krishan. 1985. "Bidi Workers: Laws, Implementation and Alternatives." In *Women Who Roll Bidis: Two Studies of Gujarat* by Renana Jhabvala, Reva Dhawan, and Krishan Mahajan. Ahmedabad: Self-Employed Women's Association.

Mies, Maria. 1982. *The Lace Makers of Narsapur: Indian Housewives Produce for the World Market.* London: Zed Press.

Onuf, Nicholas Greenwood. 1989. *World of Our Making: Rules and Rule in Social Theory and International Relations.* Columbia: University of South Carolina Press.

———. 1997. "How Things Get Normative," unpublished manuscript.

Pateman, Carole. 1988. *The Sexual Contract.* Stanford: Stanford University Press.

Peterson, V. Spike, and Anne Sisson Runyan. 1993. *Global Gender Issues.* Boulder, CO: Westview Press, 1993.

Pettman, Jan Jindy. 1996. *Worlding Women: A Feminist International Politics.* London: Routledge.

Prügl, Elisabeth. 1992. "Globalizing the Cottage: Homeworkers' Challenge to the International Labor Regime." Ph.D. Dissertation, The American University, Washington, D.C.

Ramirez, Elia. 1995. "HomeNet International: Launch of the International Network for Home-Based Workers." *News from IRENE: International Restructuring Eduction Network Europe* (Tilburg, Netherlands) (22, March): 29–30.

Rao, Rukmini, and Sahba Husain. 1987. "Invisible Hands: Women in Home-Based Production in the Garment Export Industry in Delhi." In *Invisible Hands: Women in Home-Based Production*, ed. Andrea Menefee Singh and Anita Kelles-Viitanen, 51–67. New Delhi: Sage Publications.

Scott, Joan. 1986. "Gender: A Useful Category of Historical Analysis." *American Historical Review* 91 (December): 1053–75.

Shaheed, Farida, and Khawar Mumtaz. n.d. "Invisible Workers: Piecework Labour Amongst Women in Lahore." Islamabad: Government of Pakistan, Women's Division.

Singh, Andrea M. and Anita Kelles-Viitanen, eds. 1987. *Invisible Hands: Women in Home-Based Production.* New Delhi: Sage Publications.

Sorj, Bila. 1991. "Le travail à domicile/Le travail domestique." Paper presented at the Groupe de Etude sur la Division Sociale et Sexuelle du Travail/CNRS, Paris, September.

Stienstra, Deborah. 1994. *Women's Movements and International Organizations.* New York: St. Martin's Press.

Susilastuti, Dewi Haryani. 1990. "Working for More than Salt: Female Home-based Workers in a Garment Industry." Paper presented at the Fourth International Interdisciplinary Congress on Women, New York, 2–7 June.

Sylvester, Christine. 1994. *Feminist Theory and International Relations in a Postmodern Era.* Cambridge: Cambridge University Press.

Tate, Jane. 1995. "National Group on Homeworking—United Kingdom." In *Action*

Programmes for the Protection of Homeworkers: Ten Case-Studies from Around the World, ed. Ursula Huws, 81–98. Geneva: International Labor Office.

Trivedi, Bindu. 1985. "Asian Women Homeworkers—Smashing the Myths." *Mukti* (UK) 4.

Wapner, Paul. 1995. "Politics Beyond the State: Environmental Activism and World Civic Politics." *World Politics* 47 (April): 311–40.

Whitworth, Sandra. 1994. *Feminism and International Relations: Towards a Political Economy of Gender in Interstate and Non-Governmental Institutions*. New York: St. Martin's Press.

7

Internet Governance Goes Global

Craig Simon

Architecture is politics.

—Mitch Kapor

In the architecture of content, information becomes the interface.

—Edward Tufte

The story that new ideas and technologies can transform a society and undermine established authority is a familiar one. What will make this telling different, I believe, is my use of the vocabulary of constructivism, following the works of Nicholas Onuf (1989). The framework presented by Onuf and other constructivists offers far more power than traditional International Relations (IR) frameworks to explain the rising significance of the Internet and its governing institutions. Though kindred structurationists like sociologist Anthony Giddens have been cited in various studies of Internet policy (Zurawski 1997; Uncapher 1994; Helmers, Hoffman, and Hoffman 1996), it is new territory even for constructivists engaged in IR.

I argue in this essay that the standards-making process for global telecommunications is moving out of the hands of traditional state authorities into the hands of people whose goals and loyalties are less national than commercial. States are not preparing to recapture this power. Since the nature of the newly constituted authority is inherently global, the effect, if trends continue, will be to fortify the expansion of global rule, a process which is already under way. Onuf's framework is particularly well equipped to evaluate whether Internet expansion represents a shift in effective authority, whereas other IR frameworks overlook its counterhegemonic significance. By explaining how rules make rule—how standards makers become standard bearers—constructivism draws attention to the most potent agents of global rule making.

We begin, therefore, by considering the general plan of the new system's vanguards, known to popular culture as the "digerati." This will be followed by a discussion of the different ways constructivism and competing IR perspectives approach the topic of rule making in telecommunications. The last section applies a constructivist analysis to the ongoing efforts of the Internet's creators to build new institutions and procedures for operating the Internet's addressing service, known as the domain name system (DNS). If successful, these changes would enlist the International Telecommunications Union (ITU) and other Geneva-based organizations as agents in support of global, rather than intergovernmental, goals.

The Digerati Agenda

The term *digerati*, a play on "digital literati," was coined by Nicholas Negroponte, whose *Being Digital* (1995) exalted the impact of computers on society. The word can refer loosely to anyone who has facility with computers, but is often applied to industry pioneers and opinion leaders, several of whom are glamorized in John Brockman's *Digerati: Encounters with the Cyber Elite* (1996). Given their generally high level of media savvy and skill at self-marketing, it is tempting to attribute their stardom to our society's Warholian obsession with wealth and fame. These masters of microelectronic art are ready made for celebrity, but their conspicuous station in society raises an analytical problem. Giving the digerati serious consideration as an organized movement might exaggerate their significance, imparting a substantive coherence to their views that otherwise would not exist, and thereby crediting them with an undeserved historical status.

Such concerns are outweighed by the unmistakable evidence that the digital telecommunications infrastructure reaches nearly everywhere on the globe and that, wherever it reaches, it transforms society. Moreover, many people who play key roles in designing that structure declare they are building a new order which threatens the primacy of sovereign states. Healthy skepticism demands asking whether those assertions are overblown, but we should not ignore the fact that embellished claims to power play a role in any system of social organization.

The digerati agenda is best summed up in Metcalfe's Law, a term coined by economist George Gilder in honor of Bob Metcalfe, owner of 3COM Corporation and inventor of Ethernet, the electronic protocol used by most networked personal computers. Metcalfe's Law states, "The value of a network can be measured by the square of its number of users." In short, "Connected computers are better" (Metcalfe 1996). This suggests that connecting everyone (and perhaps everything) in the world through a global network of computers would be a beneficial and desirable project. Adding members to the system would enable the network to achieve its fullest potential, and promises individual empowerment as a consequence. Metcalfe's Law is all-inclusive and imperious. It explicitly asserts that global networking is a universal social good, and implicitly challenges the exclusive norms of a world order based on states and social divisions. The explicit part of the formulation is especially interesting because of a congruence with formal theories of public goods and network externalities. Economists define public goods as things whose utility cannot be divided in a way that one person's maximum use would diminish another's benefit. Externalities refer to the ways that investors recover costs from free riders. The concept of network externalities holds that the wider use of a thing *increases* everyone's potential benefit from it, as if a lighthouse could shine more brightly when more ships find its beam, or as if the utility of a phone system improves by adding phones to it, even subsidized ones.

The implicit, *counterhegemonic* aspect of Metcalfe's Law follows from the indivisible notion of public goods. Digerati trailblazers share a tenacious and outspoken desire to overcome limits on human communication. It is considered heroic to build systems that enable escape from the binds of physical and political space. Metcalfe's 1973 invention of Ethernet, for example, was inspired by an earlier engineering feat called AlohaNet, a wireless digital data system spanning the Hawaiian islands. Tim Berners-Lee, creator of the protocols that underlie the World Wide Web, summarized his work as creating a "global information system" operating across a "seamless hypertext information space" (1992). His present activities involve developing systems of "metadata" to provide a universal content labeling standard for commercial and social applications. Jaron Lanier, who pioneered virtual reality, describes Transmission Control Protocol/Internet Protocol (TCP/IP), the underlying software of the Internet, as a political "masterpiece" which will endure as a collaborative achievement greater than the American Constitution.

> Embedded in this rather simple piece of code is a whole philosophy of life. A whole philosophy of equality among people, of equal access of people to other people. A philosophy that anything that everyone has to say is equally worthwhile. A philosophy that people should never be separated from each other, that there shouldn't be any standard hierarchy that tells them how to relate to each other. (Lanier 1997)

Consider also the Teledesic venture, a digital communications system connected through a backbone of 288 satellites in low earth orbit, allowing users to bypass the national seams now crimping land-based phone and data lines. Competing systems will also be deployed, but Teledesic is distinguished by its ambitious size and its high-profile founding investors—cell phone industry pioneer Craig McCaw and Microsoft's Bill Gates. McCaw described Teledesic to a *Washington Post* reporter as "the ultimate egalitarian product" which will "change dramatically the cultural patterns the world was built on." "We are granting people the right to interact with each other," he said. "This will have an impact on central authorities" (Mills 1997). Ironically, those same authorities are eager to compete for contracts to launch such satellites from within their presumably threatened borders.

To mix a famous phrase by Newt Gingrich with a lesser known but equally acute one by a leading constructivist, Alexander Wendt, the Information Revolution is what we make of it. Many digerati consider themselves to be revolutionaries who are particularly adept at enlisting followers to their cause. A few are becoming quite skilled at exploiting confusion and divisions among the political leaders of the world's nation-states. Telecommunication, like sovereignty or religion, can serve as a tool for anyone who seeks to manage or reorganize a society. Such tools offer a set of behaviors, institutions, and concepts of social goods that amount to a kind of grammar through which leaders and followers interact. Just as religious evangelism produces converts, just as political ideas often acquire an imprimatur of substance as they circulate, the digerati ideology advances its own self-fulfilling prophecies.

And consider how many futurologists and social soothsayers have begun to argue, quite persuasively, that acquiring and learning to use computers will advance a person's economic viability. As Gates told readers of his column in the *New York Times* syndicate, "a Web lifestyle will take hold" as people learn it is the best way of adapting to life's bothers. "You'll take the network for granted," he wrote, "turning to it instinctively without a second thought" (1997b). Within ten years, he foretells (perhaps overoptimistically), all adults will live a form of that lifestyle, and eventually everyone will rely on it to manage financial transactions. In expressing challenges to "central authority," Gates tends to be far less confrontational than his partner McCaw, but his prediction nevertheless contains a demanding admonition. The Web lifestyle will presumably offer such a reliable, trustworthy, and universally available facility for the conduct of commercial activity that it will be considered a necessity. Any individual who shuns it will be foolhardy. Any collectivity that tries to do so will be handicapping itself at great peril.

Few technologies have spurred such quick and dramatic social changes as telecommunications, but never before have the champions of an industry been so bold about seeking to build an infrastructure that can be both self-governing and not only independent of the regulatory powers of established state authorities but immune to them. This ideological position, promoting telecommunications as a means to a wider social end, is what distinguishes the digerati agenda from numerous other trade and professional associations that decry government regulation. No other social movement has dared to take such great practical strides toward transforming states into vestigial organs of the global body.

Judging this movement to be good or bad is another question. It is clear that many digerati express a desire to change the world for the better, but it is far too early to speculate about whether they can effectively remedy the kinds of injustice associated with the present system of international relations. The time is ripe, however, to formulate a critique of their normative precepts and their philosophy of action. Since inequalities are inherent in every rule-based power system, and since it is now becoming possible to sketch out the grandest features of a digerati-styled system, one can try to anticipate what types of inequalities may result if the digerati agenda reaches fruition. In other words, how will it impact the circumstances in which people find themselves?

Cyber Shockwaves

Though information technology is widely accepted to be the hallmark of our age, it is not necessarily a boon for humankind. The impact of electronic media on culture is much discussed these days, as is the rise of "internetworked" computing in business and education, and not always in glowing terms. Advanced industrial economies have experienced high investment in computers, making the machines nearly ubiquitous. Yet growth in workplace productivity has not kept pace (Sichel 1997; Thurm 1997). As cognitive psychologist Thomas Landauer demonstrated quite clearly in *The Trouble with Computers* (1995), computers are too complex for most people to use any more effectively than typewriters and regular mail. Still, we who depend on these devices feel that we could not get by without them. Despite the trials they force us to endure, and despite the degradation of our skills and investments wrought by each new generation of software and hardware, we generally feel these tools have enabled us to do new things, more quickly, and in greater quantities. We are convinced they are an essential tool for the future. Unfortunately, we have good cause to doubt whether the next version of a program will fix more than it breaks, or whether the next model of a machine will perform any more smoothly than the last. We have learned not only that we must abide by new standards as they emerge but also that the standards to which we submit may all too soon be declared obsolete. Inability to complete a task because a computer "won't take it," either because of inflexibility or flaw in design, is an increasingly familiar refrain.

Technology's benefits may be inconsistent, but its broad social impact is undeniable, especially with regard to telecommunications. Landauer's findings show that computerization of the public telephone network has brought about significant boosts in worker productivity while adding carrying capacity and switching speed at a fast pace (Landauer 1995, 169–70; also Noll 1997; 64–71). Now financial and media sectors have joined the market to create even more advanced topologies. The nerve center of the telecommunications industry has become the showcase performer of the information age. Its improvements correlate with other transformations in society, including vast changes in investment patterns and workplace organization, a steady series of giant corporate mergers, historic changes in law, and heated debates in public policy regarding censorship, monopoly, and tariff regulation. Much of the boom in telecommunications focuses on the Internet, which not only is a catch-all term for a burgeoning collection of infrastructures and applications but also may prove to be the platform through which personal communications and mass media technologies converge (Akimaru, Finely, and Zhieseng 1997).

As digital telecommunications become more pervasive around the globe, its applications are likely to intrude more and more deeply into people's lives. The current trajectory of investment invites informed speculation that, within two or three decades, innovations in the delivery of television, radio, and traditional voice phone services may transform digital data services into a qualitatively new form of technology. The scientists who are developing the prototype platform for future media convergence refer to it as Nexus (Low 1997). Prognosticating further, by the middle of the next century, basic facility with that integrated technology will likely be as essential to human socialization as mastering skills like telling time, using money, reading maps, or recalling one's address and phone number. New generations of surveillance equipment and personal information collection software will increasingly assault our concepts of privacy and autonomy, enforcing an omnipresent discipline of social monitoring that many theorists call *panoptic* (Gandy 1993; Boyle 1977; Ashley 1983). The implications of the Web lifestyle far surpass the novelty of ordering pizza through the Internet: As did the making of clocks and maps in antiquity, creation of the Web lifestyle involves the construction and application of devices that extend human knowledge and activity past local bounds of time and space. These devices free us to coordinate ourselves across those bounds in dramatically new ways, but they limit us as well. Imbued with the belief that those devices show the way to prosperity, we are forced to keep step with the world beat or else be trampled in the march. In a similar vein, Anthony Giddens uses the metaphor "Riding the Juggernaut." Modernity, unharnessed, threatens to run amok, crushing everything in its path (1990).

This raises interest in how to assess these phenomena in theoretical terms. It is one thing to identify these global drummers—the people who make "the rules." It is another to ask what they think they are doing and how they define their interests. Digerati culture has spawned its own forms of political ideology, theories of economics, and canons of literature, as well as a few martyrs. There is considerable evidence showing that the members of that culture are becoming conscious of their collective identity on the basis of their shared interest in expanding and securing the Internet. It is also possible to reveal their strategic assault on the ability of states to regulate Internet and other telecommunications activity within national borders. Therefore, my inquiry concerns the intentions of the central agents of modern technological change, recognizing that the sociopolitical implications of their work may be profound.

Let us briefly review how other observers of global affairs approach these questions.

Making Sense of the Information Revolution

Much of the current growth in the scale and scope of digital telecommunications is due to technical innovation, but the far-reaching economic initiatives of the Reagan-Thatcher era earn special credit. An apt metaphor regarding the deregulatory, pro-competitive legacy of those years was invented by *New York Times* columnist Thomas Friedman. The "golden straitjacket," he wrote, "is all the rules set down by global markets for how a country has to behave economically if it wants to thrive in today's world" (1997). The "golden straitjacket" is the tendency of political leaders to tie their hands and pledge nonintervention in their national economies, in exchange for the promises of growth and prosperity. The breakup or privatization of national telephone and telegraph monopolies has played out differently around the world, however. The contrast is especially stark between industrialized nations and underdeveloped ones. Ben Petrazzini, for example, reflects the conventional wisdom in the field of comparative politics, concluding that the "demise" of public phone monopolies in less developed countries was motivated primarily by fiscal decline, prompting political leaders to sell off national industries in exchange for infusions of foreign capital (1995). Legal scholars find themselves in rich but uncharted territory. The Information Age has spawned whole new sorts of crimes, augmented by real confusion about where such crimes occur and about who has jurisdiction in cyberspace (Kahin and Nesson 1997).

IR specialists have also begun to take notice. Joseph Nye and William Owens (1996) have written about the strategic opportunities and vulnerabilities these technologies create for the United States in the global balance of power. Jill Hills (1994), following Susan Strange, shows that advanced Western industrial states have foisted a liberal economic orthodoxy (based on open markets and monetary policy) upon the world, granting wide autonomy to large multinational corporations, while essentially privatizing international organizations. This allows such states to translate the structural power they once enjoyed (when outright coercion was more easily applied) into a relational power better suited to current circumstances. She finds these changes lamentable in that they subject weaker states to new forms of dependency.

Other studies offer practical guidance to policy makers who favor interstate cooperation. Peter Cowhey (1990) upholds the fashionable IR theories of regimes and epistemic communities. His widely read study of the norms and principles at work in intergovernmental organizations focused on the ITU's predecessor, the International Telephone and Telegraph Consultative Committee (CCITT). Cowhey rejects the functionalist notion that the telecommunications regime is a supranational technocratic exercise, describing it instead as a negotiating venue between separate entities committed to efficient national operations. Large transnational corporate consumers of telecommunications services, primarily banks seeking to reduce the cost of operations, were the first to press their governments for systemic reform in an organized way. This prompted the leading industrial states to reassess the costs of maintaining their national telecommunications monopolies, allowing them to accept privatization, competition, and the end of protectionism as a bargain that promised better payoffs.

Despite contrasts in perspectives and conclusions, all these authors work within frameworks that represent states as rationally motivated, seemingly personified, territorial-based actors. Their intent is to discuss the forces that constrain and propel those states, and how other states can perhaps be outfinessed in light of those forces. An alternative, nonterritorial perspective is presented by Craig Murphy's neo-Gramscian general study of global governance (1994). What Murphy shares with the other authors, however, is the assumption that some master script is in play, guiding if not determining the behavior of actors on the world stage. The distinction for Murphy is that the leading protagonist in this historic drama is global capitalism.

Each of these scholars seeks to understand an actor's essence by way of the actor's environment. To postulate that systemic forces like the drive for efficiency or strategic advantage can motivate transformations of the telecommunications infrastructure is to posit that such forces can rule international behavior. Following this logic, *exogenous* (external) structural forces would rule human behavior as well, caging people within fixed bars of the social world. An antithetical perspective comes from the post-modern movement. Denying that substantive material factors of the environment can exert such rule, Andrew Barry sees telecommunications technology simply as an instrument that mediates communication in society, enabling self-governance rather than constraining it (1996). By such logic, self-governance is an *endogenous* (internal) voluntary act which may foster liberation or punishment, but the devices which transmit the gaze of social discipline receive no credit or blame for the outcome.

Considering these issues as a constructivist requires formulating a position that subsumes the exogenous-endogenous dichotomy, a split that echoes in debates between positivists and the various post-positivists, post-modernists, and post-structuralists who constitute the post-modern movement. Reconciling these poles will give a clearer sense of how technology standards constrain and enable human activity, and how standards can provide the mechanisms that simultaneously regulate and constitute human society.

Constructing Standards

Unlike the authors just mentioned, constructivists rely on an interpretive scheme that explains social rule by categorizing the origins and outcomes of social rules. The axioms that "rules make rule" and "rules put resources into play" distinguish constructivism from positivist and Marxist philosophies such as realism, neo-liberalism, and historical materialism, which look first at the ways resources determine structure and then at specific social outcomes. "Post" movement authors often focus on the material oppression and feelings of meaninglessness that result from a world ruled by positivist philosophies. Critical authors of the "post" movement express a desire to develop practical strategies for emancipation from those dilemmas. We can clarify the distinctions between the philosophies of positivism and the "post" movement by recognizing that they are often taken to be equivalent to those that divide modernism and postmodernism. The former may be understood as faith in efficiency, rationality, perfectibility, the accumulation of knowledge, and collective progress. The latter insists on existential identity and self-expression, often in the context of free-floating relativism. Post-modernists regard people's imaginations as situational and unlimited, unbounded by the possibility of resolving down to a common interpretation of the world. One might say that the positivists try to see a single world by standing outside it, while the "post" movement grants the existence of infinite perspectives, placing individuals inside our own myriad worlds, looking out in endless directions.

Constructivism plays both sides against the middle, but not as a facile compromise. The challenge is to retain the positivists' scientific commitment to inquiry, probing for the fundamental structure of things while understanding that interpretation is a human act, limited by the necessity of symbol, the gravity of memory, and the imperfectibility of language. When studying society, positivists look for measurable structural variables that can be said to cause human behaviors. Their traditional research interest is the extent to which material structure makes social behavior predictable and involuntary. Constructivists, on the other hand, see human behavior and social structure as inseparable, simultaneous, *co-constituted* occurrences, but rooted in deeds of human urgency. Whereas adherents of the "post" movement are keen to celebrate that urgency, their observations often scatter into solipsistic relativism, denying that any claims about cause can be trusted. In distinction, constructivists look for the institutionalized routines of social practice that stem from human performance. One can and should seek to identify constants across social structures, with the caveat that doing so is itself an act of social construction which invents and reproduces contingent belief in that constancy. To establish habits that comport with "Reality," wrote logician Charles S. Peirce in 1877, "we seek for a belief that which we shall *think* to be true" (1955, 11). Constructivism inevitably reflects the limits of language. Like all myths and scientific theories, IR's "isms" offer grand statements about the world, instructing people how to make sense of reality so that they can comprehend it and therefore act within it. We humans are not as unfettered as the "post" movement imagines us to be, or as limited in our freedoms as the positivists expect. The point is to remember Giambattista Vico's principle of *verum factum*: what we recognize as true is what we have made.

The constructivist outlook attempts to recognize that all human deeds stand as moral choices, with constitutive effects that extend beyond immediate situations. And regardless of the mind-set reflected in an instruction, a person's acceptance of that instruction will fortify the hegemony—the authoritative influence—of its originators and its vocal proponents. For Onuf, social instructions play out in two sorts of ways. In formal organizations where the instruction might be "the boss is in charge," they situate people in offices requiring compliance with directions transmitted through a hierarchical chain of command. Alternatively, in more open social environments where the instruction might be "buy low and sell high," people will tend to behave like members of a heteronomy in which behavioral roles are regulated and constrained by commitments negotiated with others who adhere to the same instruction.

Applying constructivism means analyzing social behaviors and rules embedded in the speech acts of people who occupy some status, office, or role, within various networks, organizations, and associations. Understanding the instructive, directive, or commissive nature of those rules gives an insight into who is "in charge," and what kind of rule—hegemonic, hierarchical, or heteronomous—is being exercised. It is beyond the scope of this work to explain the source of constructivism's various trichotomies, except to note that it reveals the influence of three-part categorical schemes developed by Peirce, Giddens, and others. As a constructivist, to ask an individual who or what is "in charge" is not only to ask what meaning that ruler or rule has for them, but to appreciate that a person's interaction with a rule ascribes meaning to it. Rules arise from intersubjectivity, and cannot exist without human authorship. This formulation allows constructivism to cleave the positivist-"post" divide. We can acknowledge that the rules that define a person's identity and interest may seem fixed and persistent for that individual at a certain point in time, but such rules are transformable. An observation made by Peirce's colleague, psychologist William James, provides a useful illustration.

The antimilitarist James is still remembered for asking whether a "moral equivalent of war" could be fostered in peacetime. Intrigued by the "supremest and extremist" forms of sacrifice and effort displayed by men in battle, he wondered how to summon the passionate "spiritual energy" of soldiers for a common good, rather than internecine conflict (1972b, 295). After inquiring into the source of "martial virtues," which he admired, James concluded that the "oughts" that motivate a person stem from the individual's pride in the body (tribal, national, etc.) by which he or she is "owned" (1972b, 298). Anyone who can inculcate in others a sense of *ought* and, consequently, *obligation* in social situations is simply telling people what rules to follow (1972a, 220). More to the point, anyone who can inculcate a sense of belonging and identity in addition to this or that "ought" has made a bigger move, facilitating a system of rule. Let us say that someone's sense of being owned is equivalent to feeling part of something bigger than oneself: a faith, a nation, an institution, a club, or a meeting. To pledge allegiance to that group, to obey that group's rules, to perform some other social interaction with reference to that group, or even to say it exists is to instantiate that moment of ownership in which the institution transforms identity. James recognized that interaction as a pragmatic opening. Social construction can involve the simplest tasks of coordination or the grandest schemes of ethical unification. Society makes "man" just as "man" makes society, simultaneously, all the time.

In the case of the digerati agenda, then, it is important to investigate any canonical instruction or principle used to enlist participants a group that shares common goals. Who would adopt Metcalfe's Law as a creed worth fighting for? Self-professed Netizens (Internet citizens) are potential candidates, but their presence is small, focused around the monthly magazine *Wired* as well as a few libertarian and Left-leaning Web sites. Their current behavior resembles an unruly debating society more than a political movement. Still, even if the rights and duties associated with Netizenship are informal, vague, and unknown beyond a small circle of adherents, the notion of using the global telecommunications infrastructure to create alternative forms of political association bears watching.

The "Web lifestyle" anticipated by Gates is a considerably more potent and immediately relevant declaration. When asked how he makes such predictions, he answered, "I'm trying to draw a map that connects the present to the future" (1997b). For him to say the Web lifestyle will soon exist is to suggest it exists now, since "getting ahead" requires that we prepare for it. The prediction stands as an instruction that future human behavior will increasingly require interaction across the Internet, or a related medium. Announcing an instructive claim of such import stands as a hegemonic assertion pertinent to anyone who feels he or she belongs to modern society. Beyond his confirmed business acumen, Gates's preeminent status within global industry gives his opinions the aura of objective knowledge. For those seeking initiation into the world of wealth creation, Gates's rank as the world's richest self-made man gives him *a priori* authority, akin to the traditional authority common throughout pretechnological cultures. "[M]aternal uncles do not transmit [a] particular stock of knowledge because they know it, but they know it (that is, are defined as knowers), because they are maternal uncles" (Berger and Luckmann 1966, 70–71).

In this sense, by pronouncing an *is*, Gates urges an *ought*. That same pronouncement corresponds to a set of *directives* given to Microsoft employees and subcontractors, marshaling the organization's resources toward the goal of completing specific projects. And it also serves as a *commitment* within the marketplace, declaring that Microsoft's resources have been put at risk in the expectation that consumers and other enterprises will commit their own resources to the same project. By predicting a Web lifestyle, Gates constructs it. Those who may eventually adopt that lifestyle will also play a role in its construction, so that the institution and the person's identification with it are simultaneously co-constituted. We can think of a phenomenon and its practitioners separately, but they are not separable. One cannot exist without the other. A path cannot be called a path without the people who walk it. This is no subtle point; the notion of co-constitution is at the heart of constructivism's critique of both positivism and the post-modern movement.

Arguably, the only reality social beings can know is socially constructed, since even the most rigorously scientific disciplines of knowing are mediated by a language that explains things in terms of persistent, humanly manageable tools like logic or the study of cause and effect. To break from positivism and "postism" is to acknowledge one's conscious participation in the act of construction, while simultaneously recognizing that, without attention to social structure, there can be no meaningful way to ground identity. The issue is whether we believe we are collectively subject to a universal fate, individually masters of a uniquely private reality, or pragmatically adaptive to the world around us. It is not unusual for many people to jumble these attitudes together as it suits them on different issues, with little concern for their own discipline of thinking. The same distinctions play out in attitudes toward the social significance of the growth of telecommunications. The digerati agenda exploits this confusion, promoting the modernist impulse to herald the advent of the "New World Information Order," while celebrating post-modern desires to fabricate multi-user dungeons in virtual reality.

I intend to show that a particular virtue of the constructivist approach is its ability to explain how the claims of universalism and equality inherent in an instruction-rule like Metcalfe's Law disguise the conditions of inequality that emerge from successive waves of technological innovation. Such inequalities can privilege certain innovators or stakeholders, thereby creating or perpetuating monopoly power. Another virtue of the theory is its strength in explaining how the design and implementation of seemingly arcane electronic standards are facilitating the worldwide triumph of an institutionalized ethos in which market-style behaviors reign supreme. In other words, summoning an earlier metaphor, the freshest knots in the golden straitjackets worn by nation states have been tied by computer experts.

Of course, it is not unusual for contemporary analysts to discuss the challenges that modern forms of electronically mediated commerce present to nation-states. Legal scholar Michael Froomkin uses the term *regulatory arbitrage* to describe the ease in with which Internet-savvy traders can exploit differences in national laws to their own advantage. Yet he is optimistic about this, predicting the effect will "probably be to promote liberal democratic values of openness and freedom and not to detract from modern states' legitimate regulatory powers" (1997, 155). On the other hand, economist Stephen Kobrin worries that new technologies which enable the use of digital money (e-cash) are a "sovereignty killer." "[T]he advent of e-cash raises serious questions about the very idea of 'domestic' and 'international' as meaningful and distinct topics" (1997, 71). Constructivism allows us to take such analysis a step further, however, beyond discussions of a weakened sovereignty, toward an understanding of its co-constituted successor order. Consequently, we need to understand what sort of rules are becoming more important in people's lives.

It is appropriate here to consider the definition of the word *standard*. In the English language it derives from "stand hard," the rallying point in a battle at which a heraldic banner was raised so that field commanders could locate the source of their orders. The word now has multiple meanings, including "flag" and "a rule set up by an established authority." Every standard works literally and figuratively as a social arrangement. Cultural symbols are easy to recognize as such when people are physically assembled around a common focal point. Shared behaviors manifest such assemblies as well, the more so when people acknowledge their common practices, reflect upon them, and make them formal. When people look to a standard for instruction, they are simultaneously constituting an arrangement of people who are "pointing" to that standard. New arrivals at the scene may learn what a standard is just by pointing in the same direction as others. In that sense, the standard has regulatory power as well as constitutive effect. We organize ourselves according to the standards we acknowledge. We make standards by following them. They re-present what we do and say about them.

To shun a pervasive standard is to fall out of step with one's peers, proving one's disloyalty to a group's norms (Fletcher 1993). This invests standards with an ethical power. By stipulating what is, standards operationalize "oughts." We may refer to standards as self-enforcing or self-surveilling, but, as adherents to the various "post" movements recognize, our willing participation in a social arrangement is essential to it. Thus we may say that a rule is drawn from the consent of the people who practice it, and that every rule, to qualify as such, must incorporate one or more standards. An intriguing and practical line of questioning, then, is how people enlist support for new standards. Let us now turn to an aspect of standards making by a group of digerati that combines practical and symbolic importance, and the effects of which will be felt within a few years, rather than in many decades.

Internet Ownership and the Public Trust

The Internet has a root, technically called a root zone (often written as "." and pronounced "dot"), which serves as the authoritative directory to all locations properly registered within the system (for an exhaustive explanation, see Kahin and Keller 1997, Rony and Rony 1998). At the time of this writing in 1997, the primary root of the Internet sits on server A, a machine in Herndon, Virginia, which contains a database listing many of the names and addresses of the tips of the Internet's branches, properly referred to as *hosts,* of which there are now well over 20 million (*nw.com*). Hosts constitute the end points on which data reside, and the devices through which people access the system. Though host computers must be uniquely numbered, people prefer using memorable words and acronyms. Consequently, an important function of the root is linking *domain names* to host numbers while ensuring that no two hosts are assigned the same name.

Day-to-day responsibility for managing server A's database is currently in the hands of Network Solutions, Inc. (NSI). Additions and revisions to the host address data on server A immediately propagate to servers B through M, and then on throughout the Internet, *cached* (stored) in *name servers* around the world. Those name servers, run by Internet service providers (ISPs), from giants like America On Line down to the humblest entrepreneur, all use *routing* software, which server operators voluntarily point back up the chain to server A for instructions on how to direct traffic around the system. Therefore, when individuals send e-mail through the Internet or "surf" the Web, their transmissions are routed around the system on the basis of the contents of the root and reproduced in compliant name servers.

Responsibility for operating Internet's root is expected to change hands in 1998, either in April when NSI's five-year contract with the National Science Foundation expires, or six months later if necessary, after an optional "ramp-down" period, during which new operators will take over. But it is not yet clear who those new operators will be. A battle has been brewing for several years over how to expand the *top level* of the domain name system (DNS), and who will be in charge of adding new top-level generic suffixes, like *firm, web, arts,* and *info*. The existing generic names, *edu, org, net,* and especially *com,* are filling quickly, and are primarily an American preserve. Many digerati see the upcoming transition as an opportunity to accelerate the Internet's growth as a platform for global telecommunications convergence. Fulfillment of Metcalfe's Law requires building a system big enough to encompass world society, resulting in something far less American in character than at present. U.S. politicians, not surprisingly, have pledged to maintain control. Upon learning that the Internet's designers were planning to move the root oversight functions to Geneva, Representative Charles Pickering (R-Mississippi), head of the House Science Subcommittee on Basic Research, declared, "This is something uniquely American. That part of the [plan] is not going to sell very well—not here, not on Main Street."

To investigate this controversy is to plunge into an acronym soup of standards-making bodies, intergovernmental agencies, and other organizations which built the Internet and which claim a stake in its future. To abbreviate the story, we may begin with two groups whose leaders testified before Congressman Pickering's committee: The Internet Society (ISOC), headed by Don Heath (previously employed by MCI and British Telecom), and the Internet Assigned Numbers Authority (IANA), headed by Jon Postel (a veteran hand of Internet engineering, currently based at the University of Southern California's Information Science Institute [ISI]).

ISOC and IANA are key forces behind the effort to constitute a policy oversight committee (POC), which would take over authority of DNS management when NSI's contract expires. NSI would still be allowed to provide domain name registration services, a lucrative business, but NSI's monopoly would end, to be replaced by a globally competitive framework of registrars. These would, in turn, participate in a council of registrars (CORE), incorporated in Geneva. POC activities would be reviewed by a public advisory body (PAB), representing the interests of Internet stakeholders. The details of this plan were initially presented on February 2, 1997, by the International Ad Hoc Committee (IAHC), a group directed by Heath. The IAHC plan was formally established through an instrument known as the Generic Top Level Domains Memorandum of Understanding (gTLD-MoU, or simply MoU). Unfortunately for MoU supporters, the signing ceremony hosted by the International Telecommunications Union (ITU) in Geneva on April 29, 1997 did not go as they might have hoped.

Private industry's response was lukewarm. The MoU needed a more resounding endorsement from telecommunications companies, service providers, and other Internet businesses as an indication of legitimacy among Internet stakeholders. PSINet, an important early supporter of the IAHC, denounced the MoU and called for a global Internet convention with Vice President Al Gore as moderator. The following week, in response to mounting criticism, substantial changes were announced, removing provisions for a lottery that would have limited the number of total registrars to twenty-eight, covering seven global regions.

The public sector's initial response was also cold. Days before the ceremony, the U.S. State Department leaked a memo from Madeline Albright expressing "concerns" about the ITU secretariat's acting "without authorization of member governments" to hold "a global meeting involving an unauthorized expenditure of resources and concluding with a quote international agreement unquote" (Sernovitz 1997; Wylie 1997). The European Commission also expressed concerns. In July the U.S. Department of Commerce initiated a notice of inquiry (NOI), soliciting public comment on the expiration of NSI's monopoly. The controversy continued to escalate, prompting hearings before the Pickering's subcommittee in late September.

American critics of the MoU complain that authority for resolving disputes over contended domain names would move beyond the jurisdiction of U.S. courts. Disputes would instead be settled by administrative challenge panels (ACPs) under the administration of the Arbitration and Mediation Center of the World Intellectual Property Organization (WIPO). MoU supporters argue that clearer, more even-handed procedures are necessary to reduce the likelihood of arbitrary and inconsistent decisions. Under NSI's guardianship, registration and hosting of existing brand names like *mcdonalds.com* by third parties was allowed unless the brand owner took steps to demonstrate prior rights. NSI transferred a name to the proven owner only when the initial registrant agreed, or after litigation (InterNIC 1996), and in confusing situations, would put contended names "on hold." One notable example involved *peta.org,* a name claimed by People for the Ethical Treatment of Animals (PETA) but initially registered to the promoter of People Eating Tasty Animals (Doughney 1996). An even more vexing dispute arose over *prince.com,* a properly registered trademark of distinct companies in different countries, serving as a lesson in the challenges of regulating a global infrastructure through a patchwork of national courts (Oppedahl 1997). MoU supporters hope that expanding the range of generic top-level names will reduce the cachet of names ending in *com,* abating explosive demands for that suffix. But the MoU's success will hinge in large part on the ability of the POC/PAB/CORE/ACP institutional structure to resolve disputes over contended resources. Thus POC chose as its first president David Maher, an attorney whose speciality is international trademarks and intellectual property.

Let us now consider the DNS transition from the perspective of constructivist categories.

With regard to instruction-rule, further commercialization of the Internet would both follow and reinforce the pro-business norms that permeate modern industrial states. Adam Smith's guiding hand would become an even freer one. There are competing proposals to establish root server confederations (RSCs) that take a far less centralized, even cowboyish, approach to the question of DNS management. RSC supporters thus claim a more faithful allegiance to the free market principle. Advocates of the MoU, in turn, are likely to wave the banners of the Internet's founding mothers and fathers, asserting their legacy and status as revered authorities.

With regard to commitment-rule, breaking NSI's monopoly and creating a global market for domain registration would augment competition on the Internet, where consumers can already choose from many sources for hardware, software, and content vendors, as well as, to a lesser degree, Internet connection services. This case demonstrates the intentionality inherent in markets. To eliminate a monopoly, something must be created in its space. Moreover, students of IR who are concerned with the construction of international relations should pay close attention to the new forms of judicial association established through the MoU. Switching domain name dispute resolution venues from national courts to Geneva-based ACPs would constitute an expressly new form of commitment-rule which could eventually influence global trademark law.

With regard to directive-rule, the ability to coordinate compliant devices on the Internet is of fundamental importance for stabilizing the day-to-day operations of a "Web lifestyle." Ensuring that Internet service providers all point to a common authority like CORE for domain name information promotes that goal. Replanting the standard of the Internet's root may appear to be an obscure technical exercise, but it would have a pivotal impact, perhaps similar to those rare historical moments when new calendars or systems for calibrating time are instituted. Whether this transition will be smooth or traumatic remains to be seen.

Extending the Internet Domain

This dispute over ownership of the DNS root raises the recurring question "Who 'owns' the Internet?" Resolving the immediate battle will decide, for the time being, not only who gets to collect the Internet's equivalent of rent or tax on domain names, but, more significantly, whether the Internet's designers will be able to proliferate the use of generic names while globalizing (or at least de-Americanizing) system administration, creating a world market out of a national monopoly. The use of generic top-level names has not been widespread beyond the United States and Canada. From elsewhere in the world, NSI's distance, inconvenient business hours, and English-language orientation are often prohibitive. For anyone outside North America seeking to establish an Internet presence, registration under a national suffix usually provided an acceptable alternative. Opening new CORE-certified registries in other countries will thus make generic suffixes more appealing, especially since the new top-level domains will not be so heavily dominated by Americans. Also, the decision to incorporate CORE in Geneva affords the symbolism of a neutral, "international" city, and enhances the practical access to the root's administrative regime by Europeans, Africans, Asians, and others. If these plans succeed, worldwide investments in Internet services will continue to accelerate, and its generic spaces will take on a different, less "American" look.

Defending the MoU under pressure before Pickering's committee, Heath stated that the DNS must be treated as "an international resource subject to the public trust." Its management "must allow for true self-governance in order for the Internet to reach its fullest potential." "If one nation tries to rule it," he predicted, "others will overrule it" (Heath 1997b). Such words provide insights into the philosophy of digerati leaders. Comments related to Internet self-governance, Global Internet Governance (GIG), and global civil society all "raise flags" that indicate directions in which their thinking is headed. Heath has submitted other statements to the U.S. government regarding ISOC's global agenda.

> We believe that it is important that governments of the world should be involved in the self-governance processes that will evolve; but, they should do so in a manner so as not to control or otherwise create effective control and, thus, thwart the process of true Internet self-governance. The Internet must remain an unencumbered communications medium; it must not be used as a tool for censorship, or of controlling the free flow of information. The architecture of the Internet is based on an end-to-end philosophy. Any "controlling" activity should only be done at the end points: where content is introduced, or where it is taken off. It is with these thoughts in mind that we say government should be involved, but not in such a way to take control. (1997a)

The claim that the Internet's architecture is based on an "end-to-end philosophy" is frequently repeated among the system's designers. By declaring their intent to draw and uphold a border separating the Internet's wires and switches from the world without, the architects have become gatekeepers, pledging to maintain system security while advancing the interests of the system's users. However, in distinction to the narrow gates operated by the club of sovereign states since the inception of the Westphalian system in the seventeenth century (Österud 1997), the Internet's gates are wide and beckoning to all comers. While most serious publishers require novice authors to overcome a series of rigorous hurdles, the Internet allows anyone to publish any inanities he or she wishes, instantly, without review. While entry into a professional elite is normally granted after a process that reinforces the group's standards and reputation, the Internet's structure is intentionally open and inclusive. Therefore, it is noteworthy when the digerati target a group they wish to exclude, as they have done by seeking to deny governments a place at the Internet's head table.

Building trust in the security of Internet transactions will foster ever greater activity over that medium, increasing demand for the wiring and switches that carry its signals. The supplying industries are extremely volatile in character, though quite profitable when successful. This environment serves to reinforce the politically proactive approaches of leading players like MCI, whose corporate personalities were forged in the deregulatory heyday of the Reagan-Thatcher years and fortified by the explosive gigantism of the 1990s. Tremendous economies of scale and rapid development cycles have brought about remarkable improvements in the quality of goods, coupled with steady reductions in price. It is not unreasonable to forecast that hundreds of millions if not billions of people will be able to afford access to the system within the first decades of the next century. Under these circumstances, private industry is more likely to continue funding digerati activities than to support any effort that might threaten Internet expansion.

Many of the Internet's gatekeepers believe that new structures of social organization will form, responding to new kinds of needs, which cannot be met by the nation-state. Glenn Kowack, prior to his appointment as IANA's representative to POC, wrote a piece in the normally staid engineering journal *IEEE Communications* which lauded the Internet's engineers for deploying the "cost-implosive" economic model of the information technology industries. He echoes Peter Drucker in welcoming the rise of "societies of organizations," believing this heralds a shift of global importance. This growth will lead, however, to a "vacuum" in the "administrative environment" which cannot effectively be filled by traditional governments:

> The general direction of the Internet and the activities of its global community of users, consistent with [Thomas] Paine's concept of "natural individual propensity for society," are both philosophically legitimate and arguably superior to jurisdictional claims by nation-states. (Kowack 1997, 55)

The MoU's promoters and their adversaries both recognize that the ability to command or deny the flow of information measures their power. For rapid system growth to continue, senders and receivers must be assured that their transmissions are private and trustworthy. The digerati agenda is therefore furiously engaged in developing mechanisms to secure Internet transmissions from interference, especially in relation to issues like cryptography, free speech, and protection of intellectual property. This coincidentally provokes confrontation with states whose traditional business is also to provide security within their domain. The MoU dispute is just one of the battlegrounds but is symbolically important, because of the communicative power of names and addresses. These are constructed instruments, part of an indispensable, imperfect tool we call language. They are tags on reality which we use to mediate our contacts through a similarly constructed, mapped space. To control the domain name system in a world that rises each day greeting a Web lifestyle is to name the streets and boulevards that feed the "Information Superhighway." Those who exercise this control will acquire a tremendous power to fashion our memories of place, and to reblend our comings and goings in an entirely new way.

Today's Internet has a significant design limitation that inhibits the fulfillment of Metcalfe's Law. The current addressing scheme (Internet Protocol Version 4—IPv4) allows a theoretical maximum of 2^{32}, or 4,294,967,296 nodes on the system, well short of the population projected for the world in the next century. The practical number of addresses is far less because of inefficiencies in the allocation scheme, but an upgrade presently under development (IPv6) will create room for 2^{128}, or over $3.4*10^{38}$ addresses, a truly mind-stretching quantity, presumably enough for everyone born in the next few centuries, plus vast numbers of interconnected devices per person. The project to expand the address space is called Internet Protocol Next Generation (IPNG), and has been proceeding under a level of reasonably business-like and effective technical cooperation under the aegis of the Internet Engineering Task Force (IETF), the organization that spawned IANA and ISOC. Other IPNG priorities include adding security features that support commercial transactions, technical improvements to facilitate smooth streaming transmissions of sound and video, and management features to regulate traffic-congestion. These will all be essential elements of the Web lifestyle, regardless of the MoU's fortunes.

Postscript

Though this work refers to a digerati agenda, there is no conspiratorial *Protocols of the Elders of Cyberspace* or philosophical *Digerati Papers* which allows us to plumb their thinking. Yes, one can point to screeds like "A Magna Carta for the Information Age" (Gidari 1995), "A Cyberspace Independence Declaration" (Barlow 1996), and "Crypto-Anarchist Manifesto" (May 1992), but these stand as individual works. They present interesting insights into the culture, but they are self-consciously grandiose, and are unrepresentative of the leaders at the core. I invented the term *digerati agenda* to amplify my conclusion that the creators of global telecommunications standards are self-consciously challenging the rules and the rule of sovereign states, offering new mechanisms for coordinating economic transactions and enlisting human loyalties, and experimenting with prototypes of global government. I confess that by positing its existence I play a part in its construction. As Lao Tzu wrote in the opening of the Tao te Ching, "Naming is the origin of all particular things." By bringing the concept to a new audience, or by presenting new ways of thinking about it to those who are already interested in such ideas, I may augment it and change it. Ironically, the open-minded reader participates with me in that construction. Our effort to understand the digerati agenda reproduces it, and imparts significance to something that may soon be forgotten. Time will tell if it should have been, but there is enough intriguing evidence to warrant a continuing look. My conjectures may appear to be as grandiose as any screed, but dismissing this phenomenon out of hand risks overlooking a development of great potential consequence. People are subject to the standards and structures that they themselves have made. Thus constructivism invites its own method of analysis.

Note

Thanks go to Vendulka Kubálková, Nicholas Onuf, Michael Froomkin, Phil Agre, and Ken Goodman for their helpful comments.

Bibliography

Internet links may be accessed directly through: http://www.flywheel.com/ircw/igg.html.

Anonymous. 1994. "Magna Carta for the Knowledge Age. Release 1.2." http://crimson.com/cis/Magna-Carta.htmlhttp://www.pff.org/pff/position.html.

Akimaru, Haruo, Marion R. Finley, Jr., and Zhiseng Niu. 1997. "Elements of the Emerging Broadband Information Highway." IEEE Communications Magazine (June): 84–91.

Ashley, Richard K. 1983. "The Eye of Power: Politics of World Modeling." International Organization 37:3.

Barlow, John Perry. 1996. "A Cyberspace Independence Declaration." February 9. http://eff.org/pub/publications/John_Perry_Barlow/barlow_0296.declaration. http://www.vrx.net/declaration.html.

Barry, Andrew. 1996. "Lines of Communication and Spaces of Rule." In *Foucault and Political Reason: Liberalism, Neo-liberalism and Rationalities of Government,* ed. Andrew Barry et al. Chicago: University of Chicago Press.

Berger, Peter L., and Thomas Luckmann. 1966. *The Social Construction of Reality: A Treatise on the Sociology of Knowledge.* New York: Anchor Books.

Berners-Lee, Tim. 1992. "Summary of the World Wide Web Initiative." http://www.w3.org/summary.html

Boyle, James. 1997. "Foucault in Cyberspace: Surveillance, Sovereignity, and Hard-Wired Censors." http://www.wcl.american.edu/pub/faculty/boyle/foucault.html

Brockman, John. 1996. *Digerati: Encounters with the Cyber Elite.* New York: Hardwired.

Cook, Gordon. *Cook Report.* http://www.cookreport.com.

Cowhey, Peter F. 1990. "The International Telecommunications Regime: The Political Roots for Regimes of High Technology." *International Organization,* 44 (2) 158–76.

Doughney, Mike. 1996. "peta.org Domain Name Placed on Hold." May 12, 1996. http://www.mtd.com/tasty/editorial3.html

Fletcher, George P. 1993. *Loyalty, An Essay on the Morality of Relationships.* New York: Oxford.

Friedman, Thomas L. 1997. "France's New Jacket." *New York Times.* June 5: A21.

Froomkin, Michael. 1997. "The Internet as a Source of Regulatory Arbitrage." In *Borders in Cyberspace,* ed. Kahin and Nelson, 129–63. Cambridge: MIT Press.

Gandy, Oscar H., Jr. 1993. *The Panoptic Sort: A Political Economy of Personal Information.* Boulder: Westview Press.

Gates, William. 1997a. "Banking on a Web Lifestyle." *New York Times* Special Features. July 15, 1997. http://nytsyn.com/live/Gates2/210_072997_132203_9368.html
———. 1997b. "Q&A: Where Do Your Ideas About the Future Come From?" *New York Times,* Syndicate. September 23, 1997. http://www.nytsyn.com/live/gates2/266_092397_134025_24271.html

Gidari, Al. 1995. "A Magna Carta for the Information Age." *Seattle Times.* October 30, 1995.

Giddens, Anthony. 1990. *The Consequences of Modernity.* Stanford: Stanford University Press.

168   CRAIG SIMON

Heath, Donald M. 1997a. "In the Matter of Registration and Administration of Internet Domain Names." U.S. Department of Commerce, Docket Number 970613137–7137–01. http://www.isoc.org/whatsnew/NTIAcomments.html

———. 1997b Testimony to the House Science Subcommittee on Basic Research. September 30, 1997. http://www.isoc.org/whatsnew/hr_testimony_oral_970930.html

Helmers, Sabine, Ute Hoffman, and Jeanette Hofman. 1996. *Standard Development as Technosocial Ordering: The Case of the Next Generation of the Internet Protocol.* Social Science Research Center Berlin. http://duplox.wz-berlin.de/docs/ipng.html

Hills, Jill. 1994. "Dependency Theory and Its Relevance Today: International Institutions in Telecommunications and Structural Power." *Review of International Studies* 20: 169–86.

InterNIC on-line documents. 1996. "Domain Name Policy Dispute." ftp://rs.internic.net/policy/internic.domain.policy

James, William. (1891) 1972a. "The Moral Philosopher and the Moral Life." *Essays in Pragmatism.* In *Pragmatism and Other Essays,* ed. Joseph Blau pp. 214–35. New York: Washington Square Press.

———. (1910) 1972b. "The Moral Equivalent of War" in *Pragmatism and Other Essays,* ed. Joeseph Blau, 289–301. New York: Washington Square Press.

Kahin, Brian, and James Keller. 1997. *Coordinating the Internet.* Publication of the Harvard Infrastructure Project. Cambridge, MA: MIT Press.

Kahin, Brian, and Charles Nesson, eds. 1997. *Borders in Cyberspace: Information Policy and the Global Information Infrastructure.* Cambridge: MIT Press.

Kobrin, Stephen J. 1997. "Electronic Cash and the End of National Markets." *Foreign Policy* (Summer, 107): 71.

Kowack, Glenn. 1997. "Internet Governance and the Emergence of Global Civil Society." *IEEE Communications Magazine* (May): 52–57.

Landauer, Thomas K. 1995. *The Trouble with Computers: Usefulness, Usability and Productivity.* Cambridge: MIT Press.

Lanier, Jaron. 1997. Lecture delivered at the New Media Minds Forum Center for the Arts, San Francisco. September 11, 1997. http://www.hotwired.com/synapse/nmm/97/37/lanier0a.html

Low, Colin. 1997. "Integrating Communication Services." *IEEE Communications Magazine* (June): 164–69.

May, Timothy. (1988) 1992. "Crypto-Anarchist Manifesto." http://calweb.com/mdtate/_crypto.html

Metcalfe, Bob. 1996. "There Oughta Be a Law." *New York Times.* July 15, 1996, C5.

Mills, Mike. 1997. "Orbit Wars." *Washington Post.* August 3, 1997, W08

Murphy, Craig N. 1994. *International Organization and Industrial Change: Global Governance since 1850.* Cambridge: Polity Press.

Negroponte, Nicholas. 1995. *Being Digital.* Hotwired.

Noll, A. Michael. 1997. *Highway of Dreams: A Critical View Along the Information Superhighway.* Mahwah, NJ: Lawrence Erlbaum Associates.

NW.COM (Network Wizards). 1997. "Internet Domain Survey." http://www.nw.com/zone/WWW/report.html

Nye, Joseph S., and William A. Owens. 1996. "America's Information Edge." *Foreign Affairs* 75 (2): 20–36.

Onuf, Nicholas Greenwood. 1989. *World of Our Making: Rules and Rule in Social Theory and International Relations.* Columbia: University of South Carolina Press.

Oppedahl, Carl. "NSI Flawed Domain Name Policy Information Page." http://www.patents.com/nsi.sht

Österud, Öyvind. 1997. "The Narrow Gate: Entry to the Club of Sovereign States." *Review of International Studies* 23: 167–84.

Peirce, Charles S. (1877) 1955. "The Fixation of Belief." Reprinted in *Philosophical Writings of Peirce*, ed. Justus Buchler. New York: Dover.

Petrazzini, Ben A. 1995. *The Political Economy of Telecommunications Reform in Developing Countries: Privatization and Liberalization in Comparative Perspective.* Westport: Praeger Press.

Rony Ellen and Peter Rony. 1998. *The Domain Name Handbook: High Stakes and Strategies in Cyberspace.* Lawrence: R & D Books.

Ruthowski, Anthony. *World Internet Association.* http://www.wia.org

Semovitz, Andy. 1997. "The US Govt. Is *not* Supportive of gTLD-MoU." July 27, 1997. http://www.old.gtld-mou.org/gtld-discuss/mail-archive/4682.html

Sichel, Daniel E. 1997. *Computer Revolution: An Economic Perspective.* Washington, DC: Brookings.

Thurm, Scot. 1997. "The Productivity Puzzle." *San Jose Mercury News.* September 14. http://www.sjmercury.com/business/product091497.htm

Uncapher, Willard. 1994. "Between Local and Global: Placing the Mediascape in the Transnational Cultural Flow." http://www.eff.org/net.culture.globalvillage

Wendt, Alexander. 1992. "Anarchy Is What States Make of It: The Social Construction of Power Politics." *International Organization* 46 (2): 391–425

Wylie, Margie. 1997. "U.S. Concerned by ITU meeting." *News.com.* April 29, http://www.news.com/News/Item/0,4,10198,00.html

Zurawski, Nils. 1997. *Beyond the Global Information Frontiers: What Global Concepts ("Weltbilder") Are There on the Internet and Why?* Paper presented at the Internet Society conference, INET97. http://www.isoc.org/isoc/whatis/conferences/inet/97/proceedings/G4/G4_2.HTM.

Part IV

Construction in the Academy

8

Remodeling International Relations: New Tools from New Science?

Henry L. Hamman

The inclusion of a chapter on the application of science and mathematics in international relations (IR) in this set of essays may appear contradictory, in no small part because the constructivist approach to international relations is often seen as a subset of antipositivist or post-positivist theory, as a genre that rejects empiricism, as one of the pillars that upholds the edifice of science, and as applicable to the study of social phenomena. That this view is widely held is due to a misapprehension of the nature of constructivism, since constructivists do not follow antipositivists in rejection of empiricism. In fact, constructivist thinkers—at least those who work with Nicholas Onuf's approach—have derived their theoretical constructs precisely from the observation and analysis of the empirical.

Unlike the antipositivist or post-positivist position, which rejects the whole notion of application of the tools of science to the study of human behavior, constructivism endorses the scientific notion of formulating theory on the basis of empirical knowledge as well as the scientific view that knowledge is tentative, subject to revision, and incomplete.

A number of reasons for the rejection of science by "post" social scientists have been discussed in earlier chapters. However, another factor adding to the difficulty of discussing the possible contributions of natural science and mathematics to the understanding of the social world is the social science community's lack of awareness of developments in twentieth-century science. (To be fair, natural scientists, as a group, are hardly *au courant* with the state of the art in sociology or anthropology, either.) My conjecture is that—for social scientists at the center of their fields (men and women in their forties and fifties)—science education generally stopped with high school chemistry, or perhaps a single required natural science course in their undergraduate years. One would further suspect that most of these courses were taught by individuals who had themselves received their scientific training in the 1920s or 1930s, just as the implications of quantum physics and the special and general theories of relativity were beginning to be assimilated into the natural science canon.

Further, the research topics of international relations may well appear incompatible with the methods and data analysis techniques applied in many natural science research efforts. Natural scientists often conduct research in which observed outcomes fall not precisely on target but within a range, and they draw conclusions based upon averages of events. On the other hand, international relations tends to be concerned with specific events, and the measure of efficacy is the ability to predict a specific outcome. Given the small number of entities available for observation, the lack of appropriate experimental venues, and the inherent desire of human beings not to be shown up as wrong, it is hardly surprising that in recent decades international relations scholarship has turned away from the intractable problems of dealing with the real world and toward linguistic gamesmanship and wordplay.

The argument advanced here is that international relations scholars may find it useful to reconsider their attitudes toward the natural sciences and mathematics. First some basic considerations concerning systems and models will be summarized, and then a number of developments in the natural sciences and mathematics that appear to be of particular salience for international relations will be discussed. Additionally, the outline of a possible schema for the integration of constructivist ontology and modern mathematics and natural science will be presented.

Systems and Models

Scientific and mathematical thought is largely systematic, and the goal of much of this thought is the development of theories that can be represented as models of the subject under study. Unfortunately, becaue of the remembrance of attempts past to apply general systems theory to the study of political behavior, any suggestion that some sort of "systems theory" could advance the study of international relations is distasteful to many international relations theorists.

As Mario Bunge (1979) points out, however, we really have no choice but to study systems and their components if we wish to comprehend the workings of our world. As Bunge observes, studying components in isolation is akin to studying sawdust to understand trees—boring and of limited utility. Conversely, studying the externals of the trees without reference to their composition leaves the observer with only generalities. The difficulty with a systems-oriented approach is that it requires both breadth and depth; scholars must be both generalists and specialists. Nonetheless, whether the subject is trees or the socio-economico-political world in which we live, we cannot escape the requirement for systemic thought.

At its simplest, a system is a group of elements that are linked together in some fashion. This definition is implicit in such uses of the term as "a system of laws" and "a system of philosophy." A *taxonomy*—the simplest form of systematization—is an example of this usage. As with any other form of systematization, one of the major goals of taxonomical systems is to enable enhanced prediction (See Casti 1990, 43).

Systems may be classified as either *static* or *dynamic*. Static systems express a relationship among component parts that remains unchanged. Dynamic systems change over time.

A dynamic system is a system in which some sort of *input* is received by *components* that are in some form *interconnected* and which, in turn produce some sort of *output*. (See Howard 1991 for a clear discussion of the basic formal definition of a dynamic system.) If both input and output are contained within the system, the system is a *closed system*. To the extent that the system receives input from outside or delivers output to the outside, the system is an *open system*. An open system may have *recursive* characteristics. In such a system, output is released into the larger environment but may also feed back into the system as an input. A system that receives recursive inputs and inputs from the larger environment is a *cybernetic system*. This type of system is what we are interested in in international relations, since it is a general description of the international system and its relationship to the larger environment in which it operates.

Another important distinction is between *discrete* and *continuous* systems. In a discrete system, inputs arrive in packets, outputs are produced in the same form, and the system changes in finite increments. In continuous systems, inputs and outputs are streams.

Two other divisions among systems are important: the division between systems that treat time as an explicit variable and those that do not, and the division between systems that exhibit *entropy* and those that do not.

While time is a factor in all dynamic systems, not all systems require that the interval of time be specified. Systems that do not specify time are referred to as systems in which time is an implicit variable, while systems in which time is specified are referred to as systems in which time is an explicit variable.

The division of systems into *entropic* and *nonentropic* systems also relates to the question of time. A general thermodynamic definition of the
term *entropy* is "a measure of the capacity of an isolated macroscopic
system for change" (Coveny and Highfield 1990, 362). Left unchecked, an
entropic system will eventually move to a state of equilibrium. This may be
viewed as a form of decay, a temporal process. In the mathematical sense,
entropy is considered as a loss of information over time. As such, *entropy
may be considered a measure of the disorganization present in a system.*
The presence of entropy signifies that for the system, time is a one-way
street: the system cannot be made to run backward. Entropic systems are
also known as *dissipative* systems. Human beings are a good example of
dissipative systems, since no matter how hard we try to stem the onslaught
of old age, no one has yet managed not to get old. Even Dorian Gray
eventually disintegrated.

For nonentropic systems, to the contrary, time is viewed as reversible.
Newtonian physics and classical astronomy treat the systems they study as
nonentropic. Because they do not decay, nonentropic systems are also
known as *conservative* systems.

Since in the real world entropy is a constant, *all real-world systems are
time-dependent.*

Having declared entropy a constant, one is also asked to consider another
idea that seems diametrically opposed—evolution. Entropy argues for the
decay of systems. Evolution posits the development of increasingly complex systems. Can these two concepts coexist?

There is a body of theory and experiment that seems to support a view
that in certain conditions, systems can exhibit both evolution and entropy.
Ilya Prigogine (1984), who developed the theory of *dissipative structures*,
argues that dissipative structures develop in systems that are operating far
from equilibrium. It is within these dissipative structures that evolutionary
processes are thought to take place.

A final important division between types of systems is that between
linear and *nonlinear* systems. In essence it is the division between systems
in which there is a constant proportional relationship between the variables
in the system (linear) and systems in which changes in the values of variables are not necessarily proportional (nonlinear). Until recently, mathematics has lacked the tools to study nonlinear systems satisfactorily, so there
has been a marked tendency to attempt to produce linear models of systems,
even when these have been inappropriate.

Having accepted the idea of the system, one immediately faces a problem: to portray the system completely requires that the system itself be
studied. However, in all but the simplest systems, this is impossible: for

example, the solar system is not accessible to direct observation. Additionally, if the goal of studying the system is to understand certain aspects of it, there is considerable economy of effort to be produced by limiting the study of the system to those aspects that are of particular importance by creating models.

Bunge (1973) offers this taxonomy of models:

- *The model as object* may be defined as a hypothetically real but possibly fictitious sketch of something. The model as object may be pictorial or conceptual (e.g., a mathematical formula), but it is always partial; if it is not partial, the model is identical with the object of study. Thus, the model as object is a means of selecting the essential and ignoring the nonessential.
- *The model as theory* is a specific theory of a concrete or reportedly concrete (that is, nonreified) object. The relation between theory and model here is that a general theory that lacks the particulars supplied by the model cannot be tested; only when the theory is converted to a model is it available for empirical testing. The model as theory may be considered as a hypothetico-deductive system concerning a model object. The goal of this type of modeling is to insert the specific theory derived from the model into a comprehensive theoretical scheme.
- *The model in the æsthetic sense* is a pictorial representation.
- *The model in the heuristic sense* is an analog of a familiar object, a metaphor.
- *The model in the model-theoretic sense* is a true interpretation of a formal system.

The type of model of most immediate concern to international relations is the model as object. The hope is that through the development of enough specific model objects, it will be possible to intuit or otherwise develop the more comprehensive theoretical scheme associated with the model as theory.

In trying to produce models to serve as a test bed for theory, the sciences search for *analogons*. An analogon is something more than a simile or metaphor, something less than equivalence. An analogon is a set of parallel cases. Systems of different design that are functionally similar are considered analogous.

Formal modeling may be considered the construction of formal analogons for natural—real-world—systems. This view can be justified because the successful formal model, while without meaningful content, nonetheless produces outcomes that show a subjective similarity to the natural reality.

At this point, it may be worth a moment's digression to note that not all operations involving quantitative methods are actually modeling.

A *formal mathematical model* consists of a set of symbols, a set of transformation rules stated as well-formed formulae, and a set of inference rules that permit the construction of other well-formed formulae; when a set of axioms is allowed to operate on these elements, the result is a formal system. If it is alleged that this system is an analogon of another phenomenon, the system is said to be a formal model.

Statistical analysis is the analysis of numerical data, either descriptive or inferential. Inferential statistical analysis is a form of analysis that relies on probability theory for determining both the reliability of data and the reliability of inferences drawn from that data.

Simulation is a form of modeling in that it is an explicit attempt to produce a simulacrum of some real process in another form. The game of Monopoly is a simulation of the capitalist economic system. While a simulation may be based on a formal model, many simulations are developed heuristically.

Formal models are based on three key assumptions:

- That *quantitation* of data is possible and that these data are not reified but represent some sort of reality.
- That it is possible to express mathematically the relationship between variables represented by the data that have been gathered.
- That solving equations that express this relationship between variables sheds light upon reality.

Modeling in International Relations

A number of criticisms of modeling in international relations have emerged. Without exhausting the subject, a summary of these criticisms would include the following lines of attack:

- The generic criticism of the assumptions of Newtonian determinism. Even probabilistic models—models that introduce random or stochastic effects—are really only Newton plus an uncertainty term, since the stochastic effect is introduced on heuristic rather than theoretical grounds.
- The criticism that international relations models are based on concepts that are anarchically defined (see Ferguson and Mansbach 1988).
- The criticism that international relations models have often been produced for normative rather than scientific reasons and may well exhibit their creators' normative biases.

- The criticism that many models in international relations are particularistic.
- The criticism that because of their heuristic nature, most models in international relations remain unsubjected to the rigor of phase space analysis for validation, thus leaving open whether their variable space is coterminous with that of their real world analogons.
- The criticism that methods of scientific analysis drawn from the physical sciences are inappropriate to the study of human behavior because consciousness is not currently accessible to scientific analysis (Penrose 1989, 1994).

The basic problem with international relations models derived from classical scientific methodology is, however, one that is generally unstated: most international relations models are based on the intellectual assumptions of Newtonian physics: the clockwork, totally determined universe. Newton's physics are an attempt to explain the regular aspects of life. In international relations, though, what we are interested in is not regularity but irregularity. Thus, clockwork models are inappropriate because they do not allow for irregularities, and when irregularities appear, the models are deemed failures.

The inability of classical science and mathematics to provide tools for the significant advancement of knowledge in international relations appears to many theorists to have foreclosed advancements along these lines. But the core problem is somewhat more tractable: it is not that science has failed, but that we have emulated the wrong science, the science of the eighteenth and nineteenth centuries, rather than the science of the end of the twentieth century.

Emergent Science and Mathematics

While the term still has not been universally adopted nor comprehensively defined, one of the key aspects of current scientific thought is the notion of *emergent properties*. In shorthand terms, the notion of emergence is tied up with the question of behavior. Scientists are generally not content simply to observe and note the structure of the object of their study; they want to know what the object will do under given conditions and, if possible, the reason for that particular action. In other words, they want to know not just what "it" is, but why "it" does the things it does.

One of the ways scientists do this is by paring down the "its" they study. They try to pick out the significant feature or features of the object of their interest and to limit the variables they consider. This activity has been given the vaguely pejorative name of *reduction*, pejorative because it has been argued that reduction makes the complex overly simplistic and substitutes a pencil sketch of a tree for the reality of the forest. That line of attack was successful in raising serious doubts about the entire scientific enterprise among many who heard it, both inside and outside the scientific community. But research, discoveries, and observations over the past century, building to a crescendo in the 1960s, 1970s, and 1980s, have led to the finding that astonishingly complex and unpredicted behavior often emerges from simple—reduced—systems. This new science is a science of emergence—the unfolding of the system to reveal levels of complexity and structure that are not apparent on the surface. Emergence means that there are some properties of matter and being that emerge (or appear) only as matter and/or being develops complexity.

Marjorie Grene addresses the question of whether living systems are governed by the laws of physics—a reductionist proposition. She points out that this syllogism seems to suggest that living systems are explained by the laws of physics and that no other laws apply. She notes that such a position does not follow "unless we know ... that the laws of physics are the only laws we know." This not being the case, she proposes as a valid syllogism: "All living systems indeed obey the laws of physics, but without contravening the laws of physics they may well obey other laws as well" (Grene 1971, 21).

Today, even the most diligent defenders of the reductionist canon concede that there are properties of complex structures that do not have counterparts at lower levels. Steven Weinberg (1992) notes that there is nothing like intelligence on the level of individual living cells and nothing like life on the level of atoms and molecules. He argues that while emergence is most obvious in the biological and behavioral sciences, it also appears in physics. He cites as examples the emergent properties of thermodynamics, such as entropy and temperature, properties that are without meaning in the discussion of individual particles of matter.

Weinberg's is essentially a reductionist view of emergence. Others, like Roger Penrose (1989, 1994), have made a much broader claim, that there exists a set of rules governing—especially—human systems that are not even accessible through reduction.

Despite the contestation over the scope of the concept of emergent properties, even those who find the concept oversold agree that some aspects of reality only become visible (apparent) at certain levels of systemic development. A simple example of an emergent property might be that of color. Consider the level at which this property emerges in the element carbon:

• What color is a quark? We don't know, and even if we did, it would tell us nothing about the color of carbon.

- What color is an electron? The same answer applies.
- What color is the nucleus of a carbon atom? Again, the question is irrelevant to the color of carbon.
- What color is coal? Black.

We may know the components of a carbon atom, but the property of color emerges from the way those components interact and only above a certain level. Other examples of emergent properties in the natural world include intelligence, photosynthesis, various forms of systemic self-organization, and language. These and other emergent properties have in common that they appear only in systems that have attained a certain level of complexity. Emergence is itself a feature of the emergent science.

For international relations, what is important about the notion of emergence is that those who are studying complex system behavior are beginning to generalize about emergent properties.

One example of the generalizations that are appearing comes from the field of artificial world modeling, a computational field that uses the power of the computer to test out algorithms for the creation of virtual environments. The underlying hypothesis that legitimates the study of artificial worlds is a strange combination of reduction (in that artificial worlds are much simpler than their real counterpart) and holism (in that the entire world is the universe of study, not just a small corner of it).

Among those who have used the idea of the artificial world are economists and statisticians seeking to understand economic behavior in the real world by creating an artificial world and observing the development of economic structures in it. It is out of this work that the process of *emergent hierarchical organization* has appeared. For the current purpose, two observed characteristics are important. The first is that this emergent organization is hierarchical (see Lane 1992 for a good discussion of the implications of hierarchy).

The second important observation is that systems exhibiting emergent hierarchical organization seem to produce order from within themselves. This property is noted in physical, chemical, biological, and social systems and is often called self-organization.

Grégoire Nicolis and Ilya Prigogine (1989) point out that self-organization, though first observed in biological systems, is not a function of biology but is much more deeply rooted. They cite as examples of self-organization the order that emerges in thermal convection (a phenomenon studied in physics) and the chemical phenomenon known as autocatalysis, in which the presence of a product of a chemical reaction stimulates further production of that product.

The idea that properties like self-organization emerge as systems become more complex is interesting in itself, but more interesting is the question: What purpose do emergent properties, such as self-organization, serve? The answer to this question, offered by emergent science, is that emergent properties are the means by which complex systems adapt to their environment.

Proponents of the view of emergence as an adaptive mechanism see this as a crucial dividing point between their view of science and the more traditional position. Drawing on ideas and computer models developed by John Holland, Murray Gell-Mann stated the institutional position this way:

- There are basic rules that all systems of a given type follow.
- Historical accident is the source of other systemic parameters.
- Those features of systems that are not determined by basic rules or historical accident are the result of emergent adaptation of the system to its environment.

The trick, of course, is sorting out what is a basic rule, what is the result of historical accident, and what is the product of emergent adaptation.

Emergence's Antecedent—Uncertainty

Emergent science has been a long time in blossoming: the bud was formed in the fecund thirty-year period that started with Max Planck's proposal of the quantum theory in 1900, advanced with Albert Einstein's special and general theories of relativity (1905 and 1915), and culminated with the unification of these two theories by P.A.M. Dirac in 1929.

The notion of the quantum is perplexing: while it resolves contradictions between prediction and observation in the behavior of particles, it defies intuition and our everyday perception of reality. And yet, it is such a simple idea: the quantum is the smallest amount of energy by which a system can change. Inherent in the definition is the notion that the quantum is discrete, not continuous. The idea of the quantum is important in physics because it redefines what atomic structure is.

In classical physics, the atom resembles the solar system, with the electrons orbiting around the central atomic core of protons and neutrons. The electrons can have any orbit diameter and can, in theory, be tracked with the same precision as astronomers can track Mars. This comfortable picture is disturbed by the quantum theory, which holds that there are only certain energy levels at which the electrons (or any other particles) can exist. This feature means that when the energy level of a particle changes, it shifts immediately from one orbit to another and that unless one knows precisely what the energy level of the particle is at a given time (something that is impossible to determine), one can only give probabilities for the position of a particle. As if this were not complicated enough, researchers in quantum mechanics have shown both theoretically and experimentally that the particles appear as waves and waves as particles, depending on the conditions under which they are observed. Odd as it may seem, the results of study of the physical universe over the past ninety years have removed from physical science the matter-of-fact and the pragmatic and have elevated uncertainty to the status of a first principle.

Mathematics has added its own confirmation of ultimate unknowableness. Gödel's 1931 publication of his incompleteness theorem has made clear that no matter how hard we try, we can never produce unity of truth and proof. Gödel showed that for any given logical framework, there is at least one proposition that can be proved only by reference to a meta(logical) framework, and so on to infinity. As informally stated by John Casti (1990), Gödel's Theorem is that arithmetic is not completely formalizable. Stated even more informally, it is impossible to write down all the rules to a mathematical system. Gödel's Theorem means, for those who work with formal systems, that no matter how hard they try, some aspect of the system will escape them.

The importance of Gödel's discovery is predicated on the assumption that what is true for formal systems is also true for real, that is, nonmathematical, analogons. In Gödel's Theorem, the question is not whether the formal system mirrors the real system, but whether the formal system (which has an independent existence) provides us with information about the structure of real systems.

On a trivial level, we see the notion of incompleteness in ancient explanations of how the Earth fitted into the cosmos. In one variant, the Earth (which was thought of as a flat disk, like a tray) was said to be balanced on the backs of two turtles. The turtles, in turn, were said to stand on the backs of two birds. This system offered no explanation of where the birds perched when they became tired of flying. If Gödel's Theorem is correct (and we have no reason to assume the contrary), then we are always obliged to accept on faith some element of any system of thought.

It is, of course, one thing to acknowledge the limits of knowledge and quite another to build a scientific structure upon those limits. The former is nothing more than a negation of determinism. The latter would be a considerably greater achievement, since it would provide a means of moving forward, a means of surmounting the obstacle posed by the removal of determinism from the calculus of existence.

No doubt, few practicing scientists or mathematicians lie awake at night worrying about such issues. They have research problems to solve, articles to write, and careers to advance, just as we all do. Fortunately, though, the research they have undertaken has generated a structure that adapts to both deterministic and indeterminate phenomena. In addition, this structure accommodates notions of change, choice, and nonrationality, for which classical Newtonian determinism had been unable to account in an acceptable way.

In the popular literature dealing with aspects of this new appreciation of natural sciences and mathematics, this structure is often given the appellation "the science of complexity." This may be a misnomer, since a new understanding of complex systems is an aspect (but not the whole substance) of the new structure. It is for that reason that I have chosen the phrase "emergent science" to describe this thought structure. In the following sections, I shall touch briefly on some of the other concepts that help to delineate emergent science from the classical model.

Nonlinearity

We find it easy to incorporate into our thoughts such ideas as, "For every action, there is an equal and opposite reaction." This sort of statement appeals to us as it traces a direct path from A to B, a relationship that can be expressed as $A \rightarrow B$.

This statement says that A (whatever A may be) maps into B. But we can say much more about the relationship of A and B, drawing on our intuition. We can say that, for the statement above, it is also true that $A = kB$.

While the values assigned to A, B, and k (some constant) may change, the relationship among these three values is straightforward and directly proportional.

Relationships that do not respond proportionally (and systems that exhibit this property) are called *nonlinear*. For nonlinear systems, it is possible for two variables to be in a relationship that varies under different conditions.

Nonlinearity is an aspect of emergent science that mathematicians and scientists have only begun to explore. There are two related reasons for this. The first is the relative difficulty of solving nonlinear problems. Because they do not exhibit the regularity of response of linear problems, nonlinear problems are not susceptible to simple mathematical manipulation. Nonlinear equations are so difficult to solve that, until recently, the approach of scientists and mathematicians when confronted by nonlinear terms was to toss them out, to linearize the equation. Sometimes the equations were deliberately written to avoid nonlinear terms. For instance, the classical equation for heat flow is linear, but heat flow is nonlinear. The result of approaching nonlinear problems as if they were linear is the Hobson's choice that results: problems that are seen to be nonlinear either are left unattacked or are converted to linear problems and solved with the wrong answers.

The second reason for the recent emergence of nonlinearity in mathematics and science has to do with the relatively recent arrival on the scene of the computer, more particularly the proliferation of small but powerful individual computer workstations. As noted above, the beauty of a linear problem is that once two solutions for it are found, the path of all solutions is known. This means that, for the most part, linear problems can be solved without reference to equations because formulae are sufficient. To get the answer to a nonlinear problem, however, one must find the state of all the variables and parameters for each point at which a solution is sought. When this had to be done by hand, or even with a mechanical calculator, nonlinearity resembled the south face of the Eiger—fascinating but apparently unchallengeable.

Indeterminacy

Another block in the structure of emergent science is the notion of *indeterminacy*, or, more accurately, the notion of "apparent indeterminacy." The starting point for understanding the importance of indeterminacy is, as usual, the Newtonian worldview and, more particularly, what Gerald Holton refers to as "the delayed triumph of the purely mechanistic view in the completion of Newton's work by Laplace" (1988, 3).

Laplace is best known for his notion that a universal intelligence, aware of the position and velocity of all matter at a given moment, could accurately predict outcomes to the infinite future.

Such a notion appears amusing, naive, or arrogant today, but much of the substance of our daily lives we live as if Laplacean determinism were fact, even while bridling at the figurative straitjackets into which our free wills have been encased. It is no wonder that humanists with only limited exposure to the notions of physics rail against determinism.

Of course, as David Ruelle observes, Laplace's cosmic view is less restrictive than we are generally taught to believe. Ruelle points out that there is nothing inherently contradictory between determinism and chance, for if the state of a system at its start time is not precisely fixed but random, then the system will remain random (1991).

Despite this small comfort, the clockwork world of Laplace continued to trouble philosophers. It was only with the development of quantum mechanics in the early part of this century that relief of a sort appeared.

Two points are specially important for emergent science. The first is the introduction of the notion of *probability* into a field that had previously been characterized by the quest for precision. The second is the introduction of the notion of *the subjective role of the observer* into a field that had been characterized by an objectivist stance.

This profoundly unsettling view of the nature of the fundamental structure of the physical world has been cited as one of the intellectual roots of the relativistic philosophical movements that have assumed such importance in the intellectual tenor of contemporary Western thought. If the nature of fundamental physical reality is dependent upon the observer, then what can be determined? From another perspective, since we observers make the choice of what to look for, are we not ourselves producing deterministic results? If we cannot assert location as more than a statement of the odds, what, then, can be certain? If we can determine accurately what those odds are, is this not a form of true certainty? Paradoxes such as these have become a staple of the philosophy of science.

Conditionality, Complexity, and Chaos

As the spread of computing power focused attention on nonlinear problems, conditionality appeared as an answer to the puzzling fact that events that seemed alike often produced vastly different outcomes. Quantum mechanics gave impetus to the notion of indeterminacy. These ideas, which all share the property of "fuzziness," found unity in the rubric of chaos and complexity.

Conditionality is really nothing more than a willingness to say, "It all depends." In other words, emergent science makes explicit the well-known but too-often-ignored reality that *ceteris paribus* seldom applies. The best examples of the importance of conditions to outcomes are drawn from the subfield of emergent science known as chaos theory, but the idea is one that goes back centuries. The verse about the causal chain in which for want of a nail, the horse's shoe was lost, which caused a knight to be withdrawn from battle, which caused the tide of the battle to turn, which led to the fall of a kingdom is a clear illustration of the idea behind conditionality. Had a blacksmith tapped just a bit harder on the nail, perhaps the horse might not have lost its shoe, and so forth. Or maybe, there was a flaw in the nail or a weakness in the structure of the hoof. Such speculation can go on *ad infinitum* (not to mention ad nauseam).

The problem that chaos theory is most closely associated with in the physical sciences is an ancient one: *turbulence*. Turbulence is a specific case of a problem—the breakdown of order in deterministic systems. What makes turbulence so difficult to deal with is the unpredictability of its onset. Not only has physical science failed to devise rules for predicting the appearance of turbulence, it also has failed to develop an adequate explanation for its appearance within otherwise ordered systems. Lacking requisite theoretical tools, engineers and scientists generally deal with turbulence either by ignoring it when possible or by treating it as a problem to be approached heuristically.

Turbulent phenomena have been encountered not only in engineering, but also in a range of systems in which, despite their manifestly deterministic nature, the random and the inexplicable could appear suddenly and without warning. Since the problem of turbulence appeared incapable of solution within the scope of existing knowledge, the response was, for the most part, to ignore the issues raised, concentrating instead on the regularities, with the view that these anomalies eventually would be resolved. There is nothing shameful in this; it is the means by which the physical sciences have progressed despite the continued existence of problems that they lacked the ability to solve. The danger, of course, is that what is ignored may be treated as if it did not exist. The problem of *indeterminacy* in determinate systems, however, proved difficult to ignore, particularly after the arrival of the computer, when even the most deterministic science of all—mathematics—was increasingly troubled by stochastic intrusions. The intrusion of the random-seeming into the determinate was the cause of intellectual disquiet, as it appeared to be in contradiction to the Newtonian vision of a universe in which, when initial values were known, outcomes were assumed to be predictable.

Complexity, like chaos and like the quantum, is one of those concepts that both defies intuition and appeals to intuition. Essentially, the idea behind complexity is that the location of interesting behavior is in a region far from stability, where order is just on the verge of breaking down, at the edge of chaos. Scholars who write about complexity often refer to what they call *criticality*. When they do so, they often cite a sandpile as an example of what they are talking about.

The sandpile is a system: it consists of component grains of sand. The system receives input as more sand dribbling from above. New grains of sand organize themselves (without volition) on the top of the pile, so that the structure grows higher and higher until it can no longer remain stable. At that point, the sand slides unpredictably (chaotically) down the sides of the pile, and the system attains a new, self-organized state of criticality.

The behavior of the sandpile system is an example of how systems operate on the edge of chaos, the area of the system's phase space that is of particular interest to researchers in complex systems behavior. There are several reasons to suspect that this region is of particular interest.

First, the system is seeking to maintain itself in an organized fashion, without any outside intervention. This concept of self-organization is a core concept of theories that embrace complexity. Self-organization is the mechanism by which insect colonies arrange themselves, the mechanism by which convection currents appear in liquids and gases that have previously exhibited only Brownian motion, and (very possibly) the mechanism that underlies the creation of human societies, including states.

Second, the system at the edge of chaos is interesting because it exhibits the dynamic tension between order (self-organization) and stochastic behavior (chaos). Since the system has not slipped over the dividing line between stability and chaos, its behavior is perfectly predictable. When the boundary is crossed, it becomes impossible to say with any certainty what will happen to the structure. One cannot even say just when the boundary will be crossed, since there is exquisite sensitivity to changes in conditions at this boundary. Who can know which grain of sand, falling at which precise spot, will be the trigger for a slide? Even if the grain of sand and the precise spot were to be determined (one could figure out which grain caused the slide by simply dropping sand a grain at a time), that knowledge would not enable the observer to predict the condition of either that grain or the system when it emerges from the chaotic region.

Third, the system is interesting because the excursions into chaotic behavior vary. At some times, the slides that the falling sand triggers will be small, and only minor changes in the system will result. At other times, the excursions into chaotic realms will produce major restructuring of the system. A mathematical function called a *power law* enables an observer of the system to speak probabilistically about the chance for a major or minor restructuring to take place, although not to predict with any precision either when a given excursion into chaos will occur or how severe the excursion will be.

The Problem of Learning

Researchers have long been puzzled by questions about how complex systems seem to learn—to change their structures, their behaviors, and even their appearances—without the presence of a central directing sentient power. Of particular interest is the *genetic algorithm*, a set of instructions that modifies itself and in so doing may bring improvements to the system in which it operates.

Algorithms are nothing more than a set of rules for achieving a particular task. The benefit of an algorithm is that, once it has been developed, those who use it do not have to think about its derivation. In fact, they have no knowledge of the algorithm's presence or operation. Human beings are not aware of the embedded algorithms that govern much of their behavior. For instance, there is the algorithm that determines what happens when food reaches the stomach and the algorithm that controls what happens when a speck of dust approaches the eye. These algorithms are hardwired into our individual systems. One would imagine that algorithms, once installed, would remain the same, rote formulas, producing the same results repeatedly, ad infinitum. Yet we know that systems evolve, that new behavioral responses appear. If algorithms are rules and rules are deterministic, how can there be any change?

John Von Neumann addressed this problem. He first discussed systems, which he called *automata*, that follow algorithms to produce outputs unlike themselves, such as computers, which follow instructions but do not reproduce themselves by those instructions, and McCulloch-Pitts neurons, which produce pulses that are different from the automaton. Then he turned to automata, "which can have outputs something like themselves." Von Neumann then defined what he was interested in.

Von Neumann argued that this passage is "an axiomatically shortened and simplified description of what an organism does." He notes that the results reached by such an operation would be heavily dependent upon the way the elementary parts had been defined, their number, and so on. However, having acknowledged these limitations, he argued that it is legitimate to consider a system of self-reproducing automata "which will stand up under common sense criteria" (1966, 77).

Von Neumann made a telling point when he observed that, in considering self-reproducing organisms, one would expect to find that the organism could not produce any new organism more complicated than itself. One would expect to see a reproduction falling short of the original, so that the process would be a degenerative one. However, this is not necessarily the case, Von Neumann noted. The key to this nonintuitive result he called "complication," and the level of complication was the determinant factor for whether the process of reproductive activity would be degenerative or otherwise. The level of complication was, in turn, determined by the number of parts. Von Neumann said he did not know precisely where the break point was, but he proposed the level at between one dozen and two dozen. Then he made the following observation, which is the crucial one for this discussion:

> There is thus this completely decisive property of complexity, that there exists a critical size below which the process of synthesis is degenerative, but

above which the phenomenon of synthesis, if properly arranged, can become explosive, in other words, where syntheses of automata can proceed in such a manner that each automaton will produce other automata which are more complex and of higher potentialities than itself. (1966, 80)

The means for this production of more complex automata proposed by Von Neumann is the introduction into the system of random changes in the descriptive code that the automata use for reproduction. Some of these random changes will cause the reproductive cycle to break, and these mutations will be lethal. Others will lead to the production of more complex machines that can reproduce themselves at the new level of complexity. This is, at a basic level, precisely how genetic algorithms behave. This is also a much simplified presentation of the way in which DNA operates in the reproductive coding of living organisms.

Holland's creation of genetic algorithms is the outcome of nearly forty years of efforts to simulate evolution in a computer. His insight was that while mutations play a role in evolution, the primary engine of genetic evolution is mating, with the resultant recombination of genetic material. Holland's model for this process relies on what he calls a *classifier system*, consisting of a set of rules, each of which performs particular actions every time its conditions are satisfied by some piece of information (Holland 1992, 66). If certain parts of the output of a classifier system are tied to behaviors, then the operation of the system can trigger actions.

While the genetic algorithm clearly applies to biological systems, it can also be applied to other systems. For instance, corporate management systems evolve as managers develop new classifier systems that rate fitness in terms of corporate profit.

A Do-It-Yourself Kit for Constructivists

The picture of scientific or mathematical thought outlined above is (I suspect) considerably different from the picture held in the minds of many international relations theorists. However, this picture is remarkably consistent with constructivist ontology, enough so that it is possible, without too much imagination, to suggest a possible isomorphism between constructivism and emergent science's elaboration of complex dynamic systems. This observation may be demonstrated by the act of constructing what computer programmers call a look-up table, or a table of correspondences, such as the one presented in Table 8.1. This exercise is presented not as definitive or complete, but simply as an example of just how easily one can locate correspondences between constructivism and current scientific or mathe-

Table 8.1

Potential Isomorphisms Between Emergent Science and Constructivism

Constructivist terminology		Scientific/mathematical terminology
Agent	=	Complex automaton
Rule	=	Genetic algorithm
Institution/regime	=	Classifier system
Social arrangement/structure	=	Interconnection matrix
Social construction	=	Emergent hierarchical organization
Unintended consequence	=	Emergent property

matical thinking. While the table as it now stands is no more than a hypothesis, the relationships suggested by it are subject to experimental confirmation or rejection.

Onuf's definition of agents is at least consistent with the properties of complex automata, especially if those automata are seen as both constructing and being constructed by rules (which change over time), also known as "genetic algorithms." And just as agent-constructed and agent-governing rules generate and are generated by institutions, so too can automata-evolved sets of genetic algorithms be seen as classifier systems that generate the further evolution of the automata and the system of which they are components. A system that evolves itself (as does the international system) is by definition an emergent organization. As Onuf points out, that system, despite claims of sovereignty, does exhibit hierarchical characteristics, thus suggesting that this social construction is isomorphic with emergent hierarchical organization. Clearly, there is an isomorphism between Onuf's "unintended consequences" and emergent properties, both by definition being products of the complex interplay among the elements of the system but generated from the system itself.

Of course, pointing out potential isomorphisms is considerably less difficult than building a formal theoretical model, but the apparent goodness of fit between emergent science and constructivism is surely enough to suggest that it may be too soon for international relations theory to give up on the methods (and epistemology) of the sciences and mathematics.

If the isomorphisms suggested hold up under appropriate tests, the advance for international relations theory would be significant, since international relations would finally have in hand the tools needed to commence the construction of a model-theoretic approach to the discipline. And that would be no small achievement.

Note

Some of the material in this chapter originally appeared in a different form in my "The Emergent Scientific Epistemology and International Relations" (unpublished doctoral dissertation, Coral Gables, Fla.: University of Miami, 1993), while additional material flows from research undertaken at Sociocybernetics, Inc. I am grateful to my colleagues at Sociocybernetics, Inc., especially Bernard E. Howard, for their patience and lucidity in discussing and explaining many of the mathematical constructs used herein. I should also like to thank Vendulka Kubálková and Nicholas Onuf for many constructive suggestions. Obviously, misunderstandings or misrepresentations that remain are my responsibility alone.

Bibliography

Bunge, Mario. 1973. *Method, Model, and Matter*. Dordrecht: D. Reidel.
———. 1979. *Causality and Modern Science*, 3d rev. ed. New York: Dover.
Casti John. 1990. *Searching for Certainty: What Scientists Can Know About the Future*. New York: William Morrow.
Coveny, Peter, and Roger Highfield. 1990. *The Arrow of Time: A Voyage Through Science to Solve Time's Greatest Mystery*. New York: Fawcett Columbine.
Ferguson, Yale H., and Richard W. Mansbach. 1988. *The Elusive Quest: Theory and International Politics*. Columbia: University of South Carolina Press.
Gell-Mann, Murray. 1990. "The Santa Fe Institute." Santa Fe: The Santa Fe Institute. Photocopy.
Grene, Marjorie. 1971. "Reducibility: Another Side Issue?" In *Interpretations of Life and Mind: Essays Around the Problem of Reduction*, ed. Marjorie Grene. New York: Humanities.
Holland, John H. 1992. "Genetic Algorithms." *Scientific American* 267 (1): 66–72.
Holton, Gerald. 1988. *The Thematic Origins of Scientific Thought: Kepler to Einstein*, rev. ed. Cambridge: Harvard University Press.
Howard, Bernard E. 1991. "Dynamic Systems." Coral Gables, Fla: University of Miami. Photocopy.
Lane, David A. 1992. "Artificial Worlds and Economics." Santa Fe: The Santa Fe Institute. Photocopy.
Nicolis, Grégorie, and Ilya Prigogine. 1989. *Exploring Complexity: An Introduction*. New York: W.H. Freeman.
Penrose, Roger. 1989. *The Emperor's New Mind: Concerning Computers, Minds, and the Laws of Physics*. Oxford: Oxford University Press.
———. 1994. *Shadows of the Mind: A Search for the Missing Science of Consciousness*. Oxford: Oxford University Press.
Prigogine, Ilya. 1984. *Order out of Chaos: Man's New Dialogue with Nature*. Toronto: Bantam Books.
Ruelle, David. 1991. *Change and Chaos*. Princeton: Princeton University Press.
Von Neumann, John. 1966. *Theory of Self-Reproducing Automata*, edited and completed by Arthur W. Burks. Urbana: University of Illinois Press.
Weinberg, Steven. 1992. *Dreams of Final Theory*. New York: Pantheon.

9

Reconstructing the Discipline: Scholars as Agents

Vendulka Kubálková

Since Nicholas Onuf introduced the approach in 1989, "constructivism" has spread like a forest fire. Unfortunately most scholars took only the label. They attached it to many things and rarely defined it. Worse still, it became a vacuous cliché: as the post–Cold War order is being reconfigured, the term *constructivism* has an air of being appropriate for the occasion.

This book was not written to reclaim rights to a particular word. If in the world of academe it were possible to register a trademark for any "original" term or concept, the legal profession would have to move to campuses and the flood of academic publications would be reduced to a trickle. We want to reattach the term to the meaning its author originally intended for an entirely different reason.

Constructivism as Onuf conceived it was designed to convey a distinct message. If someone cries that there is a fire when there is no fire, then eventually the word will no longer convey alarm when it would be warranted. When people falsely cry "fire," the word loses its meaning and association. As this book shows, *constructivism* does not refer to instances of states signing international agreements, joining an international organization, or observing rules of a particular international regime. *Constructivism*, in this book, refers to a universal human experience of living in both smaller and larger social contexts. Expanded ontological guidelines to how the world is put together do not necessarily exclude or diminish the centrality, in the present world, of states and interstate relations. Yet the redescription of the world leads to a very different understanding of states and states' relations. Reclaiming the word *constructivism* saves it from being drowned in so many parallel meanings that the original message is not heard.

Addressing the issue raised by the title of this chapter with constructivism in mind provides ample justification for moving beyond endless esoteric debates into something more constructive. How do scholars in IR function as agents? How does the discipline as an institution constitute agency? How, in short, can constructivism be turned to an analysis of this discipline itself? Answering these questions from a constructivist perspective reveals the multiple agencies and their often conflicting rules that the academic discipline, and individual scholars, must reconcile.

Agents are participants in the social process, individuals whose acts materially affect the world. Not all individuals can intervene in every kind of world-making, social arrangement-constituting process. Rules constituting a society define the conditions under which individuals, institutions, or associations can intervene in the affairs of society.

Each of us, in our profession as scholars, is an agent. Indeed, we can be many sorts of agents at once, and we are part of multiple social arrangements in which, by definition, we could or should be intervening in the world. In this chapter, I count five such social arrangements in which we can, as a profession and/or as individuals, make a difference: in the culture of society broadly construed, in the culture of international politics, in the foreign policy of the United States in particular, in the discipline of IR, and in the classroom. To put it differently, how IR as an institution in the United States functions as an agent depends on the intersection of a number of social processes, all of which affect or are affected by academic IR: society, its foreign policy, the international society and its agents, the IR discipline itself, and the teaching that trains future agents. The requirements of these agencies are intertwined, sometimes mutually reinforcing, often conflicting. In the following discussions I will try to address them as if they were isolated from each other.

1. Guardians of Western Culture in Academic Disciplines

Society determines the guardians of its culture. For that purpose, the educational system is established and charged with the analysis and codification of rules and norms, and with their legitimization, justification, elucidation, and explication. Education provides knowledge both of these rules and of overt and covert sanctions for noncompliance. Universities educate the future public elites, educators, journalists and other media specialists, and future policy makers.

According to established practice in the Western universities, rules keep the guardians of education away from agents in "real life." Until recently, the question of whether IR could become "an agent" in international politics would have been beyond the bounds of reasonable debate, and one who raised the question would be dismissed as a disciple of Noam Chomsky, Joe McCarthy, or of Soviet Marxist-Leninist propaganda. In the liberal tradition, academics and practitioners have been regarded as two distinct ethnic groups with only limited intermingling, as with the exception of few Kissingers defecting to diplomacy and lapsed diplomats seeking careers in academe. The prevailing view, as Stanley Hoffmann put it, was that you cannot expect "a cherry tree to grow apples any more than an apple tree can grow cherries." Academics as guardians of knowledge were to be *protected* from political interference in their relentless search for the truth. This positivist separation of scholar and subject matter was reinforced by the more sophisticated positivism of behavioralism: in their pursuit of objective truth and value-free knowledge, the academic discoverers of knowledge were *isolated* (Alker 1982) to preserve their quest from the contaminating influence of "outside" interests. The separation has developed into a big "gap" in need of bridging. Alexander George (1994) reports that policy makers concede the usefulness of putting things in a larger context. George concluded, however, that the academic version of knowledge is perceived as very different from "policy relevant knowledge" (the more heuristic wisdom sought by policy makers). Can the distinction between academics and policy makers be defended in the information age, in an era of unprecedented democratization of access to data requiring interpretation? If the universities do not help to make sense of the world, where else do policy makers turn?

Other custodians of Western culture, of which the discipline of IR is a part, are scattered: they are in the media, the publishing world, different government agencies, and think tanks. The circumstances under which they are eligible to become "agents" depend also on the internal norms and rules established in the intellectual community of a country.

In principle, university professors, as both scholars and teachers, have been called upon to rationalize and legitimize the assumptions of their culture. As such they can serve as prime agents of social construction. But often it is the unintended effects of their primary activities that become more important.

For example, the IR discipline has been constructed as a discipline with the mandate to study war and conflict in international relations so that future wars may be avoided. Nobody would dismantle a discipline for failing to fulfill that mission, which is no doubt harder than finding a cure for cancer. If IR has failed in its main mission, then inadvertently it has performed to perfection a much easier role, namely the reaffirmation of the mainstream realist understanding of international relations.

States as social arrangements require and receive constant reminders and confirmations, constant displays of symbols and rituals reinforcing the social process called state or nation. The understanding of the world as taught in international relations courses assisted these processes. A state-centric view and an understanding of "anarchy" on the "outside" contrasted with the safety of the "inside" reinforce personal allegiances to the state. As has frequently been pointed out, the international or global awareness of young students and citizens generally is low, and the blind acceptance of norms and rules for national behavior on the world stage is incredibly high. Citizens question internal policies in minute detail but accept the image of international relations as received. Thus they accept passively the existence of and need for immigration regulations, carry passports, and subject themselves to visa controls. The state's flags fly proudly, and soldiers are celebrated and honored for dying or killing for their country, the most incredibly powerful of social constructions.

2. Guardians of the Culture of the International Society of States

The public elites of other countries are similarly engaged in shaping the rules and norms of their societies. IR scholars have acted on the assumption that because the theory and practice of IR are supposed to be universally valid, the practice of IR and the codifications of norms and rules of IR published by American presses will be universally accepted. The worldwide use of the English language has reinforced this myth. This approach denies a role to local circumstances in different countries and to local "agents" who are inevitably engaged in the process of co-construction.

Reacting to this flawed assumption of universality, many perceive cultural imperialism, hegemony, and parochialism in the practice of American intellectuals. American scholars of IR reassure themselves that they are doing a good job in teaching a realist view of the world, in an effort to represent the "truth," since the states system is so well institutionalized across the planet. There is no meaningful way to live outside states (except in rather inhospitable areas on the ocean and underwater or in the air). How was this arrangement constructed? Who set the rules and norms?

Anglo-American textbooks portray academic IR and its understanding of this process as part of a universal human experience. This contrasts sharply with perceptions of the process elsewhere. IR does not exist as a separate academic area of study in most parts of the world. Yet in the Anglo-American context, it has been portrayed as being on a par with natural sciences such as biology or physics, of universal relevance.

Onuf's analytical scheme makes it easier to recognize—indeed, it leads us to expect—that the rules and norms of IR are not uniform across the world. The practice of diplomacy originating in the West appears to have gained universal currency. Yet not all rules and norms related to IR are shared or universalized. States accept international law and international organizations, and in their international intercourse behave in a similar manner (Hedley Bull thought this constituted what he called international society). Onuf's constructivism acknowledges that there are multiple sources of rules and norms constructing the world's social structure. Both local identity and culture are crucial influences on the interpretation and creation of rules by agents. The analysis of norms and rules in world politics reveals that they reflect national, ethnic, religious, and other identities, brought to bear on social processes by particular cultures.

The conduct of international relations makes sense only within a cultural context. Unfortunately, because of the assumption of universality, the cultural context has been a blind spot (or indeed a consciously excluded subject) in the discipline of IR. And yet, members of Western societies do assume that ideas count, that rules guide conduct, that people can make real choices, and that differences can be reconciled. By contrast, in the former Soviet bloc (in which culture retains a strong legacy of the communist way of thinking and understanding the world), new rules have not always replaced the old. The culture of the former Soviet bloc still assigns a primary position to material factors and treats rules in a strictly instrumental fashion. It may appear to offer meaningful choices, but the rule has not yet been established that choices can be made. It is indeed possible that rules will continue unchanged on one level and will change on another, as happened when the Soviet Union fell apart.

IR scholars seldom appreciate that the majority of the world does not speak or think in the language of modernity. IR experts therefore confront an insurmountable problem with the current debate about "de-Westernization," "desecularization," or "Islamization" of the world; "religious wars"; or *revanche du Dieu*. The missing common denominator is a need to recognize that frighteningly complex world affairs require an understanding of many systems of thought, whether religious or secular. Each of these systems carries its own attitudes and values about good and bad, right and wrong, the world and God, individual, family, society, state, nation, wealth, authority, equality, justice, conflict, violence, and war.

The cause of the problem can be found in Western culture. Most post-Enlightenment Western thinkers, in the spirit espoused by many academics to this day, assume that religions are superstitions to be phased out in the age of "modernity" and "progress" by a "secular humanism" and by science. Exposed by a diminished preoccupation with the Cold War, the error of this assumption is being revealed. Stimulated by migration, social mobility, trade, and the electronic and print media, religion has expanded explosively within many societies and has reemerged as an international force. Religions are increasingly recognized as one of the most significant forms of social organization and ideology, the codifications of norms and rules. Religiously inspired people are agents too. The world is disrupted with increasing frequency in the name of religion, at both the domestic and the international level. Indeed, some religions do not include among their values a territorial principle that respects state boundaries and nonintervention across them. Religions define values and struggles over values, in addition to struggles for security and wealth, and will very likely play a central role in the next century. Many observers now view religion as an important predictor of peace and war, just as ideology was during the Cold War. Yet the study of religions is totally absent from IR studies. In the most recent book heralding the return of the identity and culture to international relations, there is no index entry referring to religion per se and there are only several pages dealing with Islam (Lapid and Kratochwil 1996).

3. Advisors to Foreign Policy Makers

IR need not be irrelevant to foreign policy making. The lack of relevance is expressed in the deepening disdain with which policy makers approach research and advice proffered by academics. For policy makers, the ready-made substitute for scholarly advice is at hand in the Information Age: access through information superhighways to "knowledge" without the benefit of formal training in IR. If academic IR does not perform this role, if the debates become too esoteric or impossible to understand, then sanctions (often too subtle to be regarded as such) will come into play: funding for professors and job opportunities for graduates will flow elsewhere, and the status and the profile of the profession will be lowered. The franchise will be taken over by whoever else is capable of performing the relevant tasks: print media, television commentators, and journalists.

Academics may console themselves that these are people whom we prepared to be agents and whose role we constructed. But did we? If we examine the rendition of the world as we find it in the media, the conclusions are disturbing: awareness of the "outside" has not been enhanced and international affairs take a distant second place to national and particularly local events. Reporting and editorials in public affairs journals reflect a strong degree of statecentrism but none of the increasingly arcane conceptual apparatus that IR scholars use to make sense of the world. We do hear voices that speak in the language of constructivism, without knowing what it is, like Moliere's M. Jourdain, who never knew that he spoke in prose.

4. Members of Academic Disciplines

Certain rules and norms govern the American academic community as it engages in the social processes discussed so far. Crucial in this regard is the hierarchy of the American IR community, the internal rules it abides by, and its ability to regenerate, evaluate itself, and adjust. Also important are the rules and norms that establish qualifications and seniority in the field, define scholarship, and identify the "mainstream," marking the rest as outside the mainstream.

The distinction between mainstream and nonmainstream does not have an obvious parallel in the British Commonwealth countries or Europe. There, terminal degrees are awarded with the participation of a diverse academic community. Doctoral examiners are selected (and their identity is kept secret from the candidate) from any other university in the same (or even another) country. Thus a standard is maintained that does not necessitate the tremendously strict pecking order in the American academy, whereby degrees are judged and awarded internally by each institution. Academe in the United States is therefore very hierarchical, with very limited "upward mobility." Perhaps the reason is the tremendous size of the U.S. educational system. IR is taught in most of the 3,200 degree-awarding institutions, which would make it difficult to follow the British and Continental model. The consequence of the U.S. system is that only the elite in the IR field, a handful of "experts" located in the most respected U.S. universities, are "agents." What is published in the main scholarly journals (with editorial boards "manned" by the same group) and by the main publishing houses is controlled by these experts. The rest of the field is left simply to instruct students in mainstream wisdom.

5. Teachers of Students in a Relation as Individuals

Most scholars are teachers. Teaching remains the most pedestrian form of agency for most of us, but the main or the only one in which we are not anonymous. We devise syllabi that reflect our professional opinions about knowledge, and we stand in front of classes to convey it.

It is from these pedagogical concerns and ambitions that this volume has grown. On one hand, IR is one of the most important subjects taught in the social sciences. On the other hand, we worry about whether our pronouncements qualify as knowledge to impart to students. We have two choices.

One is to present the student with a smorgasbord of approaches and debates encouraged by the notion that IR is multiparadigmatic. Thus graduate students are left with the problem of deciding to what paradigm their research should be attached, and undergraduate students are left with xenophobic ideas about the increasing inhospitability of the world "outside." Professional students, combining IR with preparation for work in business or other professions with a "global" component, will be left without much help and with little idea about what to expect when confronting the globe.

The second choice is to pick and teach an approach that each of us regards as the most sensible one, playing down or ignoring all the others. This is easy for scholars who teach the results of their own research. Yet the sharp distinction between mainstream and nonmainstream makes it irresponsible for nonmainstream scholars to pursue this path since their students would be seriously disadvantaged by ignorance of mainstream texts should they proceed to other institutions for other degrees. Neither option is attractive to the teacher who is disenchanted with current debates. Not everyone finds it easy to teach tenfold classifications and increasingly incestuous delusionary "debates" over "schools of thought" (of often one or two people) explaining an imaginary world populated by abstract and nonhuman but often reified creatures such as states, anarchies, structures, levels, units, and balances. The creatures are accorded their own logic that people cannot hope to influence.

A reorientation is obviously overdue. A glance at a handbook for teachers (LaBarr and Singer 1977) published twenty years ago reveals that we are adding without cumulating and repeating without deepening. Most of the texts this handbook lists still appear in footnotes. The list could now be augmented by including younger scholars, but newer books are more and more polemical and assume a broader and broader range of shallower knowledge diffused within a larger and larger body of literature. Nothing ever seems to be pruned out. Amazingly not even the "hurricane" of the Cold War's end managed to do the pruning job.

However, it is the accumulation of irrelevancies, in all five social processes discussed above, that gives hope that change is possible. Pressures for change come also from outside the discipline. Many academic fields, social sciences as well as natural sciences, are now adding global concerns to their agenda. Interest in the global context is obvious not only among economists (who populate a subfield of IR) but also in sociology, historical sociology, sociology of religion, anthropology, demography, and geography. It seems to follow logically that as the world becomes increasingly global, the subject matter of these disciplines will spill across traditional boundaries. The natural sciences also work with the global perspective in mind, particularly those sciences that address environmental degradation or the Information Age—by definition global in scope. It is too late to stop them from encroaching on our turf. What then does the future of IR hold? What will happen next?

Reconstructing IR?

Nothing. Certainly not soon. There are only two processes, both social, that might intervene to bring about a change in due course. First, the discipline of IR might cease to be an agent in any of the senses discussed above. Before that happens, however, a second process might intervene: IR might well take on ideas and concepts from other fields. This process of absorption would be at the same time a process of dissolution. IR would not cease to exist but would assume a new role—a role pioneered in the study of the environment. IR would coordinate an influx of social and natural sciences into global studies without insisting on its own distinct turf. Just as ecology has become an organizer and integrator of many disciplines (indeed, *ecology* is derived from the Greek *oikos*, for "house"), so too IR might house the "social ecology of global society."

Unlike realism, constructivism is not threatened by such potential developments. On the contrary, it can provide valuable assistance in reconstructing the discipline. Those who are aware of these processes are more likely to take steps forward ahead of the mainstream.

Note

Paul Kowert has very kindly helped me to rewrite this chapter. My thanks go to him for this assistance, as well as to both Paul Kowert and Nicholas Onuf for their comments. I take responsibility for the chapter's conclusions.

Bibliography

Alker, Hayward R. 1982. "Logic, Dialectics, Politics: Some Recent Controversies." In *Dialectical Logic for the Political Sciences*, ed. H.R. Alker, Poznan Studies in the Philosophy of the Sciences of Humanities, vol. 7, 65–93. Amsterdam: Rodopi.

George, Alexander L. 1994. *Bridging the Gap: Theory and Practice in Foreign Policy.* Washington, DC: United States Institute of Peace.

LaBarr, Dorothy F., and J. David Singer. 1977. *The Study of International Politics: A Guide to the Sources for the Student, Teacher, and Researcher.* Santa Barbara, CA: Clio Books.

Lapid, Yosef, and Friedrich Kratochwil, eds. 1996. *The Return of Culture and Identity in International Relations Theory.* Boulder, CO: Lynne Rienner.

Pettman, Ralph. 1994. "What We Think About World Politics, What We Don't Think, and Why?" Paper presented at the U.S. International Studies Association Conference, March.

Index

Adorno, Max, 45
Adler, Emmanuel, 8
academic disciplines. *See* disciplines
academics and practitioners, 195
act, acting. *See* deed
action-structure. *See* Carlsnaes;
    morphogenesis
actions, class of. *See* rules
administrative challenge panels
    (ACPs), 162, 163
agency, 59–61, 64–77
  co-constitution of, 128
  theory of, 128
agent(s), 5, 6, 7
  as institutions, 72–73
  as observers, 61–62, 64, 71, 73
  autonomy, independence of, 65, 77
  control over, 63, 74–5
  defined, 80–81
  individual as, 83
  International Relations as, 195
  imputing structure, 83
  scholars as, 194–201
  singular, collective, 64, 66
  state as, 83
  See also rule
agent-structure problem/debate, 62,
    79–99, 62, 79, 82, 83, 89
  and levels of analysis, 88–89
  ontological and methodological
    nature of, 83
Albright, Madelaine, 161
algorithm, genetic, 188–90
Alker, Hayward, 31, 195
  See also Alker, H. and Biersteker, T.
Alker, H. and Biersteker, T., 30, 31,
    36, 48

Allen, Roger, 111
Allport, Gordon, 107
Alperovitz, Gar, 44
Althusser, Luis, 6, 45
  See also Marxism, structural
analytic dualism, 91–92
anarchy, 196
  in structural realism, 90
  interactions within, 90
  condition of. *See* rule
Anderson, Perry, 41, 44
anthropology, 9
anti-epistemology. *See* Foucault, Michel
anti-positivist, 173
approach/paradigm, 48
  discourse, 39
archaeology of knowledge. *See*
    Foucault, Michel
Archer, Margaret, 91–92
Aristotle, 30
arrangements. *See* structure
artificial world, 181
Ashley, Richard, 35, 36, 37, 41, 48, 49
associations, as institutions, 72–76
Aswan High Dam, 113, 114, 116, 118
attribution error, 107, 110, 114, 116
Austin, J.L., 45
authority. *See* control legitimate;
    hegemony
autonomy. *See* agents, autonomy of

Baghdad Pact, 110, 111
balance of power, 20
  as institution, 70-71
  global, 153
  See also consequences, unintended
Banks, Michael, 36